Regional Advantage

REGIONAL ADVANTAGE

CULTURE AND COMPETITION IN
SILICON VALLEY AND ROUTE 128

ANNALEE SAXENIAN

HARVARD UNIVERSITY PRESS

CAMBRIDGE, MASSACHUSETTS, AND LONDON, ENGLAND

To Jamie, who set the deadline

And to Marty, who helped me meet it

Fourth printing, 1996
First Harvard University Press paperback edition, 1996

Library of Congress Cataloging-in-Publication Data

Saxenian, AnnaLee.
Regional advantage : culture and competition
in Silicon Valley and Route 128 / AnnaLee Saxenian.
    p.   cm.
Includes bibliographical references and index.
ISBN 0–674–75339–9 (alk. paper)
ISBN 0–674–75340–2 (pbk.)
1. High technology industries—California, Northern.
2. High technology industries—Massachusetts.
3. United States—Economic conditions—1981–
—Regional disparities.
I. Title.
HC107.C22N677   1994
338.4'762'000979473—dc20   93-39416

Designed by Gwen Frankfeldt

CONTENTS

PREFACE TO THE
PAPERBACK EDITION

▶ In early 1995, a journalist from Boston suggested that *Regional Advantage* was already outdated. He claimed that the book offered an accurate, if painful, portrayal of the experience of the Route 128 economy through the 1980s—but that the situation had fundamentally changed since 1990. He pointed to several recent software and networking start-ups, the formation of new business associations, and the restructuring of large firms like the Digital Equipment Corporation (DEC) as evidence of a turnaround of the regional economy.

This view, common in the Boston area today, poses a deeper challenge to the argument advanced in this book than may be evident at first glance. If the Route 128 technology industry has rebounded, then either the original claims of the book were wrong or the region's culture and institutions have been transformed. The former, of course, is more likely. After all, *Regional Advantage* concludes that nothing less than an opening of the boundaries among technology businesses and between these firms and surrounding financial, educational, and public sector institutions will enable the region to compete effectively with Silicon Valley. It is difficult to imagine a business community overcoming in such a brief time the culture and practices of secrecy, self-sufficiency, and risk-aversion consistently displayed by firms and other institutions in Route 128. Indeed the mechanisms of social and institutional change would need to be far more flexible than I have argued for such a change to occur.

The available data, however, do not support the notion of a regional turnaround. In fact, in the period from 1990 to 1992 (the most recent data available at this writing), Route 128 lost some 9,375 jobs in technology sectors ranging from computers and communications equipment to electronic components, aerospace, and instruments, and added only 1,048 new jobs in software (see Historical Data).

Even if the data do not indicate a recovery, is there other evidence that the Route 128 region is reinventing itself? Layoffs at the minicomputer firms have spawned a new generation of companies, many of which are rejecting the management models of their predecessors. Chipcom Corporation, a manufacturer of networking hardware, for example, was started in 1983 by veterans of Data General and DEC. While capitalizing on local expertise in computer networking, Chipcom's founders assiduously avoided vertical integration and maintained open corporate boundaries. Yet as with the region's other start-ups, the question remains whether even enlightened firms like Chipcom can compete without the advantages of a supportive regional environment, particularly when their competitors draw on an industrial infrastructure and culture that both demands and facilitates rapid change, openness, and learning.

Several other computer networking firms were started in the Route 128 region during the 1980s. By the early 1990s, however, the dominant players in the business—Cisco, 3Com, and Bay Networks—were based in Silicon Valley. And in 1995, Chipcom was acquired by 3Com. The merged company is now the second largest player in a $10 billion market that is growing more than 30 percent annually. Once again in the computer networking sector, as with semiconductors in the 1960s and microprocessor-based computers in the 1980s, the center of gravity in a dynamic new sector has shifted decisively to the west.

Chipcom is not an isolated example. Firms that were hailed as the upcoming stars of Route 128, from Powersoft to Wellfleet, have been acquired by or merged with Silicon Valley companies; others like Thinking Machines and Kendall Square Research have gone out of business. Even Lotus Development, the region's only nationally recognized software company, was acquired by IBM. These acquisitions of east coast companies by Silicon Valley competitors further slow cultural change in Route 128. When east coast companies are acquired the center of gravity for management invariably shifts to the west, diminishing the local supply of managers. Today there are very few people in the Boston area who are experienced in running big healthy technology companies.

Nor is this trend likely to change. Today Silicon Valley boasts far more start-ups in key areas like networking, wireless communications, multimedia, and internet applications. As in the 1980s, more than three times as many venture capital dollars are being invested in Silicon Valley technology start-ups than in New England ventures. Moreover, the conservatism of the east coast venture capital community makes it very difficult for companies that boldly define new markets to gain funding: entrepreneurs with good ideas on Route 128 are either forced to scale down their vision quickly or hook up with venture capital from the west and are convinced to move to the Valley. This helps explain why, aside from Lotus, it is difficult to name a nationally successful Route 128 software company, while Silicon Valley has produced market leaders like Netscape, Oracle, Intuit, and Adobe.

The formation of the Massachusetts Software Council and the Massachusetts Telecommunications Council are positive signs of change in the region. These groups have rejected the oppositional politics of the Massachusetts High Technology Council and instead provide support services and networking opportunities for local firms. Most significantly, they have distanced themselves from the short-sighted tax cutting agenda that has impoverished the region's public institutions. The question remains whether these new associations and others will be able to create a broader culture of collaboration in the region.

It is perhaps telling that while *Regional Advantage* has provoked significant interest among regional policy-makers and business executives from Oregon to New Mexico, the response of the Route 128 community to the book has been largely indifferent, if not hostile. In part, this reflects the insularity of an old-line industrial community—the very problem the book describes. But it exposes a deeper problem as well: the absence of opportunities in the region for collective discussions. In Silicon Valley a myriad of forums bring together individuals from different firms and industries, from public and private sectors, and from financial, educational, and training institutions. These gatherings, both formal and informal, enable individuals—often determined competitors—to discuss common problems, debate solutions, and define the shared identities that enable an industrial community to transcend the interests of independent firms. Only such an industrial community can create and recreate regional advantage in today's competitive global economy.

The Japanese response to *Regional Advantage* remains most striking. Although the book barely mentions Japan, it has generated remarkable and sustained attention from Japanese policy leaders and industry executives—a group that has repeatedly demonstrated its ability to learn quickly from foreign industrial experience.

The greatest long-term threats to the Silicon Valley economy are not simply from Japan (and the rest of Asia), however. Closer to home, continued reductions in public funding for California's educational institutions—from its elementary and secondary schools to the sophisticated network of community colleges, state universities, and the University of California system—jeopardize the rich supply of technical talent and the research base that have historically supported the regional economy.

Nonetheless, Silicon Valley continues to flourish in the 1990s. By 1994, twenty of the region's technology companies boasted more than $1 billion in sales (compared to only five in the Route 128 region) and collectively Silicon Valley technology firms surpassed $106 billion in sales. These firms are expanding their ties with the Pacific Rim—exploiting their access to its booming markets and a highly skilled Asian workforce. Moreover, the three-year-old Joint Venture: Silicon Valley Network has engaged literally hundreds of policy-makers, entrepreneurs, executives, consultants, and educators in ongoing efforts to enhance the region's collaborative advantage.

In short, important organizational and cultural differences continue to define the divergent fortunes of the Silicon Valley and Route 128 economies. This does not mean that change is not possible. Cultures and institutions are not static, they are continually created and recreated through conflict and struggle as well as routines, habits, and practices. As a native of the Boston area, I may wish that the Route 128 region turns itself around quickly; as a scholar, I know that it is likely to take decades to overcome the management practices, culture, and institutions that have hindered the region in the past.

San Francisco
August 1995

Prologue

▶ Jeffrey Kalb resigned from the Digital Equipment Corporation in the spring of 1987. Kalb was one of the minicomputer giant's rising stars, and his departure was yet another blow to a company that had recently lost dozens of talented executives. Frustrated and burned out, Kalb returned to his native California, joining the exodus of engineers from the technology region around Route 128 in Massachusetts to its West Coast counterpart, Silicon Valley.

Kalb's move reflected more than a desire for a sunny climate. By the late 1980s the locus of technological innovation in computing had shifted decisively to the West. Experienced engineers moved to Northern California to join a new generation of companies or, like Kalb, to try their hand at entrepreneurship.

Kalb founded the MasPar Computer Corporation in early 1988. MasPar was typical of a wave of specialized start-ups that were fueling an economic boom in Silicon Valley. The firm concentrated on massively parallel computing, an architecture that increased the speed and power of computer systems by having tens of thousands of processors work in parallel, rather than sequentially, to process information.

In an interview in 1991, Kalb looked back on his decision to start MasPar in Silicon Valley:

> There's a fundamental difference in the structure of the industry between Route 128 and here. Route 128 is organized into large companies that do their own thing. At Digital, we had our own capabilities for everything, not just little things, but boards, chips, monitors, disk drives, everything. It's very difficult for a small company to survive in that environment, where you can't get components easily. It's not any one individual thing. It's the amount of energy it takes to get everything . . .

There are a large number of experienced people here who have retired but are still active in the industry and are available as consultants, members of boards of directors, or venture capitalists. There is a huge supply of contract labor—far more than on Route 128. If you want to design your own chips, there are a whole lot of people around who just do contract chip layout and design. You want mechanical design? It's here too. There's just about anything you want in this infrastructure. That's why I say it's not just one thing. It's labor, it's materials, it's access to shops, and it's time.

You can get access to these things back there sooner or later, but when you're in a start-up mode, time is everything. Time-to-market is right behind cash in your priorities as a start-up. When things are right down the street, decisions get made quickly. It's not one thing, but if you spend lots of time on airplanes and on the phone, playing phone tag, you can get an overall 20–30 percent slowdown in time-to-market . . .

The Valley is very fast-moving and start-ups have to move fast. The whole culture of the Valley is one of change. We laugh about how often people change jobs. The joke is that you can change jobs and not change parking lots. There's a culture associated with that which says that moving is okay, that rapid change is the norm, that it's not considered negative on your resume . . . So you have this culture of rapid decisions, rapid movement, rapid changes, which is exactly the environment that you find yourself in as a start-up.

In the early days of the semiconductor industry there were certain places that everybody frequented and the standing joke was that if you couldn't figure out your process problems, go down to the Wagon Wheel and ask somebody. Well there's still a lot to that. We talk about the information sharing in Japan, with these major programs that cause information to be shared. There's a velocity of information here in the Valley that is very high, not as high as it used to be, but I can assure you that it is much higher than it is in most other areas of the country. This means that relationships are easier to develop here than in the East. Unless you've actually worked in it, you don't really recognize how very different the Silicon Valley infrastructure is.

Silicon Valley and Environs

Route 128 and Environs

Within the map:
ESSEX

Lowell

MIDDLESEX

Burlington
Route 128
Lexington

Maynard

Waltham
Cambridge
Boston

Marlborough

SUSSEX

NORFOLK

INTRODUCTION:
LOCAL INDUSTRIAL SYSTEMS

▶ During the 1970s Northern California's Silicon Valley and Boston's Route 128 attracted international acclaim as the world's leading centers of innovation in electronics. Both were celebrated for their technological vitality, entrepreneurship, and extraordinary economic growth. With common origins in university-based research and postwar military spending, the two were often compared. They were also widely imitated. As traditional manufacturing sectors and regions fell into crisis, policymakers and planners around the world looked to these fast-growing regions and their "sunrise" industries as models of industrial revitalization and sought to replicate their success by building science parks, funding new enterprises, and promoting links between industry and universities.

This enchantment waned during the early 1980s, when the leading producers in both regions experienced crises of their own. Silicon Valley chipmakers relinquished the market for semiconductor memory to Japanese competitors, while Route 128 minicomputer companies watched their customers shift to workstations and personal computers. Both regions faced the worst downturns in their histories, and analysts predicted that they would follow the path of Detroit and Pittsburgh to long-term decline. It appeared that America's high technology industry, once seen as invulnerable, might not survive the challenge of intensified international competition.

The performance of these two regional economies diverged, however, in the 1980s. In Silicon Valley, a new generation of semiconductor and computer start-ups emerged alongside established companies. The dramatic success of start-ups such as Sun Microsystems, Conner Peripherals, and Cypress Semiconductor, and the continued dynamism of large companies such as Hewlett-Packard and Intel, were evidence that Silicon Valley had regained its former vitality. Route 128, in contrast, showed few signs of reversing a decline that had begun in the early 1980s. The once-hailed "Massachusetts Miracle" ended abruptly, and start-ups failed to compensate for continuing layoffs at the region's established minicomputer companies, Digital Equipment Corporation, Data General, Prime, and Wang. By the end of the 1980s, Route 128 producers had ceded their longstanding dominance in computer production to Silicon Valley.

Silicon Valley is now home to one-third of the 100 largest technology companies created in the United States since 1965. The market value of these firms increased by $25 billion between 1986 and 1990, dwarfing the $1 billion increase of their Route 128–based counterparts.[1] Although the two regions employed workforces of roughly the same size in 1975, between 1975 and 1990 Silicon Valley firms generated some 150,000 net new technology-related jobs—triple the number created on Route 128 (see Figure 1). In 1990 Silicon Valley–based producers exported electronics products worth more than $11 billion, almost one-third of the nation's total, compared to Route 128's $4.6 billion.[2] Finally, Silicon Valley was the home of 39 of the nation's 100 fastest-growing electronics corporations, while Route 128 claimed only 4. By 1990 both Southern California and Texas had surpassed Route 128 as locations of fast-growing electronics companies.[3]

Why has Silicon Valley adapted successfully to changing patterns of international competition while Route 128 appears to be losing its competitive edge? Despite similar origins and technologies, these two regions evolved fundamentally distinct industrial systems after World War II. Their different responses to the crises of the 1980s revealed differences in productive organization whose significance had been unrecognized during the rapid growth of earlier decades—or had been seen simply as superficial disparities between "laid back" California and the more "buttoned up" East Coast. Far from superficial, these differences illustrate the importance of the local determinants of industrial adaptation.

Silicon Valley has a regional network–based industrial system that promotes collective learning and flexible adjustment among specialist producers of a complex of related technologies. The region's dense social networks and open labor markets encourage experimentation and entrepreneurship. Companies compete intensely while at the same time learning from one another about changing markets and technolo-

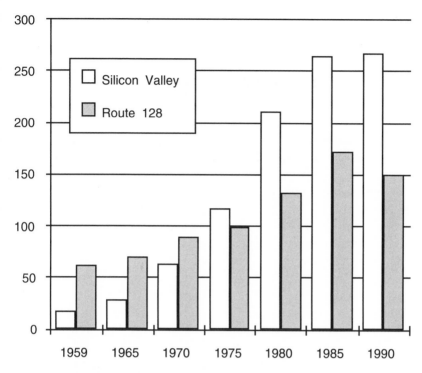

Figure 1. Total high technology employment, Silicon Valley and Route 128, 1959–1990. Data from *County Business Patterns*.

gies through informal communication and collaborative practices; and loosely linked team structures encourage horizontal communication among firm divisions and with outside suppliers and customers. The functional boundaries within firms are porous in a network system, as are the boundaries between firms themselves and between firms and local institutions such as trade associations and universities.

The Route 128 region, in contrast, is dominated by a small number of relatively integrated corporations. Its industrial system is based on independent firms that internalize a wide range of productive activities. Practices of secrecy and corporate loyalty govern relations between firms and their customers, suppliers, and competitors, reinforcing a regional culture that encourages stability and self-reliance. Corporate hierarchies ensure that authority remains centralized and information tends to flow vertically. The boundaries between and within firms and between firms and local institutions thus remain far more distinct in this independent firm–based system.

Networks versus Independent Firms

The Silicon Valley and Route 128 economies are not isolated examples of the two types of industrial systems. Independent firm–based systems dominate the industrial geography of the United States and large parts of Europe. They are typically associated with capital-intensive industries such as oil, rubber, machinery, and automobiles, and they have been analyzed by students of the large-scale corporation. These analyses have little to say about the organization of regional economies, however, primarily because the traditional vertically integrated corporation tends to internalize most local supplies of skill, technology, and other resources. As a result, even when regional theorists examine large corporations, few link the social, institutional, and technical fabrics of different localities.[4]

There is, in contrast, a growing literature on the dynamics of regional network–based industrial systems, which have been identified in many parts of the world and in many historical periods.[5] In these systems, which are organized around horizontal networks of firms, producers deepen their own capabilities by specializing, while engaging in close, but not exclusive, relations with other specialists.[6] Network systems flourish in regional agglomerations where repeated interaction builds shared identities and mutual trust while at the same time intensifying competitive rivalries.

The most studied contemporary examples of regional network–based systems, the small-firm industrial districts of the Third Italy, specialize in traditional industries such as shoes, textiles, leather goods, furniture, and ceramic tiles. Germany's Baden-Württemberg is known for its mix of small and medium-sized makers of machine tools, textile equipment, and automobile components alongside giant electronics corporations. Similar flexible industrial clusters have been identified in Denmark, Sweden, Spain, and Los Angeles.[7] While each of these variants of network systems reflects distinctive national and regional institutions and histories, their localized social and productive interdependencies are comparable to those in Silicon Valley.

The successes of Japanese industry are similarly attributable, at least in part, to network organizational forms. The Japanese corporation is more internally decentralized and more open to the surrounding economy than the traditional large American corporation. Producers of electronics, autos, and machine tools, for example, rely on extensive networks of small and medium-sized suppliers, to which they are linked through ties of trust and partial ownership. Although Japan's large firms historically exploited suppliers, many increasingly collaborate with them, encouraging them to expand their technological capabilities and organizational autonomy. Like their Silicon Valley counterparts, these producers tend to be geographically clustered and depend heavily on informal information exchange as well as more formal forms of cooperation.[8]

As the case of Japan suggests, there are large- as well as small-firm variants of network-based systems. Large corporations can integrate into regional networks through a process of internal decentralization. As newly independent business units are forced by competition to achieve the technical and productive standards of outsiders, they often draw on the social and technical infrastructure of the local economy and collaborate with external suppliers and customers.[9]

Of course all economic activity does not cluster within a single regional economy. Firms in network systems serve global markets and collaborate with distant customers, suppliers, and competitors. Technology firms, in particular, are highly international. However, the most strategic relationships are often local because of the importance of timeliness and face-to-face communication for rapid product development. Moreover, nonlocal suppliers succeed in part by integrating into regional economies that specialize in similar lines of business. Paradoxically, the creation of regional clusters and the globalization of production go hand in hand, as firms reinforce the dynamism of their own localities by linking them to similar regional clusters elsewhere.

REGIONAL ADVANTAGES

The experience of Route 128 and Silicon Valley in recent decades suggests that there are important regional sources of competitive advantage. Neither standard accounts of industrial adaptation as a national or a sectoral process nor traditional theories of regional development, which treat Silicon Valley and Route 128 as comparable concentrations of skill and technology, can account for Silicon Valley's superior adaptive capacity during the 1980s. Producers in these two regions compete in the same technology-related markets and are located in the same nation, yet they have fared quite differently in the competitive turmoil of recent decades. Their differences in performance cannot be explained by approaches that view firms as separate from the social structures and institutions of a local economy.[10]

Historical evidence emerging from the United States and other advanced industrial nations confirms that variations in local institutions and corporate forms shape regional capacities for adaptation.[11] The recognition that differences in economic performance within nations can be as great as those between nations has spurred growing interest in regions. However, the concepts traditionally used to analyze regional economies provide little assistance in accounting for the differences in performance of Silicon Valley and Route 128.

Students of regional development rely on the concept of external economies to assess the sources of comparative advantage that lie outside the individual firm.[12] They view Silicon Valley and Route 128 as classic examples of the external economies that derive from industrial localization: as cumulatively self-reinforcing agglomerations of technical skill, venture capital, specialized suppliers and services, infrastructure, and spillovers of knowledge associated with proximity to universities and informal information flows.[13] But the concepts of agglomeration and external economies cannot explain why clusters of specialized technical skill, suppliers, and information produced a self-reinforcing dynamic of increasing industrial advance in Silicon Valley while producing stagnation and decline along Route 128.[14] The simple fact of spatial proximity evidently reveals little about the ability of firms to respond to the fast-changing markets and technologies that now characterize international competition.

The notion of external economies assumes that the firm is an atomistic unit of production with clearly defined boundaries. Treating regions as collections of autonomous firms has led some observers to conclude that Silicon Valley suffers from excessive, even pathological, fragmentation.[15] This view overlooks the complex of institutional and social relationships that connect the producers within the region's fragmented industrial structure. Although the broadest interpretations of technological external economies recognize that firms learn from one another through flows of information, ideas, and know-how, they do so only by denying the initial theoretical distinction between internal and external economies—between what is inside and what is outside of the firm.[16]

EMBEDDING THE ECONOMY

Far from being isolated from what lies outside them, firms are embedded in a social and institutional setting that shapes, and is shaped by, their strategies and structures.[17] The concept of an industrial system illuminates the historically evolved relationship between the internal organization of firms and their connections to one another and to the social structures and institutions of their particular localities.[18]

It is helpful to think of a region's industrial system as having three dimensions: local institutions and culture, industrial structure, and corporate organization.[19] Regional institutions include public and private organizations such as universities, business associations, and local governments, as well as the many less formal hobbyist clubs, professional societies, and other forums that create and sustain regular patterns of social interaction in a region. These institutions shape and are shaped by the local culture, the shared understandings and practices that unify a community and define everything from labor market behavior to attitudes toward risk-taking. A region's culture is not static, but rather is continually reconstructed through social interaction.

Industrial structure refers to the social division of labor—the degree of vertical integration—as well as to the extent and nature of links between customers, suppliers, and competitors in a particular sector or complex of related sectors. Students of regional development have analyzed this aspect of industrial systems the most extensively—but often at the cost of neglecting its close relationships to the other two dimensions of an industrial system. The final dimension, internal firm organization, includes the degree of hierarchical or horizontal coordination, centralization or decentralization, and the allocation of responsibilities and specialization of tasks within the firm.

The three dimensions are closely interconnected. No single dimension adequately accounts for the adaptive capacity of a regional economy, nor is any single variable prior to or causal of the others. Regional culture, for example, is important, but it is not decisive in promoting particular industrial forms. During the 1970s Silicon Valley's chipmakers embraced the dominant management models and pursued self-sufficient business strategies despite a regional culture that promoted open exchange and informal cooperation.

Differing combinations of the three dimensions of an industrial system are possible, although they tend, in practice, to become mutually reinforcing components in coherent regional economies. Dense networks of social relations play an important role in integrating the firms in Silicon Valley's fragmented industrial structure. Elsewhere, however, the small, specialized firms in regional clusters remain isolated, linked only by arms-length market relations.[20] Moreover, apparently analogous institutions can play different roles in different industrial systems. Universities, for example, are widely viewed as sources of knowledge and information for their regional economies. But Stanford University, which actively promoted local technology start-ups during the years following World War II, is far more deeply integrated into its regional surroundings than the Massachusetts Institute of Technology (MIT). Thus it is not sufficient to consider institutions in isolation; they too are parts of the broader industrial systems in which they are embedded.

ADAPTING TO CHANGE

Understanding regional economies as industrial systems rather than as clusters of factors of production, and thinking of the two regions as examples of the two models of industrial systems—the decentralized regional network–based system and the independent firm–based system—illuminates the divergent trajectories of the Silicon Valley and Route 128 economies since World War II. The histories of these two regions also provide a striking illustration of the relationship between regional networks and the process of industrial adaptation.

Silicon Valley's producers continued to adapt to the leading edge of electronics technologies, while Route 128 companies repeatedly stumbled—often losing out to the West Coast. In the early 1960s Silicon Valley established itself as the nation's center of semiconductor innovation, overtaking Route 128's initial leadership in transistors and other solid state devices. Although several large Route 128 companies eventually began producing semiconductors internally, the region never developed an independent semiconductor business.

A second opportunity emerged for Route 128 when it became a center of minicomputer production in the late 1970s. Most observers at the time described an emerging division of labor between Silicon

Valley and Route 128, with the former specializing in semiconductors and the latter in computers. But Route 128 producers failed to make the transition to smaller workstations and personal computers, and in the late 1980s the locus of innovation in computing shifted from the East to the West, just as it had in semiconductors two decades earlier.

In a network-based industrial system like that in Silicon Valley, the region—if not all the firms in the region—is organized to adapt continuously to fast-changing markets and technologies. The system's decentralization encourages the pursuit of multiple technical opportunities through spontaneous regroupings of skill, technology, and capital. Its production networks promote a process of collective technological learning that reduces the distinctions between large and small firms and between industries or sectors.

The independent firm–based industrial system flourished in an environment of market stability and slow-changing technologies because its leading producers benefited from the advantages of scale economies and market control. It has been overwhelmed, however, by changing competitive conditions. Corporations that invested in dedicated equipment and specialized worker skills find themselves locked in to obsolete technologies and markets, while hierarchical structures limit their ability to adapt quickly as conditions change. Their inward focus and vertical integration also limit the development of a sophisticated local infrastructure, leaving the entire region vulnerable when the large firms falter.[21]

In the case of semiconductors and again with computers, Silicon Valley's network-based system supported a decentralized process of experimentation and learning that fostered successful adaptation, while Route 128's firm-based system was constrained by the isolation of its producers from external sources of know-how and information. Route 128 firms continued to generate technological breakthroughs but were not part of an industrial system that would have enabled them to exploit these successes as a region. In Silicon Valley, as in comparable localities elsewhere, regional networks promote the collective technological advance that is increasingly essential to competitive success.

1

GENESIS: UNIVERSITIES, MILITARY
SPENDING, AND ENTREPRENEURS

Marching to war, M.I.T. and its myriad scientists and technicians helped bring closer the inevitable peace and became a catalyst for the renaissance of a Boston that had already begun to stir, to shake off more than a generation of fitful sleep.

—Russell B. Adams, Jr.

▶ The Second World War and the ensuing Cold War recast the economic landscape of the United States. The federal government spurred the growth of new industries and regions by channeling resources to university labs to develop war-related technologies. Researchers at the Massachusetts Institute of Technology (MIT) and Stanford University, as leading beneficiaries of defense and aerospace contracts, spearheaded the economic transformation of Eastern Massachusetts and Northern California. Their pioneering research in radar, solid state electronics, and computing created localized pools of technical skill and suppliers that attracted established corporations and supported the formation of new enterprises. Fueled initially by federal funds, the process of entrepreneurship and technology advance became self-sustaining by the early 1970s and ensured the position of Route 128 and Silicon Valley as the nation's leading centers of electronics innovation and production.

More than two centuries of industrialization laid the foundation for the postwar surge of activity in electronics in the Boston area. Several leading technology firms were formed in Massachusetts during the nineteenth century; by the 1940s the region was home to a sizeable group of electronics manufacturers. The Santa Clara Valley, by contrast, remained an agricultural region as late as the 1940s, famous primarily for its apricot and walnut orchards. Aside from a handful of small electrical firms, the only local industry was small-scale food processing and distribution.

While both regions were transformed by the war and the massive flows of military funds for electronics research and production during the 1950s and 1960s, these different starting points shaped their future trajectories. Silicon Valley's pioneers sought to overcome the region's status as an industrial latecomer by replicating Boston's technology complex. But in attempting to imitate this model they unwittingly transformed it. Unhampered by the constraints imposed by preexisting industrial traditions, the region's founders created a distinctive technological community.

Relations between universities and local industry during the war and postwar years offer early evidence of these differences. While both Stanford and MIT encouraged commercially oriented research and courted federal research contracts in the postwar years, MIT's leadership focused on building relations with government agencies and seeking financial support from established electronics producers. In contrast, Stanford's leaders, lacking corporate or government ties or even easy proximity to Washington, actively promoted the formation of new technology enterprises and forums for cooperation with local industry. This contrast—between MIT's orientation toward Washington and large, established producers and Stanford's promotion of collaborative relationships among small firms—would fundamentally shape the industrial systems emerging in the two regions.

ROUTE 128

Technological innovation was not new to Massachusetts in the postwar period. New England companies pioneered manufacturing techniques and equipment in the textile, armaments, and machine tool industries during the nineteenth century. As these industries declined or moved out of the region, Eastern Massachusetts became a center of automobile and electrical manufacturing.[1] The region experienced prolonged decline during the first half of the twentieth century, however, as it continued to lose traditional manufacturing industries to lower-wage regions and as financial services shifted from Boston to New York.

The foundation of a regional recovery was laid before the decline itself had become fully apparent. The establishment of MIT in 1861 as a technical university had reflected the region's long industrial tradition. Unlike neighboring Harvard University, which maintained a calculated distance from the industrial world, MIT encouraged research and consulting for private industry.[2] The chair of the electrical engineering department, Donald Jackson, wrote in 1910 that MIT stood "ready to undertake some of the more distinctively commercial investigations under the patronage or support of the great manufacturing or other commercial companies." He appointed an advisory committee made up of top executives from major corporations such as General Electric (GE) and Westinghouse.[3]

In 1918, MIT established a Technology Plan to encourage large corporations like GE, Eastman Kodak, and Dupont to become continuing sources of financial support. The university also created a Division of Industrial Cooperation and Research during the 1920s to solicit corporate research contracts and keep companies apprised of MIT research findings. The Technology Plan was discontinued by 1930, but the Division of Industrial Cooperation and Research (later the Office of Sponsored Projects) maintained its capacity to solicit and manage corporate contracts.[4]

In addition to building ties with established corporations, MIT was at the center of a new wave of electronics activity in the first decades of the twentieth century. Electrical engineering professor Vannevar Bush helped start the American Appliance Company—later the Raytheon Manufacturing Company. Founded to make refrigerators, the firm changed its name to Raytheon in 1925 after acquiring the rights to a new kind of vacuum tube that would permit radios to run on household current rather than on bulky batteries. Raytheon was funded with investments from J. P. Morgan and an informal group of wealthy Bostonians. Other technology start-ups during this period such as Polaroid and the National Research Corporation also relied on local individuals for financing.[5]

This private investment was soon dwarfed by federal funding of research in electronics. MIT became the nation's leading center of research during the war, performing more military research than any other U.S. university, largely due to the efforts of Vannevar Bush. Bush went to Washington in 1940 to serve Roosevelt in the national defense effort; in 1941 he was named director of the newly formed Office of Scientific Research and Development (OSRD), the first federal agency dedicated to science and research. In this role, Bush revolutionized the relationship between science and government by funding universities rather than government labs to pursue basic military research. He also cemented the ties between MIT and Washington by using his friends in the local industrial and research communities to ensure that MIT graduates dominated the OSRD's committees.

MIT laboratories received one-third of the $330 million in contracts awarded by Bush's OSRD during the 1940s and 1950s.[6] Other universities in the Boston area, including Harvard and Tufts, also received millions of dollars for research in such emerging fields as radar, missile guidance and navigational systems, and submarine warfare. This massive government funding fueled the industrial revitalization of the New England economy.

MIT used its OSRD contracts to establish the Radiation Laboratory (Rad Lab), the first large-scale interdisciplinary and multifunctional R&D organization at a U.S. university, to perform crucial wartime research on radar and navigation systems. Harvard's labs pioneered work on submarine warfare and anti-radar systems. These research units drew top physicists and electronics engineers from across the country, and many remained as university researchers and faculty, or as employees in local companies, after the war. When the Rad Lab was disbanded, for example, it had close to four thousand employees, of whom more than one thousand were scientists and engineers.[7]

Local industry benefited directly from the war effort as well. Raytheon was awarded a stream of government contracts to produce tubes and magnetrons for radar devices. The company, tiny among the ranks of its established competitors such as General Electric (GE), Westinghouse, RCA, and Bell Labs, grew dramatically through wartime military contracts. Sales grew from $3 million to $173 million (to equal those of GE) between 1940 and 1945, while employment jumped from 1,400 to 16,000. This wartime experience with high-volume production also allowed Raytheon to bid successfully for missile guidance systems contracts during the 1950s.[8]

As the war drew to a close, the greater Boston area's so-called Research Row—composed of MIT, Harvard, and other local universities and a growing concentration of industrial laboratories—offered an intellectual and technological labor pool unsurpassed in the nation, if not in the world. Frederick Terman, Dean of Engineering at Stanford, would later recall his days as one of Vannevar Bush's doctoral students at MIT: "There was always an industry around Cambridge and Boston and MIT was right in the middle of it. It was easy for a professor to find things to do in industry where his specialized knowledge was of value to them, and it would be kind of fun for him to apply some of his knowledge to real world activities. Every place you looked, you would find guys doing something with some company."[9]

In an era of regional markets for corporate debt and equity, Boston also benefited from maturing industries that were generating more investable capital than they consumed. While wealthy individuals and families had occasionally invested in speculative technical enterprises before the war, most of Boston's capital was tied up in insurance companies and investment trusts. This began to change in 1946, when a group of New England financiers and academics, including MIT President Karl T. Compton, organized the American Research and Development Corporation (ARD) to supply capital to research-based enterprises seeking to exploit the new technologies developed during the war.

Under the leadership of General George Doriot, a Harvard Business School professor, ARD became the first publicly held venture capital company in the nation. The company actively pursued investment opportunities at MIT and its labs. The first recipients of ARD investments, High Voltage Engineering Co. and Tracerlab, were formed by the university's faculty and alumni. ARD's most successful investment, the Digital Equipment Corporation (DEC), was started in 1957 by a graduate of MIT, Ken Olsen.[10]

Despite its early pioneering role, however, MIT curtailed its financial support for ARD in 1955. Articulating the conservatism of New England universities and financial institutions of this era, MIT concluded that investing in start-up companies was too risky and not consistent with how "men of prudence, discretion, and intelligence manage their own affairs."[11] This calculated distancing from the region's new technology enterprises would typify MIT's relationship to Route 128. In spite of the university's commitment to commercially relevant research, it kept firms at arm's length.

The early successes of ARD-funded enterprises did, however, encourage the region's banks and insurance companies to invest in technology firms. Private investment also increased significantly after the war, with the First National Bank of Boston serving as an intermediary between aspiring entrepreneurs and wealthy families such as the Rockefellers, Whitneys, and Mellons. The First National Bank also formed its own investment company in 1957 and became the nation's first Small Business Investment Corporation (SBIC) in 1958 after the passage of the Small Business Investment Act provided tax benefits for companies that invested in small businesses. Several new venture funds were in turn formed by departing employees of ARD and the First National Bank of Boston (now the Bank of Boston).[12]

The emergence of new sources of capital for technology enterprises supplemented the continued flow of government funds to local labs and universities. At the request of the Air Force, MIT established the Lincoln Laboratory in 1951 to develop long-range radar, air defense warning systems, and high-speed digital data processors. MIT's Instrumentation Lab (now the independent Charles Stark Draper Lab), which had developed aircraft and missile navigational equipment, began devising missile guidance systems for the space race. The MITRE Corporation, a spin-off of MIT's Lincoln Lab, was formed as a nonprofit corporation to work on air defense and missile warning systems. The Air Force Cambridge Research Laboratories, which grew out of the breakup of the Rad Lab, focused on radar and air defense. By the mid-1960s, these labs jointly employed some 5,000 scientists and engineers.

The completion in 1951 of the first twenty-seven-mile stretch of the Route 128 highway created space for this burgeoning research and industrial activity. The circumferential highway linked some twenty towns in the greater Boston area and provided a prestigious and attractive location for technology firms—one that was ideally situated within a short drive of MIT, Cambridge, and several desirable suburban communities.[13]

While early critics referred to Route 128 as "the road to nowhere," local boosters soon renamed it "America's Technology Highway." Within a few years, Route 128 attracted a diverse mix of research labs, branches of established corporations, and start-ups—and the highway was so congested that it was widened from six to eight lanes. By 1961, there were 169 establishments employing 24,000 people located directly on the highway, and at least as many again nearby that considered themselves Route 128 firms. In 1965, MIT researchers counted 574 companies in the region, and the number more than doubled in the following eight years.[14]

The branches of national corporations such as Sylvania, RCA, Honeywell, Clevite, and Avco became a part of the area's growing technology complex, as did numerous distributors and professional service providers. But technology start-ups were the most important new source of industrial activity in this period. MIT engineering departments and research labs spawned at least 175 new enterprises during the

1960s, including 50 from Lincoln Lab and another 30 from the Instrumentation Lab. Raytheon, whose defense contracts had made it the state's largest employer, was the source of close to 150 start-ups, and the electronics division of Sylvania spawned another 39.[15]

These start-ups, like the region's established electronics producers, were heavily supported by military and aerospace contracts.[16] The Transitron Electrical Corporation, for example, was founded in 1952. When the Navy authorized the use of Transitron's gold-bonded diodes in a fire control system, the firm took off and became one of the nation's leading semiconductor producers.

Funding for defense-related research and development grew dramatically with the onset of the Cold War, the Korean conflict, and the space race. Boston area firms, like the labs at MIT, used well-established ties to Washington to capture a disproportionate share of this growing military largesse. Massachusetts firms received more than $6 billion of Department of Defense (DOD) prime contracts during the 1950s, and more than $1 billion annually during the 1960s. In 1962, federal government purchases accounted for fully half the sales of Route 128 firms.[17]

By 1970, the Route 128 region had established itself as the nation's leading center of innovation in electronics. Local firms specialized in the production of electronic components such as radar transmitting tubes, telecommunications, industrial control and computing, and missile control and guidance systems. The region never attracted high-volume manufacturers of standard electronic equipment or consumer electronics, such as televisions and radios, primarily because of its remoteness from U.S. population centers.[18] Instead, Route 128 producers focused on the technologically sophisticated components and military electronics that required high levels of skill and constant innovation.[19]

It took a severe regional recession to reduce the reliance of Route 128 producers on defense and aerospace markets. As the Vietnam war ended and the space race slowed in the early 1970s, military contracts to the region fell precipitously. Close to 30,000 defense-related jobs were lost between 1970 and 1972, and the unemployment rate in the high tech sector reached 20 percent. Raytheon alone laid off 10,000 workers, or 40 percent of its workforce. Many of these firms, which had grown accustomed to the low-risk, cost-plus world of defense contracting, discovered that they lacked the organization and skills needed to compete in civilian markets. After a painful economic down-turn, compounded by the final demise of the Massachusetts textile, shoe, and apparel industries, many Route 128 technology firms were forced to shift toward commercial markets. By the time the defense business rebounded in the late 1970s, its importance was overshad-owed by the growth of the minicomputer industry.[20]

The minicomputer pulled Route 128 out of its downturn. By the late 1970s, the region was booming as the center of the fastest-growing sector of the computer industry. These mid-sized computers—with ca-pacity, performance, and prices falling between those of mainframe and personal computers—accounted for 34 percent of the nation's $26 billion computer industry in 1980. Firms located in the Route 128 region generated more than two-thirds of the value-added in mini-computers.[21]

Like other important postwar technologies, the minicomputer was developed through the combined efforts of federal military funding and university research. Once a commercial market emerged, it attracted private capital. While basic computing research was carried out at MIT in the postwar decades, the task of refining the concept for military application passed to MIT's Lincoln Laboratory, where re-searcher Ken Olsen was finding ways to make computers smaller and more versatile. In 1957 Olsen and two partners left Lincoln Lab to start DEC. The company's plan to build electronic modules to design and test computers gained an initial investment of $70,000 from ARD.[22]

Despite its limited initial mandate, in 1959 DEC introduced the Pro-grammed Data Processor (PDP)-1, the first commercially available gen-eral-purpose computer. With a price tag of $120,000, only fifty-three of these computers were sold. By 1967, however, the firm was produc-ing low-cost minicomputers in large volumes. By 1977, with revenues exceeding one billion dollars, DEC easily led the market with 41 percent of worldwide minicomputer sales.[23]

Several other minicomputer firms were started in the region during the 1950s. An Wang, a researcher at Harvard's Computation Lab, started Wang Laboratories in 1951 to manufacture electronic calcula-tors and word processing systems. In 1955, the Computer Control Corporation, a Raytheon spin-off that pioneered minicomputer design, was purchased by Minnesota-based Honeywell Corporation.

The formation of computer ventures based in Massachusetts accelerated during the 1960s and 1970s. Twenty-five were started during the 1960s, compared to only six in prior years, and another twenty-three were founded during the 1970s. As spin-offs from existing high tech firms increased, successful firms became role models for others hoping to try their hand at entrepreneurship. An executive who decided to start his own minicomputer firm put it this way: "Those guys were just like you and me. There was nothing unique or special about them. So I figured if they can do it, why can't I?"[24]

Edson DeCastro left DEC in 1968 to start the Data General Corporation (DG), the region's most publicized minicomputer start-up. DG quickly emerged as DEC's principal competitor. By 1980 it was the third-largest minicomputer company in the nation, after DEC and Silicon Valley–based Hewlett-Packard. The region's other leading minicomputer producers, Prime Computer and Computervision, were started during the 1970s. In 1972 William Poduska left his executive position at Honeywell's minicomputer division to found Prime. Around the same time, Philippe Villers started Computervision to manufacture minicomputers as components of Computer Aided Design/Computer Aided Manufacturing (CAD/CAM) systems. Poduska and Villers each went on to start two more firms and became the leading role models for entrepreneurs in the Route 128 region.

As these fast-growing minicomputer firms took their place alongside the producers of military electronics and instrumentation, they expanded the local supplier base. This technical infrastructure consisted of job shops supplying the custom circuit boards, electronic components, precision machinery, metal parts, and subassemblies that are critical for developing prototypes and short product runs. The region also became the home of scores of technical and management consulting firms and other providers of business services. This infrastructure was an important resource that supported both established firms and start-ups.

By 1975 the technology complex along Route 128 employed close to 100,000 workers and was poised for a decade of explosive growth. This economic turnaround, which would be associated with the "Massachusetts Miracle," was fueled primarily by the expansion of the minicomputer manufacturers and a continuing flow of military contracts to firms like Raytheon. The region's producers were only vaguely aware of the threat posed by a technology region in California that already employed as many people and was growing much faster. Confident in the present, with markets exploding, Route 128 industry focused its attention inward.

Silicon Valley

Silicon Valley's origins are typically traced to the founding of the Hewlett-Packard Company (HP) in 1937. The small Palo Alto garage where two Stanford graduate students started an electronics instrumentation business has become a Silicon Valley landmark. The legend surrounding the company's origins captures the key elements of the region's ascent, particularly the distinctive role played by Stanford University and the value placed on entrepreneurship.

Frederick Terman, who moved to Stanford to become an electrical engineering professor after his graduation from MIT, encouraged his graduate students William Hewlett and David Packard to commercialize an audio-oscillator that Hewlett had designed while working on his master's thesis. In fact, he lent Hewlett and Packard $538 to start producing the machine, he helped them find work to finance their initial experiments, and he arranged a loan from a Palo Alto bank which allowed them to begin commercial production.[25] This episode foreshadowed Stanford's active role in the Silicon Valley economy.

HP's fortunes, like those of many of its East Coast counterparts, were shaped by the war. Although the firm's first major sale was a contract for eight audio-oscillators for the Walt Disney studios, HP took off during the war. Military contracts for its electronic measuring devices and receivers that were used to detect and analyze enemy radar signals boosted sales from $37,000 in 1941 to over $750,000 in 1945. Yet these were minuscule sums relative to those garnered by the established East Coast producers such as Raytheon. With only 130 employees, HP was dwarfed by GE, RCA, Westinghouse, and Raytheon, each of which employed thousands.

A small cluster of prewar technology firms—many actively encouraged and supported by Stanford's Terman—grew up alongside HP to provide a foundation for the region's emerging electronics industry. Charles Litton, a Stanford graduate, founded Litton Engineering Laboratories in 1932 to produce glass vacuum tubes. During the war it was the nation's leading source of glass-forming machinery, and subsequently it became Litton Industries, a major manufacturer of military electronics systems. When brothers Sigurd and Russell Varian invented the klystron, a flexible microwave receiver and transmitter, at Stanford in the late 1930s, the university gave them $100 of materials and free use of its physics laboratory in exchange for a 50 percent interest in any resulting patents for applications of the technology.[26] Their klystron tube became central to U.S. antiaircraft and antisubmarine radar during the war, and in 1948 the brothers formed Varian Associates, which became a major electronic instrumentation manufacturer.

The early commercial successes of firms such as HP, Litton, and Varian consolidated Northern California's position as an emerging center of electronics production. There were, to be sure, antecedents. A handful of fledgling hydroelectric power and electrical firms had located in the Bay Area in the early twentieth century. However, the scale of industrial activity was insignificant compared to that of the Boston area at the time. In fact, some of the region's leading companies moved east during the 1930s when radio became a national medium.[27]

As it had for Boston, the Second World War marked a turning point for the Santa Clara Valley. The war attracted large numbers of people to war-related industries in the San Francisco Bay area. Santa Clara County was well positioned to take advantage of this growth; it was convenient to military installations and industrial centers in Richmond, Oakland, and San Francisco, the gateway to the Pacific theater. The Moffett Field Naval Air Station alone drew thousands of military personnel. Local industry, from vegetable canneries to electronics companies, geared up for war production.[28]

While military demand dramatically improved the fortunes of Northern California firms, the government awarded the majority of the wartime military electronics contracts to large East Coast companies. The West Coast Electronics Manufacturers Association (WCEMA) was formed in 1943 in response to an announcement by the War Production Board of a drastic cutback in the contracts to West Coast firms. The twenty-five California electronics manufacturers (thirteen from the north, twelve from the south) that formed this forerunner of the American Electronics Association sought to promote their industry, particularly by lobbying for a share of the defense contracts that were going to eastern companies.[29]

After the war, Terman intensified his efforts to promote the development of the region's base of technology and industry. He left his faculty position at Stanford in the early 1940s to take up a wartime post as director of Harvard's Radio Research Laboratory, and returned to Stanford in 1946 as Dean of Engineering. Terman's experience in the East had exposed him to military electronics research and convinced him of the weaknesses of West Coast industry and universities. Not only was there little industry on the San Francisco peninsula, but, in Terman's words: "Stanford emerged from World War II as an underprivileged institution. It had not been significantly involved in any of the exciting engineering and scientific activities associated with the war." Impressed by the technological dynamism of the Boston area and determined to stop the loss of his best students to the East, Terman dedicated himself to developing Stanford and local business in tandem:

> The West has long dreamed of an indigenous industry of sufficient magnitude to balance its agricultural resources. The war advanced these hopes and brought to the West the beginnings of a great new era of industrialization. A strong and independent industry must, however, develop its own intellectual resources of science and technology. For industrial activity that depends on imported brains and second-hand ideas cannot hope to be more than a vassal that pays tribute to its overlords, and is permanently condemned to an inferior competitive position.[30]

Terman sought to strengthen the role of the university in supporting technology-based industries by building a "community of technical scholars" in the area around Stanford. In his words: "Such a community is composed of industries using highly sophisticated technologies, together with a strong university that is sensitive to the creative activities of the surrounding industry. This pattern appears to be the wave of the future." In keeping with this program, Terman built the electrical engineering program at Stanford into one of the best in the country by recruiting promising engineering faculty and expanding its graduate programs. By 1950, Stanford was awarding as many doctorates in electrical engineering as MIT, despite its much smaller faculty.[31]

The war experience also provided Terman with important academic and government contacts. Like his MIT mentor, Vannevar Bush, Terman used his relationships in Washington to attract federal contracts for both university labs and local firms. Stanford's research and development programs benefited directly from the growth of federal spending for the Korean conflict and the space race, as did local electronics producers. However, the distance from Washington often gave Boston area firms an advantage over California companies when dealing with federal officials.

Terman's most extensive efforts thus went to building collaborative ties between Stanford and local industry. He was convinced that "If western industry and western industrialists are to serve their own enlightened and long-range interests effectively, they must cooperate with western universities wherever possible, and strengthen them by financial and other assistance." Terman encouraged faculty and students to become acquainted with the region's businesses and learn of opportunities there. He arranged field trips for students to the region's electronics firms, and he spoke regularly at industry meetings to encourage businessmen in the area to learn what Stanford was doing and how its research might help their companies.[32] Terman also urged the members of WCEMA to work together for the common good, reinforcing a spirit of cooperation among local manufacturers.

Three institutional innovations during the 1950s reflect the relationships that Terman pioneered in the region. First, Stanford established the Stanford Research Institute (SRI) to conduct defense-related research and to assist West Coast businesses. It was charged with "pursuing science for practical purposes (which) might not be fully compatible internally with the traditional roles of the university."[33]

Second, Stanford opened its classrooms to local companies through the Honors Cooperative Program. The university encouraged engineers at electronics companies to enroll in graduate courses directly or through a specialized televised instructional network which brought Stanford courses into company classrooms. This program—which had no parallels at MIT—strengthened ties between firms and the university and allowed engineers to keep up-to-date technically and to build professional contacts. By 1961 there were thirty-two companies participating in the program, with about 400 employees pursuing advanced degrees in science and engineering on a part-time basis. Enrollment increased dramatically in subsequent decades.

Third, Terman promoted the development of the Stanford Industrial Park, one of the first such parks in the country. While initially a source of income to support the rapid growth of the land-rich but cash-poor university, the industrial park helped to reinforce the emerging pattern of cooperation between the university and electronics firms in the area. The first tenant, Varian Associates, chose to move its administration and R&D operations closer to Stanford in the late 1940s in order to "bring the company closer to old friends, ease ongoing collaborations, and improve access to graduate students in physics and electrical engineering."[34]

As the university granted more acreage for industrial use, other firms such as GE, Eastman Kodak, Admiral Corporation, HP, and Watkins-Johnson followed. Terman described how he enlisted his former student David Packard to help promote the industrial park: "He and I began playing a little game. People would come to see me about locating a business in the park, and I would suggest they also talk to Packard to find out what it meant to be close to a cooperative university. When people came to him first, he would reciprocate. Our goal was to create a center of high technology." The park was located a short walk from Stanford classrooms, and leases were granted only to technology companies that might benefit the university. As a result, park companies frequently hired Stanford faculty members as consultants and graduates as employees. They also became involved in research projects that were relevant to their own activities. In 1955 the Stanford Industrial Park covered approximately 220 acres. By 1961 it had grown to 652 acres and was home to 25 companies that together employed 11,000 people.[35]

The cluster of industrial activity around Stanford grew rapidly during the 1950s, its growth fueled in part by continued military spending. Terman encouraged national aerospace and electronics firms to locate facilities in the Palo Alto area, stressing the area's growing concentration of skill and knowledge as well as its pleasant climate and natural beauty. He persuaded the Lockheed Aerospace Company to set up a research laboratory in the Stanford Industrial Park in 1956, and to locate its new Missile and Space Division in Sunnyvale one year later. In a classic deal, Stanford agreed to provide faculty members to advise the division and to train its employees, while Lockheed in turn was instrumental in rebuilding Stanford's aeronautical engineering department.[36]

Other established firms, including Westinghouse and Philco-Ford, located research labs or manufacturing facilities in the area during the 1950s and 1960s, as did corporations such as Sylvania, Raytheon, and ITT. IBM, which had established a punch-card plant in San Jose in 1943, set up a research center during the 1950s.[37] And in 1970 Xerox Corporation established its Palo Alto Research Center (PARC). The National Advisory Committee for Aeronautics (later NASA) also leased property on Moffett Field for its Ames Research Center, which soon became a hub of aerospace research. These research facilities and branch plants substantially enlarged the technical infrastructure and skill base of Silicon Valley by drawing engineering talent into the region and supporting the expansion of local suppliers.[38] They were also a prolific source of start-ups in technologies ranging from lasers and microwaves to medical instrumentation. Although the region's industrial base remained small relative to its East Coast counterpart throughout the 1950s, it grew rapidly. WCEMA moved its headquarters from Los Angeles to Palo Alto in 1964 in recognition of the emerging center of technical activity in Northern California. By the late 1960s Santa Clara County was recognized as a center of aerospace and electronics activity. Its most explosive growth, however, was driven by the emergence of an industry that had not even existed until 1951.[39]

The Santa Clara Valley was dubbed Silicon Valley in the early 1970s after the main ingredient in the semiconductor.[40] The industry had taken root in California with the location of Shockley Transistor in Palo Alto in 1955. By 1970 it was the largest and most dynamic sector of the regional economy and Santa Clara County had established itself as the nation's leading center of semiconductor innovation and production, surpassing even the early industry cluster around Route 128.

The origins and subsequent splintering of Fairchild Semiconductor powerfully shaped the evolution of Silicon Valley. William Shockley, a Stanford graduate and one of the inventors of the transistor, left AT&T's Bell Laboratories in 1954 to commercialize his invention. After an unsuccessful effort to establish a transistor firm in Massachusetts under the auspices of Raytheon, he returned to Palo Alto with the backing of Beckman Instruments to start the Shockley Transistor Corporation.[41] Shockley hired a team of top-caliber engineers but proved to be an inept manager. Two years after the firm's founding, eight of its leading engineers, later known as the "traitorous eight," decided to leave and form a competing venture. With the help of the New York investment banker Arthur Rock, they gained the backing of the Fairchild Camera and Instrument Corporation of New York and founded Fairchild Semiconductor Company.

Fairchild Semiconductor quickly outgrew its parent. The company's first order, from IBM for one hundred mesa silicon transistors, came when the firm had barely moved out of a garage. But Fairchild's real growth was fueled by government contracts, first from the Air Force and later from NASA.[42] By 1963 Fairchild sales reached $130 million, most of which was for military markets.

Fairchild spawned ten spin-offs in its first eight years. Even as the firm began to falter, partly because of the problems of control by a distant corporate parent that did not understand the semiconductor business, it continued to generate some of the industry's most innovative spin-offs. By 1968 all eight of the firm's original founders had left. Some went on to start new ventures, including Robert Noyce, Gordon Moore, and Andy Grove, who, without a written business plan, convinced Arthur Rock to invest $2.5 million in the Intel Corporation. Jean Hoerni started more than a dozen firms after leaving Fairchild in 1961. Others of the "traitorous eight," including Eugene Kleiner, went on to become some of the valley's most prominent venture capitalists.

Thirty-one semiconductor firms were started in Silicon Valley during the 1960s, and the majority traced their lineage to Fairchild. Only five of the forty-five independent semiconductor firms started in the United States between 1959 and 1976 were located outside of Silicon Valley. An emerging infrastructure of suppliers provided an important advantage to start-ups in the region. Early semiconductor enterprises had little choice but to produce their own manufacturing equipment. By the late 1960s, however, they could rely on the region's fast-growing, independent equipment sector. In a spin-off process that was increasingly common in the region, engineers left more established companies to start new ventures that produced the capital goods and materials needed for semiconductor design and fabrication. Older instrumentation firms such as Varian also began producing manufacturing equipment. When Raytheon abandoned its own efforts at semiconductor production in the early 1960s, its executives justified the purchase of Rheem Semiconductor in Palo Alto—the first Fairchild spin-off—by the need to "establish a base in the important West Coast in order to share in its expanding equipment manufacturer's market."[43]

Military and aerospace markets accounted for a diminishing share of the semiconductor business as the growth of the computer industry fueled demand for transistors and integrated circuits. Government purchases, which had accounted for half of total semiconductor shipments during the 1960s, dropped to only 12 percent in 1972, and continued to fall throughout the decade. Silicon Valley, never as dependent on defense markets as Route 128, thus managed to achieve a gradual transition to commercial production during the 1960s and 1970s.[44]

Venture capital replaced the military as the leading source of financing for Silicon Valley start-ups by the early 1970s. Independent investors, encouraged by the favorable tax treatment of investments in small businesses, established SBICs and partnerships in California during the 1950s and 1960s. The growth of the venture capital business mirrored that of the local semiconductor industry, as successful entrepreneurs chose to reinvest their earnings in promising new companies. By 1974 the region was home to more than 150 active venture capitalists. Stanford University—in marked contrast to MIT—also regularly invested a portion of its endowment in venture activities.

In three decades the Santa Clara Valley had transformed itself into a dynamic technology complex, on a par with the older electronics capital in Massachusetts. A combination of university research, military spending, and entrepreneurial risk-taking stimulated a self-reinforcing dynamic of localized industrial development. By 1975 the region's technology enterprises employed well over 100,000 workers, and Silicon Valley's agglomeration of engineers, electronics firms, specialist consultants, venture capitalists, and supplier infrastructure was paralleled only by that of its East Coast counterpart. The two regions were widely recognized as the nation's leading centers of electronics innovation and production, with Route 128 specializing in minicomputers and Silicon Valley in commercial semiconductors.

Despite these similarities, the two regions were already developing along divergent trajectories. Silicon Valley's lack of a prior industrial history and its distance from established economic and political institutions facilitated experimentation with novel and productive relationships. In his efforts to transfer the model of a technological community from Massachusetts to California, Frederick Terman promoted more open and reciprocal ties between Stanford and local industry than existed in the Route 128 region. This was just the tip of the iceberg. Although the process was rarely conscious, the producers in the West were creating an industrial system that operated very differently from the older one on the East Coast.

SILICON VALLEY:
COMPETITION AND COMMUNITY

Corporations in the East adopted a feudal approach to organization . . . There were kings and lords, and there were vassals, soldiers, yeomen, and serfs, with layers of protocol and perquisites, such as the car and driver, to symbolize superiority and establish the boundary lines . . . Noyce . . . rejected the idea of a social hierarchy at Fairchild . . . Everywhere the Fairchild emigres went, they took the Noyce approach with them. It wasn't enough to start up a company; you had to start a community, a community in which there were no social distinctions, and it was first come, first served in the parking lot, and everyone was supposed to internalize the common goals. The atmosphere of the new companies was so democratic, it startled businessmen from the East.

—Tom Wolfe

▶ Silicon Valley and Route 128 quickly came to be viewed as industrial counterparts, comparable centers of electronics entrepreneurship and innovation located on opposite coasts. There were the often-noted superficial differences: Easterners wore jackets and ties and Californians preferred jeans and T-shirts. But if these contrasts made for colorful journalism, scholars and policymakers regarded them as minor distinctions between otherwise comparable industrial agglomerations. The rapid growth and technological dynamism of the two regions appeared to vindicate Frederick Terman's efforts to transfer to the West Coast the lessons of Boston's technology region.

But the differences between these economies ran deeper than variations of style and attire. While Silicon Valley and Route 128 companies advanced similar technologies and competed in similar markets, the organization of production in the two regions diverged from the earliest days. Initial differences in social structures and industrial practices laid the foundation for the creation of two distinct industrial systems.

From the outset Silicon Valley's pioneers saw themselves as outsiders to the industrial traditions of the East. The geography of the region, too, encouraged the development of a distinctive industrial pattern. Companies initially located near Stanford and its industrial park in Palo Alto, but quickly spread to the cities to the south—Mountain View, Sunnyvale, Santa Clara, and eventually San Jose. The natural boundaries of the peninsula, a relatively narrow stretch of land hemmed in by the San Francisco Bay to the east and the foothills of the Santa Cruz mountains to the west, ensured a density of development that minimized physical distances between companies and facilitated intensive informal communications.[1]

Drawn together by the challenge of geographic and technological frontiers, the pioneers created a technical culture that transcended firm and function. They developed less formal social relationships and collaborative traditions that supported experimentation. They created firms that were organized as loosely linked confederations of engineering teams. Without intending to do so, Silicon Valley's engineers and entrepreneurs were creating a more flexible industrial system, one organized around the region and its professional and technical networks rather than around the individual firm.

A TECHNICAL COMMUNITY

The early entrepreneurs of Silicon Valley saw themselves as the pioneers of a new industry in a new region. They were at once forging a new industrial settlement in the West and advancing the development of a revolutionary new technology, semiconductor electronics. The shared challenges of exploring uncharted technological terrain shaped their view of themselves and of their emerging community.

This collective identity was strengthened by the homogeneity of Silicon Valley's founders. Virtually all were white men; most were in their early twenties. Many had studied engineering at Stanford or MIT, and most had no industrial experience. None had roots in the region; a surprising number of the community's major figures had grown up in small towns in the Midwest and shared a distrust for established East Coast institutions and attitudes.[2] They repeatedly expressed their opposition to "established" or "old-line" industry and the "Eastern establishment."

As newcomers to a region that lacked prior industrial traditions, Silicon Valley's pioneers had the freedom to experiment with institutions and organizational forms as well as with technology. Having left behind families, friends, and established communities, these young men were unusually open to risk-taking and experimentation.

The experience of working at the Fairchild Semiconductor Corporation also served as a powerful bond for many of the region's early semiconductor engineers. During the 1960s it seemed as if every engineer in Silicon Valley had worked there: fewer than two dozen of the four hundred men present at a 1969 semiconductor industry conference held in Sunnyvale had never worked for Fairchild. Many of the region's entrepreneurs and managers still speak of Fairchild as an important managerial training ground and applaud the education they got at "Fairchild University." Similar shared professional experiences continued to reinforce the sense of community in the region even after individuals had moved on to different, often competing, firms.[3]

To this day, a poster of the Fairchild family tree, showing the corporate genealogy of the scores of Fairchild spin-offs, hangs on the walls of many Silicon Valley firms. This picture has come to symbolize the complex mix of social solidarity and individualistic competition that emerged in the Valley. The tree traces the common ancestry of the region's semiconductor industry and reminds engineers of the personal ties that enabled people, technology, and money to recombine rapidly into new ventures. The importance of these overlapping, quasi-familial ties is reflected in continuing references, more than three decades later, to the "fathers" (or "grandfathers") of Silicon Valley and their offspring, the "Fairchildren."[4]

At the same time, the family tree glorifies the entrepreneurial risk-taking and competitive individualism that distinguish the region's business culture. Silicon Valley's heroes are the successful entrepreneurs who have taken aggressive professional and technical risks: the garage tinkerers who created successful companies. These entrepreneurial heroes are celebrated for their technical achievements and for the often considerable wealth that success has brought them.[5]

One of the earliest observers of the Palo Alto semiconductor industry, the journalist Don Hoefler, was amazed by the juxtaposition of competitive rivalries and quasi-familial loyalty that distinguished the area. His series of articles in *Electronic News* in 1971 coined the term "Silicon Valley" and offered an early description of the emerging industrial community: "This common ancestry makes the semiconductor community there a tightly knit group. Wherever they go, ex-Fairchilders retain an awesome respect and emotional attachment to their Alma Mater.

The wives all know each other and remain on the friendliest terms. The men eat at the same restaurants; drink at the same bars, and go to the same parties. Despite their fierce competition during business hours, away from the office they remain the greatest friends."[6]

The habits of informal cooperation among Silicon Valley engineers predate the semiconductor industry. Just as Terman's support of his engineering students far exceeded the traditional limits of professorial encouragement, former engineering students extended assistance to other firms in the region, providing new entrepreneurs with encouragement, advice, computer time, space, and even financing. A San Jose journalist later noted that "As their company grew, both Hewlett and Packard became very involved in the formation and growth of other companies. They encouraged entrepreneurs, went out of their way to share what they learned, and were instrumental in getting electronics companies to work together on common problems . . . Largely because of them, there's an unusual spirit of cooperation in the local electronics industry."[7]

A *Fortune* magazine writer who visited Silicon Valley in the early 1970s described the "technological community" he found there in similar terms: "A surprising degree of cooperation among companies, almost Japanese in its closeness, has added further impetus to Santa Clara's ascendancy. It begins on a personal level. Transplanted Easterners are sometimes startled by the openness and lack of abrasiveness in relationships among people in the Far West." He went on to attribute this openness to the shared educational backgrounds and experiences of local entrepreneurs and to the geography of the area:

> Many of the executives in the area got to know each other as students at Stanford or as participants in local business and political affairs. The relatively close proximity of companies makes associations easier . . . That kind of a close-knit community where a meeting affecting, say, the semiconductor industry brings out company presidents by the dozens was unlikely to arise in sprawling Los Angeles or in the Boston area, where companies are widely scattered.[8]

The informal socializing that grew out of these quasi-familial relationships supported the ubiquitous practices of collaboration and sharing of information among local producers. The Wagon Wheel bar in Mountain View, a popular watering hole where engineers met to exchange ideas and gossip, has been termed "the fountainhead of the semiconductor industry."[9] As Tom Wolfe described it:

Every year there was some place, the Wagon Wheel, Chez Yvonne, Rickey's, the Roundhouse, where members of this esoteric fraternity, the young men and women of the semiconductor industry, would head after work to have a drink and gossip and brag and trade war stories about phase jitters, phantom circuits, bubble memories, pulse trains, bounceless contacts, burst modes, leapfrog tests, p-n junctions, sleeping sickness modes, slow-death episodes, RAMs, NAKs, MOSes, PCMs, PROMs, PROM blowers, PROM blasters, and teramagnitudes, meaning multiples of a million millions.[10]

By all accounts, these informal conversations were pervasive and served as an important source of up-to-date information about competitors, customers, markets, and technologies. Entrepreneurs came to see social relationships and even gossip as a crucial aspect of their businesses. In an industry characterized by rapid technological change and intense competition, such informal communication was often of more value than more conventional but less timely forums such as industry journals.

Information exchange continued on the job. Competitors consulted one another on technical matters with a frequency unheard of in other areas of the country. According to one executive: "I have people call me quite frequently and say, 'Hey, did you ever run into this one?' and you say 'Yeah, seven or eight years ago. Why don't you try this, that or the other thing?' We all get calls like that." The president of the Western Electronics Manufacturers Association (WEMA) compared the openness of Silicon Valley to the East: "Easterners tell me that people there don't talk to their competitors. Here they will not only sit down with you, but they will share the problems and experiences they have had." According to an experienced semiconductor executive: "This is a culture in which people talk to their competitors. If I had a problem in a certain area, I felt no hesitation to call another CEO and ask about the problem—even if I didn't know him. It was overwhelmingly likely that he'd answer (my question)."[11]

Another veteran executive stressed the importance of personal ties: "Local engineers recognize that the quality of the feedback and information obtained through their networks depends upon the credibility and trustworthiness of the information provider. This sort of quality is only assured with individuals with whom you share common backgrounds and work experiences."[12]

A variety of more and less formal gatherings—from trade association meetings and industry conferences to trade shows and hobbyists' clubs—also served as specialized forums for information exchange. One local executive notes: "There are people gathered together . . . to discuss every area of common scientific interest in the Valley. Around every technological subject, or every engineering concern, you have meeting groups that tend to foster new ideas and innovate. People rub shoulders and share ideas."[13]

The Homebrew Computer Club, for example, was founded in 1975 by a group of local microcomputer enthusiasts who had been shaped by the counterculture ethic of the sixties. They placed a notice on bulletin boards inviting those interested in computers to "come to a gathering of people with like-minded interests. Exchange information, swap ideas, help work on a project, whatever." Within months, the club's membership had reached some five hundred regular members, mostly young hackers, computer users who came to meetings to trade, sell, or give away computer hardware and software and to get advice. The club became the center of an informal network of microcomputer experts in the region, which survived even after the group itself folded. Eventually more than twenty computer companies, including Apple Computer, were started by Homebrew members.[14]

The region's social and professional networks were not simply conduits for the dissemination of technical and market information. They also functioned as efficient job search networks. Gathering places like the Wagon Wheel served as informal recruiting centers as well as listening posts; job information flowed freely along with shop talk. As one engineer reported: "In this business there's really a network. You just don't hire people out of the blue. In general, it's people you know, or you know someone who knows them."[15]

Such labor market information was essential in Silicon Valley, where engineers shifted between firms so frequently that mobility not only was socially acceptable, it became the norm. The preferred career option in Silicon Valley was to join a small company or a start-up, rather than an established company. The superiority of small, innovative firms over large corporations became an article of faith among many of the region's engineers.

Silicon Valley was quickly distinguished by unusually high levels of job-hopping. During the 1970s, average annual employee turnover exceeded 35 percent in local electronics firms and was as high as 59 percent in small firms. It was rare for a technical professional in Silicon Valley to have a career in a single company. An anthropologist studying the career paths of the region's computer professionals concluded that job tenures in Silicon Valley averaged two years. One engineer explained: "Two or three years is about max (at a job) for the Valley because there's always something more interesting across the street. You don't see someone staying twenty years at a job here. If they've been in a small company with 200 to 300 people for 10 or 11 years you tend to wonder about them. We see those types coming in from the East Coast."[16]

In the words of an engineer who was leaving the computer firm he had started to help launch a new disk drive venture: "Three years is enough at one place. I accomplished everything I set out to do there. My old company is profitable. If I stayed it would become a job, sort of like maintenance. Here there are new challenges." Or another engineer: "A man who has not changed companies is anxious to explain why; a man who has (changed companies) perhaps several times, feels no need to justify his actions. Mobility has become the norm."[17]

These high rates of mobility forced technology companies to compete intensely for experienced engineering talent. Headhunters became common in Silicon Valley during the 1970s, and firms began to offer incentives such as generous signing bonuses, stock options, high salaries, and interesting projects to attract top people. Early efforts to take legal action against departed employees proved inconclusive or protracted, and most firms came to accept high turnover as a cost of business in the region. In fact, employees often left for new opportunities with the blessings of top management, and the understanding that if it didn't work out, they could return.[18]

The geographic proximity of the region's firms facilitated occupational mobility. Moving from job to job in Silicon Valley was not as disruptive of personal, social, or professional ties as it could be elsewhere in the country. According to one engineer:

> If you left Texas Instruments for another job, it was a major psychological move, all the way to one coast or the other, or at least as far as Phoenix. Out here, it wasn't that big a catastrophe to quit your job on Friday and have another job on Monday and this was just as true for company executives. You didn't necessarily even have to tell your wife. You just drove off in another direction on Monday morning. You didn't have to sell your house, and your kids didn't have to change schools.

As another local executive put it, "People change jobs out here without changing car pools." Ironically, many Silicon Valley "job-hoppers" may well have led more stable lives than the upwardly mobile "organization men" of the 1950s who were transferred from place to place by the same employer.[19]

As individuals moved from firm to firm in Silicon Valley, their paths overlapped repeatedly: a colleague might become a customer or a competitor; today's boss could be tomorrow's subordinate. These relationships transcended sectoral and occupational boundaries. Individuals moved both within and between industry sectors: from semiconductors to personal computers or from semiconductor equipment to software. They moved from established firms to start-ups, and vice versa. And they moved from electronics producers to service providers such as venture capital or consulting firms—and back again. In the words of the anthropologist Kathleen Gregory: "Negotiating a career in Silicon Valley is best viewed as an intricate free form dance between employees and employers that rewards continuous monitoring, but cannot be fully choreographed. Careers in computing do not take place by design, but are emergent and negotiated between ever changing individuals and employers."[20]

Professional loyalties and friendships generally survived the turmoil. In fact, this continual shuffling and reshuffling tended to reinforce the value of personal relationships and networks. Few presumed that the long-term relationships needed for professional success would be found within the four walls of any particular company. Many came to rely on trade shows, technical conferences, and informal social gatherings to maintain and extend their professional networks.[21]

As a result, Silicon Valley's engineers developed stronger commitments to one another and to the cause of advancing technology than to individual companies or industries. According to a semiconductor executive who has worked in the region for three decades: "Here in Silicon Valley there's far greater loyalty to one's craft than to one's company. A company is just a vehicle which allows you to work. If you're a circuit designer it's most important for you to do excellent work. If you can't in one firm, you'll move on to another one." Another executive who worked on Boston's Route 128 before coming to Silicon Valley describes these personal networks: "The network in Silicon Valley transcends company loyalties. We treat people fairly and they are loyal to us, but there is an even higher level of loyalty—to their network. I have senior engineers who are constantly on the phone and sharing information with our competitors. I know what my competitors say in their speeches and they know what I say in private conversations." Or in the words of Wilf Corrigan, founder of LSI Logic: "There are a lot of people who come to work in the morning believing that they work for Silicon Valley."[22]

This decentralized and fluid environment accelerated the diffusion of technological capabilities and know-how within the region. Departing employees were typically required to sign nondisclosure statements that prevented them from revealing company secrets; however, much of the useful knowledge in the industry grew out of the experience of developing technology. When engineers moved between companies, they took with them the knowledge, skills, and experience acquired at their previous jobs.

This localized accumulation of technical knowledge enhanced the viability of Silicon Valley start-ups and reinforced a shared technical culture.[23] One engineer claims that a distinct language evolved in the region and that many of the technical terms used by semiconductor production engineers in Silicon Valley would not be understood by their counterparts in the East: "The language of East Coast silicon is not the same as that of the West Coast. If I say that I'm doing CMOS n angstroms, everybody in the West will understand what I mean. In the East they'll mean something different. There is a community here, with a shared language and shared meanings."[24]

By the early 1970s Silicon Valley was distinguished by the speed with which technical skill and know-how diffused within a localized industrial community. The region's social and professional networks operated as a kind of meta-organization through which engineers, in shifting combinations, organized technological advance. Individuals moved between firms and projects without the alienation that might be expected with such a high degree of mobility because these relationships remained intact. In Silicon Valley, the region and its networks, rather than individual firms, became the locus of economic activity.

COOPERATION AND COMPETITION

The technological and financial opportunities offered in Silicon Valley proved irresistible to many local engineers. New generations of successful role models—such as Intel's Robert Noyce and, later, Apple's Steven Jobs—legitimized the risks and rewards of entrepreneurship.[25] As a result, the pace of formation of new firms accelerated dramatically during the 1960s and 1970s. The successive generations of semiconductor start-ups depicted by the Fairchild family tree were repeated in sectors ranging from computers and software to disk drives and networking equipment.[26]

The many examples of engineers with humble origins who became millionaires by starting successful companies simply had no parallel in the more stable social structures of the East. Jerry Sanders, founder of Advanced Micro Devices, was an extreme example. Sanders grew up in south Chicago, the son of a traffic light repairman. By the time he was fifty years old, Sanders counted two Rolls Royces among his seven cars, maintained a mansion in Bel-Air, a beach house in Malibu, and an apartment in San Francisco, and boasted a celebrity-like affinity for diamond jewelry.[27] Few were as extravagant as Sanders, but Silicon Valley's newly made millionaires did not hide their wealth: they drove expensive imported cars, built custom homes in exclusive neighborhoods, and flew private airplanes.

Although many Silicon Valley entrepreneurs became millionaires, most appear to have been motivated less by money than by the challenge of independently pursuing a new technological opportunity. The culture of the Valley accorded the highest regard to those who started firms; status was defined less by economic success than by technological achievement. The elegantly designed chip, the breakthrough manufacturing process, or the ingenious application was admired as much as the trappings of wealth—and the emerging electronics industry offered manifold opportunities for such accomplishments.

The region's culture encouraged risk and accepted failure. An entrepreneur who moved to Silicon Valley from Route 128 to start a computer company describes this culture: "Start-ups here tend to move very fast. The culture of the Valley is a culture of change: the peer pressures and social pressures support risk-taking and people changing jobs a lot. The velocity of information is very high—much higher than the rest of the country. Rapid change is the norm. That's exactly what's needed for start-ups." The founder of a semiconductor equipment and fabrication consulting business based in Silicon Valley reports that it took him only six days to finance his company. This was possible in part because of professional networks that extended back to his days at Fairchild, and in part because of the willingness of the region's venture capitalists to move very rapidly on promising opportunities.[28]

Not only was risk-taking glorified, but failure was socially acceptable.

There was a shared understanding that anyone could be a successful entrepreneur: there were no boundaries of age, status, or social stratum that precluded the possibility of a new beginning; and there was little embarrassment or shame associated with business failure.[29] In fact, the list of individuals who failed, even repeatedly, only to succeed later, was well known within the region.

New ventures were typically started by engineers who had acquired operating experience and technical skills working in other firms in the region. The archetypical Silicon Valley start-up was formed by a group of friends and/or former colleagues with an innovative idea that they could not realize in their current workplace. They drew up a business plan, sought funding and advice from local venture capitalists (often former engineers and entrepreneurs themselves), and relied on an expanding circle of university researchers, consultants, and specialized suppliers for additional assistance in starting the new enterprise.

The venture capital industry was the financial engine of this entrepreneurial process. Not only were venture capitalists a critical source of capital for many start-ups, they were also central actors in the region's social and professional networks. Contrary to popular belief, Silicon Valley's venture capital industry emerged out of the region's base of technology enterprises, not vice versa. As successful entrepreneurs like Fairchild's Eugene Kleiner and Don Valentine reinvested their capital in promising local start-ups, they created a new and different kind of financial institution.

Venture capitalists brought technical skill, operating experience, and networks of industry contacts—as well as cash—to the ventures they funded. Silicon Valley's venture capitalists become unusually involved with their ventures, advising entrepreneurs on business plans and strategies, helping find co-investors, recruiting key managers, and serving on boards of directors. A Stanford finance professor and former Wall Street executive characterized the difference between local venture capitalists and traditional investors: "In New York, the money is generally managed by professional or financial promoter types. Out here, the venture capitalists tend to be entrepreneurs who created and built a company and then sold out. When problems occur with any of their investments, they can step into the business and help out."[30]

Geographic proximity helped build and sustain these relationships. The office complex at 3000 Sand Hill Road in Menlo Park, just a few miles from Stanford University, became the de facto headquarters for venture capital activity on the West Coast. Because most enterprises that sought venture funding were supported by two or more investors, venture capitalists met frequently to exchange information on potential deals and to collaborate in the formation of new enterprises. As in the relations between the firms they funded, however, cooperation among Silicon Valley's venture capital community was always tempered by the reality of intense competition. In the words of Tom Perkins, a leading venture capitalist and a former Hewlett-Packard executive: "you can't really call us a cabal because sometimes we work together and sometimes we compete."[31]

An expanding network of specialist suppliers and service providers also facilitated the start-up process. The semiconductor equipment and materials industry flourished in the 1970s as engineers left established semiconductor companies to start firms that manufactured capital goods such as diffusion ovens, step-and-repeat cameras, and testers, and materials and components such as photomasks, testing jigs, and specialized chemicals. The structure of the semiconductor equipment manufacturing industry soon mirrored that of the merchant semiconductor industry. Like their customers, these firms tended to be highly competitive and innovative small enterprises. This independent equipment sector promoted the continuing formation of semiconductor firms by freeing individual producers from the expense of developing capital equipment internally and by spreading the costs of development. It also reinforced the tendency toward industrial localization, as most of these specialized inputs were not available elsewhere in the country.

A similar process occurred a decade later as independent suppliers of disk equipment and materials grew up alongside the region's flourishing disk drive industry. In addition, hundreds of small design firms, contract manufacturers, metalworking shops, software developers, and prototyping operations made their homes in Silicon Valley to serve its electronics producers.

This localized technical infrastructure allowed the region's start-ups to focus on specific areas of expertise, without the burden of manufacturing every part of a product or performing every organizational function. As Robert Noyce put it: "In spite of press to the contrary, we are going to less and less vertical integration. In contrast to the situation of 25 years ago, all electronics companies now do not feel that they must make their own semiconductor devices; nor do all semiconductor companies feel they must grow single crystals, make their own masks, build their own furnaces, assembly equipment, or test equipment."[32]

Service providers specializing in the problems of technology industry—lawyers, market research firms, consulting companies, public relations companies, and electronics distributors—played a similar role in Silicon Valley. Like the venture capitalists, the region's professional service firms were often run by individuals with experience in local technology industry. They served as valuable intermediaries and offered expertise that could not be found elsewhere. Dataquest, a market research firm founded in 1971, for example, brought business leaders together for regular conferences and informal meetings. Because they attracted a broad cross-section of the Silicon Valley business community, Dataquest meetings offered business contacts and information about competitors as well as market information. The public relations and marketing firm Regis McKenna, Inc., also counted many leading Silicon Valley firms as its clients, and held frequent seminars, open houses, and receptions. These events were designed to bring local managers, analysts, and media and university representatives together to promote "matchmaking and deal making" between different parts of the industrial community and to provide a forum for the discussion of trends in the region and in the technology industry.

The region's leading law firms similarly specialized in areas that were important to technology firms, such as intellectual property, licensing, incorporation of start-ups, and trade law. Like the market research and venture capital firms, Silicon Valley lawyers frequently brokered business connections as well. According to one study of the Silicon Valley legal community: "It may well be that one of their most important contributions has come from the fact that they know all the venture capitalists personally and could set up lunches with them for their scientist and engineer clients." The study concluded that the style of law practiced in the region was "informal, practical, result-oriented, flexible and innovative, keyed to high-trust business relationships— that matches the business culture of Silicon Valley." This is not to suggest that lawsuits were absent in Silicon Valley, only that the region was far less litigious than other parts of the country.[33]

Educational institutions were also critical to Silicon Valley's burgeoning technical infrastructure. By increasing enrollment in its Honors Cooperative Program, for example, Stanford offered an important advantage to small companies that sought to attract top talent but were unable to provide the continuing education and training needed in a fast-changing technological environment. Stanford's Industrial Affiliates program promoted research collaboration between individual faculty, departments, and outside companies, further expanding the university's role in the region.

The University of California at Berkeley, located thirty miles north of Stanford, also became an important technological resource for Silicon Valley industry during the 1960s and 1970s. While its engineering programs were small in the 1950s, Berkeley rapidly expanded its master's and doctoral programs in electrical engineering. By the mid-1970s, it was training almost as many electrical engineers as Stanford and MIT, which meant that the two West Coast universities together were granting close to twice as many doctoral degrees as MIT annually.[34] In addition to dramatically increasing the supply of state-of-the-art engineers in the Bay Area, Berkeley became an important center of research in the fields of semiconductors and computer science. The presence of two world-class scientific and engineering research universities that were actively involved in Silicon Valley industry created a technological milieu unparalleled elsewhere in the nation.

The California state university and community college systems were also important—but often overlooked—elements in Silicon Valley's technical infrastructure. By the 1970s San Jose State University trained as many engineers as either Stanford or Berkeley and the region's six community colleges offered technical programs that were among the best in the nation. Foothill College in Los Altos Hills, for example, offered the nation's first two-year A.S. degree in semiconductor processing, and the mandate of Mission Community College in Santa Clara was to coordinate programs with the neighboring electronics complex. De Anza College in Cupertino similarly became known for its extensive electronics training programs and links with local firms.[35]

The community colleges were particularly responsive to the needs of local business: they contracted with local companies to teach private courses for their employees, even holding courses at company plants to enable employees to attend after hours. Local technology firms in turn provided consultants to develop the electronics curricula as well as large numbers of part-time and moonlighting teachers. Many firms also contributed equipment to local schools, while some allowed community college students to use their equipment during the evenings. When Tandem Computers donated more than $1 million in computer equipment to Foothill College, for example, the school was able to triple the number of students in its computer courses to more than five thousand.

A sign of the importance of this localized industrial infrastructure was the growing number of research labs or branch plants of national technology firms in the region. In a keynote address to the International Solid State Circuits Conference in 1978, industry veteran Ian MacKintosh explained: "It is abundantly clear that the existence of Silicon Valley confers important advantages on the IC companies that operate within it, particularly in regard to the high (but informal) level of localized communication and debate, and to the availability of the strong common services industry which has developed in the area."[36] As more firms located in the region they further enhanced the environment for start-ups by expanding the skilled labor pool, the capacity of shared services, and the intensity of localized communications and debate.

The industrial structure that emerged in this environment was highly fragmented. Silicon Valley's start-ups exploited the apparently limitless opportunities offered by electronics technology to differentiate their products, processes, and applications. Products and services became increasingly specialized as each firm sought to define and dominate a particular niche of a broader industry. By the late 1950s, for example, the region was already populated by more than 100 high technology establishments, most with a distinctive market or technical focus. Horizontal specialization thus accompanied vertical specialization in the region's semiconductor industry, breeding a continuing process of industrial diversification.[37]

As this process of industrial specialization and fragmentation repeated itself, the region developed a diverse and adaptable industrial ecology. The difficulties of any single firm could no longer destabilize an entire industry; the failure of an industry could no longer threaten the entire region. Noyce compared this phenomenon to the principles of chip design: "Redundancy is the most effective method of assuring the reliability of the system, or the yield of a device. If there are many potential paths from sand to useful electronic equipment, the failure of one segment of one path can be compensated for by increased traffic on the others. In the same way, a bridge out on the highway is not necessarily a block to reaching the final objective if there are other, parallel roads."[38]

The richness and complexity of the industrial system that resulted are difficult to describe. By the end of the 1970s Silicon Valley was populated by close to three thousand electronics manufacturing firms, including producers of semiconductors, computer systems, software, peripherals, capital equipment, test and measurement instruments, telecommunications equipment, medical electronics, and military and aerospace equipment; and a variety of prototyping operations, metal-forming companies, machine shops, and contract manufacturers. The vast majority of these firms were small: 70 percent had fewer than 10 employees and 85 percent had fewer than 100.[39] And there were at least as many nonmanufacturing firms, including research and development labs, product-design houses, headhunting firms, venture capitalists, market researchers, consultants, and a wide range of related support services.

In Silicon Valley industrial fragmentation did not lead to competitive vulnerability or economic weakness. In fact, it appears to have contributed to the flexibility and resilience of the industrial fabric. While the region's small, specialized firms might, in theory, have generated mutually destructive forms of competition or been unable to undertake complex or long-term investments, Silicon Valley's supportive social structures, institutions, and collaborative practices provided a framework for mutual learning and adjustment. Thus, while competitive rivalries spurred technological advance among local producers, the regional economy was far from the simple free market of economic theory.

Silicon Valley's decentralized industrial system was integrated in part by a variety of informal and formal cooperative practices and institutions. Many of these cooperative practices were simply attempts to be neighborly. One semiconductor-executive-turned-venture-capitalist recalls that in the early days of the industry it was not uncommon for production engineers to call their friends at nearby competing firms for assistance when quartz tubes broke or they ran out of chemicals. Another executive describes how technicians in competing factories cooperated: "When the gas line stopped at 2 A.M., you just called your buddies at the company across the street and shared their gas. Or if the epi-reactor was down, your friend did your chips on his second shift and you helped him out the next week with his ion implants. This all happened without any legal paperwork." One of Silicon Valley's few women entrepreneurs, who was starting a software business and couldn't afford the big mainframes and minicomputers of the day, reports that friendly Hewlett-Packard executives allowed her team to work on the HP computers in the wee hours of the night. She recalls showing up at HP with sleeping bags.[40]

In other cases, cooperation was a carefully calculated business decision. Cooperation among Silicon Valley firms took many forms—from cross-licensing and second-sourcing arrangements to technology agreements and joint ventures. Semiconductor firms, following the model set by AT&T's Bell Labs with the transistor, liberally cross-licensed their patents to competitors during the industry's first three decades. This pooling of inventions and devices ensured that technical advances diffused quickly and the industry as a whole progressed, regardless of the fate of any individual firm. In Robert Noyce's words: "Without so doing [cross-licensing patents], no firm could be using the latest technology in all areas. One might be using epitaxy without diffusion, another oxide masking but not planar techniques, yet another making MOS transistors without the possibility of making integrated circuits."[41]

Second-source arrangements, in which producers ensured that alternative suppliers of their products existed, similarly spread technological capabilities within the region's industrial community. Second-sourcing was initially required by the Pentagon to ensure backup supply of critical military components, particularly from the small and often untried semiconductor firms in Silicon Valley. The practice continued even after the defense market declined because civilian customers also wanted a guarantee of a competitive source of components. Even more than cross-licensing, these second-source arrangements helped upgrade the capabilities of the region's engineering community. They required that competitors share not only technical specifications but also details of manufacturing processes with competing producers. Many ventures began in the 1960s and 1970s as second sources for other semiconductor firms and, with time, developed the skill to introduce products of their own.

Technology exchange agreements and joint ventures were also commonplace in Silicon Valley long before they became staples of American industry. Such arrangements were struck between firms participating in the same market, between suppliers and customers seeking a detailed understanding of one another's problems and needs, and between firms wishing to share financial risk. Some were short-lived and others more lasting, but all served to pool resources or capabilities and furthered the partners' efforts in new technology or new markets.

Imitation and reverse engineering (copying) of devices were also common, if less conventional, ways for firms to keep up with technical advances. While typically done without the original manufacturer's permission or cooperation, reverse engineering was pervasive during the early decades because the imitated company rarely had legal recourse. There were even firms in Silicon Valley that specialized in "documenting" products for clients considering imitation or reverse engineering.

These cooperative arrangements seem unusual in part because of the intensity of competition in Silicon Valley. Competitive rivalries were often highly personalized, since status was defined by technical excellence and innovation as much as by market share. The surpassing need to bring products or technologies to market ahead of competitors produced an unusually hard-driving work ethic. Intense peer pressure among an ambitious and talented professional community forced engineers to work extraordinarily long hours and contributed to high rates of drug use, divorce, and burnout in the region.[42]

Even under relentless competitive pressure, an underlying loyalty and shared commitment to technological excellence unified members of this industrial community. Local firms both competed for market share and technical leadership and simultaneously relied on the collaborative practices that distinguished the region. The paradox of Silicon Valley was that competition demanded continuous innovation, which in turn required cooperation among firms. Nothing was prized more than individual initiative and technological advance, and these depended on the information, technology, and experience that resided in the Valley's social and professional networks. Knowledge of the latest techniques in design, production, and marketing diffused rapidly among this community; the ease of recombining existing skill and know-how with new ideas and technologies ensured that firms in the region pursued a multiplicity of technological paths—many of which would have been bypassed under a more stable industrial regime.

Business associations played an important role in Silicon Valley's decentralized industrial system as well.[43] By the late 1970s Silicon Valley was feeling the effects of nearly four decades of explosive, unconstrained growth. Rapidly inflating housing prices, severely congested roadways, and environmental degradation threatened the activities of local manufacturers and aroused community groups to call for a halt to industrial expansion in the region. Caught between pressure from local governments and community activists to control growth on the one hand and shortages of skilled technical workers on the other, local business founded an umbrella association that could serve as the voice of industry in the region.

David Packard, chairman of Hewlett-Packard Corporation, led the formation of the Santa Clara County Manufacturing Group (SCCMG) because of his strong belief that the future of the electronics industry was directly related to the future of Silicon Valley.[44] The twenty-six founding members of the SCCMG included older electronics companies like IBM and HP, new firms like Intel, and nonelectronics companies and banks. Its stated aim was to work "side-by-side" with representatives of county government in solving social and political problems. Confronting the problems of rising housing prices and traffic congestion, for example, the SCCMG worked out accommodations with government and environmental groups that relied on voluntary targets and indicative plans. Member firms also committed financial resources and the time and expertise of its members to devise solutions to land use, transportation, and environmental problems. As a result of these initial successes, cooperation between industry and government became the model for local policymaking.

Industry associations such as the Western Electronics Manufacturers Association (WEMA, the forerunner of the American Electronics Association) and the Semiconductor Equipment and Materials Institute (SEMI) also helped integrate the region's decentralized industrial structure. When WEMA moved to Palo Alto in 1964, it explicitly identified with the region and its small technology firms. Unlike the older, Washington-based Electronic Industries Association, which focused its energies on lobbying for the large, established radio and consumer electronics companies, WEMA made a commitment to "be where the companies are" and to build a solid base in California before expanding elsewhere. The association quickly forged an identity among its West Coast membership that was distinct from the "old-line" electronics businesses of the East.[45]

WEMA focused on providing services to assist the management of small, emerging technology firms, rather than on lobbying for established corporations. It sponsored seminars and educational activities that encouraged the exchange of ideas and information, including management training sessions on subjects ranging from finance and technology marketing to production and export assistance. These sessions proved valuable to managers of many of the region's small and medium-sized firms, who typically had technical rather than managerial backgrounds.

WEMA, which became the American Electronics Association (AEA) in 1978, also strengthened the region's social and professional networks by hosting meetings for managers and CEOs. In the words of a local business journalist:

> Electronics companies are uniquely systems-oriented. Almost no firm manufactures from the ground up a stand-alone product. A company either draws on other people's components or makes products that fit with other people's products into a system. Friendships made through the AEA help the companies develop products that work together . . . Perhaps the AEA's most significant contribution to the electronics industry is what it did to foster networking. Most top executives of young, fast-growing electronics companies are relatively inexperienced in some important management areas. The AEA, with its frequent seminars and monthly meetings of company presidents, provides an excellent opportunity for those executives to meet and learn from their peers.[46]

This integrative role was confirmed by many Silicon Valley managers who reported finding customers or business partners at AEA functions, who saw the AEA as a source of market and technical information, or who simply valued the opportunity to stay in touch with friends and colleagues. When WEMA expanded outside California, its leaders recognized the importance of these networks and developed regional councils, which replicated the structure of the original Silicon Valley model.[47]

The Semiconductor Equipment and Materials Institute (SEMI) was founded in Silicon Valley in 1970 by three semiconductor equipment vendors who were dissatisfied with the lack of attention they were receiving at WESCON, the regional electronics trade show. Like WEMA, SEMI explicitly avoided the lobbying and pressure-group politics of traditional trade associations. Rather, it sponsored trade shows, coordinated standard-setting activities, and organized education and market research programs for the small firms in an industry that, even by Silicon Valley standards, was highly fragmented, technologically sophisticated, and fast changing.[48]

Many firms in the semiconductor equipment industry depended upon trade shows for survival, as they could not afford the cost of marketing to distant customers. The annual SEMICON trade show enabled them to exchange technical ideas, expand their range of professional contacts, and socialize with industry colleagues. These trade shows effectively compress social and professional networks in time and space and provide opportunities for informal exchange that formerly occurred only within and between large companies.

Technical standards are especially important in industries such as semiconductor equipment that are fragmented and technically complex. SEMI invested considerable effort in building consensus among its members concerning industry technical standards. In 1973, for example, approximately 2,000 specifications for silicon wafers were in use by scores of U.S. silicon vendors, and the wafers were manufactured in a variety of different shapes. This lack of uniformity created problems of waste, inventory, and planning for vendors and customers alike. Despite the initial opposition of semiconductor manufacturers, a SEMI standards committee defined and publicized specifications for emerging three-inch wafer lines. By 1975, more than 80 percent of all new wafers met SEMI specifications.

SEMI's standards-setting process involved the volunteer efforts of more than 3,000 industry professionals who defined specifications for virtually all materials, processes, and equipment used in semiconductor manufacturing. This process was coordinated by more than 100 international committees, subcommittees, and task forces meeting more than 200 times a year. It culminated in the annual publication of a Book of Semiconductor Standards (BOSS) containing volumes on chemicals, equipment automation, materials, micropatterning, and packaging.

SEMI's efforts validated the importance of standards to prevent duplication and waste. Their standards also allowed customers to choose among competing sources of supply, rather than becoming dependent on a single vendor. In addition, many Silicon Valley engineers reported that the process of standard setting was as important as the standards themselves, because it helped build close understandings and working relationships between suppliers and end-users.

SEMI activities also included education and information programs. Volunteer committees of SEMI members organized technical symposia, dinner meetings, information seminars, and conferences to inform members of research and technological advances; to promote interchange between SEMI members, customers, capital providers, and engineering faculty; and to provide market forecasts for various segments of the industry. In short, SEMI, like WEMA, offered a range of services that allowed small firms to stay abreast of fast-changing technologies and markets and to continually refresh their networks.

THE "HP WAY"

While the engineers and professionals of Silicon Valley were creating an industrial community that blurred the boundaries between firms, they were also eliminating the traditional boundaries between employers and employees and between corporate functions within the firm. In their place, they were creating interdependent confederations of project teams that were linked by intense, informal communications and that mirrored the region's decentralized industrial structure.

In an environment that lacked indigenous industrial traditions and experienced managers, Silicon Valley's pioneers explicitly sought to avoid the hierarchical structures of East Coast companies. Long before it was fashionable, William Hewlett and David Packard, and later Intel's Robert Noyce, pioneered management styles based on teamwork, openness, and participation. Even as their firms grew large, they strove to preserve the openness, intensity, and sense of purpose that had characterized working life in early Silicon Valley start-ups. This management style, which was characterized by trust in individual motivation, a high degree of professional autonomy, and generous employee benefits, came to be known as the HP Way. As a Harvard Business School case describes the HP Way: "It includes a participative management style that supports, even demands, individual freedom and initiative while emphasizing commonness of purpose and teamwork . . . According to this style, the company provides employees direction in the form of well-defined negotiated goals, shared data, and the support of necessary resources. Yet employees are expected to create their own ways of contributing to the company's success."[49]

Hewlett and Packard themselves played a central role in creating this corporate culture. They remained deeply involved in the day-to-day operations of their company, even as it grew large. They made a point of striking up informal lunch and hallway conversations with employees at all levels, and they encouraged managers to "wander around," spending part of each day initiating unplanned discussions. An HP salesman who later helped found 3Com recalled: "On my first day at HP in 1967, I met Bill Hewlett in the lunchroom. After lunch, he invited me up to meet the engineers working on desktop computers and calculators. He became my mentor, and I learned early on about 'management by wandering around.'"[50]

The physical setting at HP also encouraged informal communications:

company facilities were designed to be easily accessible to teams solving problems together. As an HP executive described it: "We aren't really sure what structure is best. All we know for certain is that we start with a remarkably high degree of internal communication, which is the key. We have to preserve that at all costs."[51]

By institutionalizing the notion that good ideas could come from anywhere, Hewlett and Packard also pioneered a decentralized organizational structure that represented an important departure from traditional corporate organization. In an effort to preserve the flexibility and responsiveness of start-ups, they established product divisions as semi-autonomous business units. Each of the original instrument market segments was managed as a self-sustaining division with full responsibility for product development, engineering, manufacturing, marketing, and personnel. As one of these quasi-independent businesses got too big, it would be broken down into smaller units. This structure not only increased the organization's attention to markets and responsiveness to customers, it also greatly reduced the decisionmaking authority of senior management. In place of the centralization that characterized the traditional hierarchical American corporation, HP created a corporate office that provided strategic vision and shared administrative infrastructure for the firm and did so in collaboration with the business units.

HP also eliminated most traditional corporate symbols of hierarchy and status, including private offices, reserved parking spaces, and differentiated attire and office furniture—replacing them with symbols of teamwork and California living. All employees were given the same profit sharing and eligibility for stock options. The company sponsored a first-rate company cafeteria that was open to employees of all ranks, intramural sports teams, Friday beer busts, and a park for employees and their families in the Santa Cruz mountains.

The company's self-image was, not surprisingly, that of a family. Through the HP Way and "management by wandering around," HP management sought to build a humanistic culture that promoted creativity, initiative, and teamwork. While many of these innovations were symbolic, they contributed powerfully to a culture that was far more open and participatory than the traditional low-trust management that characterized virtually every major American corporation at that time.

Intel Corporation also came to be known within Silicon Valley for its attention to managing people as well as technology. Both companies were seen as models of good management and both were widely imitated, but HP was perceived as the more familial culture, while Intel came to be known as a hard-driving company that encouraged excellence through competitive achievement. One observer described the distinction between HP and Intel management styles as the difference between the ancient Greek cities of Athens and Sparta.[52]

Intel cofounders Robert Noyce, Andy Grove, and Gordon Moore brought a decade of management experience at Fairchild Semiconductor to their start-up. Noyce, who had been responsible for developing a management plan and philosophy at Fairchild, chose to recruit recent graduates of engineering schools rather than hire experienced managers. He often gave them responsibilities commonly held by people twice their age. He believed that if employees developed a passionate commitment to the firm's goals they would make appropriate decisions unencumbered by layers of management.

Noyce also insisted that all Intel engineers and office workers receive stock options in order to encourage them to identify with the firm and its vision. He worked hard to create a "corporate community" at Intel, one that avoided all manifestations of social hierarchy—from reserved parking spaces and executive suites to the executive dining room—and rules of dress (except the unwritten rule that dress should be modest) Work spaces were spartan, set in a big shed-like room. "Offices" were modular particle-board partitions that could easily be rearranged. Everyone, including the founders, worked from the same secondhand metal desks. Top managers met frequently with front-line employees to discuss ideas and resolve problems.

Differences between levels of management were also minimized at Intel, and individuals were given a degree of autonomy and responsibility unheard of in the East. Under Noyce and Moore, Intel was divided into autonomous "strategic business segments." Each segment was run like a separate company, giving managers at Intel more autonomy than executive vice presidents at most traditional corporations. Noyce believed that large organizations were naturally prone to inertia and, like management at HP, he sought to break the firm into smaller units with the flexibility and control of start-ups. In his words: "A small organization can turn on a dime and change direction. You suggest another way to do things and you can get it implemented in a week or two When you have 10,000 people to change the direction of, it just doesn't happen that way. What you do, or hope you can do, is to break the organization down into small manageable units so that you can change the direction of one unit at a time."[53]

A major purpose of these organizational structures was to facilitate the exchange of ideas and information. Openness and confrontation were encouraged at Intel. In the early days, Noyce and Moore had lunch every Thursday with a random group of employees. Employees were expected to "say whatever they think": a new engineer was expected to challenge Noyce or anybody else with differing ideas. Sparta was no place for the meek: Intel also developed a "we're the toughest" work attitude, which often included "voluntary" overtime (those who did not participate were considered "unpatriotic"), report-card-like performance ratings, and a publicly posted Late List, recording those who arrived after 8 A.M.

During the 1960s and 1970s, technology firms in Silicon Valley assimilated different aspects of the HP and Intel models. Some firms adopted no-layoff policies. Many provided generous stock options for all employees—the rank and file as well as top managers. According to one venture capitalist: "Stock is the mother's milk of Silicon Valley. It's important to give people equity here. If they don't have ownership in the company, it just doesn't work very well."[54]

In some cases, these efforts were primarily symbolic. Managers might extend stock options and other benefits to professional employees alone, neglecting the region's largely female and minority production workforces. Other firms paid minimum wages or demanded that employees perform tedious work under dangerous or unhealthy conditions. These firms became known as "sweatshops" and were characterized by little sense of community. Many eventually failed or left the area in search of low-cost labor.

More commonly, however, these efforts created a work environment that was less formal and centralized, and more open and egalitarian than traditional East Coast corporations. A recent study of the business culture of Silicon Valley confirms both the prevalence and distinctiveness of this new management model. Andre Delbecq and Joseph Weiss interviewed local electronics managers in the early 1980s and concluded that even as Silicon Valley firms grew larger, they preserved many of the informal and entrepreneurial qualities of start-ups.[55]

Their survey documents the highly intuitive and casual decisionmaking styles in Silicon Valley firms, the absence of concern with organization charts, procedures, or other formal mechanisms for control, the elimination of status barriers, and the general informality of workplace procedures, dress, and work styles. Delbecq and Weiss conclude that stock options enabling employees to share in the wealth created by important breakthroughs are far more prevalent in Silicon Valley than traditional pension plans. And they note the importance of the (often charismatic) entrepreneur in enabling a company to respond rapidly to markets and technologies.

Local executives described these distinctive organizational practices:

It's possible for a Bob Noyce and a Gordon Moore to walk around Intel in open shirts. John Sculley can wear a plaid shirt to work and walk among the crazies. Having visited most of the companies in this valley, I am always struck with the continuous interaction between senior executives and their people at all levels of the organization.

The most important communications that occur in our company are informal, the ad hoc meetings that occur when we walk around the plant. Structured meetings held between 2:30 and 3:30 P.M. on specific topics really are atypical.[56]

Some executives compared the Silicon Valley business culture with that of other places:

The communication patterns are clearly different in Silicon Valley. There is far more openness and much less worrying about whether someone goes around you. There's not only a tendency not to follow channels, there is a deliberate attempt to stimulate a wide variety of ideas. Innovations bubble up in unexpected places. Champions receive support from unexpected sponsors. People have less of a sense of an organization chart in Silicon Valley.

I think it's very difficult in some of the large East Coast companies to know what's happening. Communication is formal. There is so much staff work done before top managers see anything, so much report generation that you're not really involved intuitively in key decisions . . . There is an absolute desire to be highly informal on the West Coast. Individuals find it easy to communicate quickly. This informality allows us to share consensus and move rapidly.[57]

Managers also commented on the openness and fluidity of the business environment, which includes not only the mobility of people but even the impermanence of physical structures:

The mobility among people strikes me as radically different than the world I came from out East. There is far more mobility and there is far less real risk in people's careers. When someone is fired or leaves on the East Coast, it's a real trauma in their lives. If they are fired or leave here it doesn't mean very much. They just go off and do something else . . . the impermanence that you see in the walls of offices, the mobility of the physical ecology is (also) very different. One of the things that struck me when I came to Silicon Valley was the impermanence of all the facilities. The walls are all temporary because everyone knows that the configurations will be changed six months later. And my experience at Apple has been that everything does change in six month increments. The idea of permanent walls with windows and doors that was part of corporate America is not part of Silicon Valley.[58]

At its best, this business culture encouraged intense involvement and enthusiasm among the Silicon Valley workforce. The system rewarded performance rather than seniority. It ensured the diffusion of understanding and knowledge of both the firm and the industry among all levels of the workforce, from the lowest technicians to senior engineers. One engineer who moved from a semiconductor firm in the Boston area to Silicon Valley in the early 1960s described the sense of community within firms: "It was totally different out here . . . We were all treated well, and there was a sense that everyone knew what was going on and everyone could get a piece of the wealth through stock options. Our attitude was 'we're all in this together, so let's work hard and let's play hard.'"[59]

In Delbecq and Weiss's view, the critical unit of production in the region is not the firm but the loosely coupled engineering team, which they define as "a set of individuals with a strong sense of entrepreneurship, joined around a project mission associated with a technology-driven change, who remain in contact frequently and informally with multiple levels and functions within the company through intense informal communications."[60] This model of shifting and horizontally linked confederations of work teams describes not only life inside Silicon Valley companies but also the wider organization of the regional economy.

There is little doubt that this management model has contributed to the absence of labor unions in Silicon Valley's technology firms. There are approximately 200,000 union members in the four-county region, but virtually none work in high technology industries. No high technology firm has been organized by a labor union in Silicon Valley during the past twenty years, and there have been fewer than a dozen serious attempts.[61]

Most Silicon Valley entrepreneurs regard unions much as they view East Coast corporations—as relics of a dying industrial order which they are determined to transcend. The novelist Tom Wolfe describes how Robert Noyce's experience working for Fairchild Corporation in New York influenced his thoughts about these issues:

> Noyce disliked many things "back east" . . . there was no one back east who knew how to run a corporation in the United States in the second half of the twentieth century. Back east they had never progressed beyond 1940. Consequently they were still hobbled by all of the primitive stupidities of bureaucratism and labor-management battles. They didn't have the foggiest comprehension of the Silicon Valley corporate community.
>
> Labor-management battles were part of the ancient terrain of the East. If Intel were divided into workers and bosses, with the implication that each side had to squeeze its money out of the hides of the other, the enterprise would be finished. Motivation would no longer be internal; it would be objectified in the deadly form of work rules and grievance procedures.[62]

Traditional corporate hierarchies, with internal job ladders that defined predictable career paths, were far less prevalent or meaningful in Silicon Valley than elsewhere. These "ladders" were often reorganized before any individual could climb them. The centralized authority of senior management was frequently minimized as autonomous business units related to one another and to the center as peers; differences between workers and managers engaged in a shared technological project were likewise reduced.

Without fully recognizing the consequences, Silicon Valley's pioneers were creating the foundations of a decentralized industrial system that blurred the boundaries between social life and work, between firms, between firms and local institutions, and between managers and workers. This model, though hardly universal even in Silicon Valley, has influenced the organization and workplace practices in many other industries faced with rapid changes in markets and technology.

Paradoxically, however, while the region's engineers saw themselves as different from the rest of American business, they failed to recognize the importance of the networks they had created. Silicon Valley's entrepreneurs failed to recognize the connection between the institutions they had built and their commercial success. They saw themselves as the world did, as a new breed of technological pioneers, and they viewed their successes as independent of the region and its relationships.

What appeared to both the actors and the outside world to be the outcome of individual entrepreneurial achievement and competitive markets was in fact the result of a complex, highly social process rooted in an industrial community. While they competed fiercely, Silicon Valley's producers were embedded in, and inseparable from, these social and technical networks. Lacking a language to describe this unusual mix of cooperation and competition, they saw themselves through the lens of American individualism. They attributed their spectacular growth and unchallenged dominance of world markets to individual technical prowess and entrepreneurial risk-taking. Just as the vocabulary of rugged individualism, entrepreneurship, and free markets blinded Silicon Valley's engineers to the institutional and social underpinnings of their industrial strength, it also left them unable to ensure their own survival. Assuming that the dynamism of free markets would be self-perpetuating and self-governing, they saw no need to attend to the institutional foundations of their vitality. This lack of self-understanding would lead them to make choices that would threaten the long-term dynamism of the industrial region they had created.

3

ROUTE 128: INDEPENDENCE AND HIERARCHY

On the East Coast, everybody's family goes back generations. Roots and stability are far more important out here. If you fail in Silicon Valley, your family won't know and your neighbors won't care. Out here, everybody would be worried. It's hard to face your grandparents after you've failed.

—William Foster, Stratus Computer

▶ That electronics production would flourish along Route 128 was almost inevitable. Massachusetts boasted a long history of industrial innovation and an unparalleled concentration of capital, skill, and technology. In the 1950s, the region was home to several of the nation's leading semiconductor producers—well before William Shockley located his transistor company in Palo Alto. And during the 1960s and 1970s, dozens of established electronics producers located facilities on or near "America's Technology Highway" alongside a proliferation of start-ups with names like Unitrode, Teradyne, and Computervision.

As Silicon Valley's entrepreneurs created an industrial system based on the region and its social and technical networks, their counterparts along Boston's Route 128 inherited and reproduced an industrial order based on independent firms. Route 128's technology enterprises adopted the autarkic practices and structures of an earlier generation of East Coast businesses. Secrecy and territoriality ruled relations between individuals and firms, traditional hierarchies prevailed within firms, and relations with local institutions were distant—even antagonistic. The regional economy remained a collection of autonomous enterprises, lacking social or commercial interdependencies.

To be sure, some of the region's entrepreneurs rejected the practices of their industrial predecessors. MIT's early computer pioneers developed a "hacker" tradition that favored openness and free technical exchange, while several local companies, including the Digital Equipment Corporation (DEC), experimented with nonhierarchical organizations. However, the networking and collaborative practices that typified Silicon Valley never became part of the mainstream business culture of Route 128, and the region's new management models only partially departed from traditional corporate practices.

The geography of the two regions reflected and reinforced these divergent industrial systems. Technology companies in Massachusetts were scattered widely along the Route 128 corridor and increasingly along the outer band, Interstate Route 495, with miles of forest, lakes, and highway separating them. Unlike Silicon Valley, where firms clustered in close proximity to one another in a dense industrial concentration, the Route 128 region was so expansive that DEC began to use helicopters to link its widely dispersed facilities.

This independent firm–based industrial system offered the advantages of scale and stability, but it was slow to respond to changing markets and technologies. While the region was a hotbed of semiconductor activity in the 1950s—well before the industry took root in the West—Silicon Valley's network-based system quickly surpassed it. This early reversal in semiconductors reflected the differing adaptive capacity of the two industrial systems and foreshadowed the events of the 1980s.

PURITAN INDUSTRY

The origins of the Digital Equipment Corporation (DEC) in the two-hundred-year-old Assabet Mill of the American Woolen Company are symbolic of the weight of the past in the Route 128 region. While radical new technologies were being developed by the region's electronics companies, the identities and practices of its engineers reflected the legacy of centuries of industrial history.

New England society in the middle of the twentieth century was characterized by conservative traditions that dated from the seventeenth century. The hierarchical and authoritarian ethic of Puritanism—in which identities were shaped largely by family and class backgrounds and by location in a well-defined social hierarchy—continued to influence the regional culture centuries after its arrival.[1] Most of the New England population resided in stable communities and neighborhoods that were often home to three generations; many of these families could trace their genealogies in the region back more than ten generations.

These longstanding ties to families, neighborhoods, and communities ensured a strict separation between work and social life among the engineers of Route 128. Silicon Valley's entrepreneurs, lacking local roots or family ties, developed shared identities around the project of advancing a new technology, barely distinguishing between their professional and social lives. The social world of most New England engineers, by contrast, centered on the extended family, the church, local schools, tennis clubs, and other civic and neighborhood institutions. Their experiences did little to cultivate the strong regional or industry-based loyalties that unified the members of Silicon Valley's technical community. Most were from New England, many had attended local educational institutions, and their identities were already defined by familial and ethnic ties.

The blurring of social and professional identities and the practices of open exchange of information that distinguished Silicon Valley in the 1960s and 1970s never developed on Route 128. Interviews with engineers in the electronics enterprises of Eastern Massachusetts suggest a far more traditional suburban professional lifestyle. Engineers generally went home after work rather than getting together to gossip or discuss their views of markets or technologies. The social gathering places that were common in Silicon Valley do not appear to have existed on Route 128. According to Jeffrey Kalb, who worked in the Massachusetts minicomputer industry for more than ten years before moving to Silicon Valley: "I was not aware of similar meeting spots in Route 128. There may have been a lunch spot in Hudson or Marlboro, but there was nothing of the magnitude of the Silicon Valley hangouts." Another former DEC employee put it more bluntly: "I lived and worked for DEC in Maynard [Massachusetts] for more than five years, and I still can't tell you where 'Route 128' is."[2]

When engineers did socialize with colleagues, it was usually with spouses for a game of bridge, a dinner party, or a tennis match, and the discussion rarely turned to work. One professional who has spent time on both coasts noted:

> In Boston, breakfast table talk in city restaurants turns to politics, religion, sex, and business of all types. In Santa Clara, the people to your left and right are almost universally talking about semiconductors, operating systems, networking typologies, interfaces, high technology start-ups, and high technology rocket drops.
>
> It's constant. It's everywhere. In the malls, at church (if you have time to go and haven't given up that eastern custom), in the newspapers, on

the television, in the bank queue. It is a 24-hours-a-day, seven-days-a-week activity.[3]

The computer culture that developed in Cambridge and the surrounding MIT's Kendall Square during the 1950s and 1960s stands out as an exception to these norms. A community of counterculture "hackers" from the labs of MIT worked on computers day and night and developed a radical ethic of open information sharing, free and unlimited access to computers, and meritocracy—regardless of degrees, age, race, or position.[4] This area was later dubbed Technology Square for its concentration of small software firms, but it had little impact on the business mainstream along Route 128.

The founder of Digital Equipment Corporation, Ken Olsen, attributes the social conservatism of Route 128 employees and managers—and their corresponding reluctance to share information or rely on outsiders—to the influence of the Puritan traditions of self-reliance and self-reflection. Olsen himself was well known for his modest lifestyle and deep religious commitment: one biography refers to him as a "modern day puritan." In spite of his millions, Olsen preserved an intensely private and unpretentious personal life. He avoided social gatherings, abstained from drinking, smoking, and cursing, lived in a modest home, and drove an old Ford to work. He also let it be known that he mowed his own lawn, shoveled his own walk, and did his own grocery shopping.[5]

As the most visible business leader in the Route 128 region, Olsen offered a role model that differed radically from Silicon Valley's more conspicuous, outgoing, and sometimes extravagant entrepreneurs. Other local entrepreneurs were similarly known for their modesty and rejection of the material trappings of status.[6] This meant that the region's technology leaders developed neither the public profile nor the sense of community found in Silicon Valley.

The conservative social traditions and attitudes of New England also shaped the organization of local labor markets and patterns of entrepreneurship. Stability and company loyalty were valued over experimentation and risk-taking in the Route 128 region. Whereas interfirm mobility became a way of life in Silicon Valley during the 1960s and 1970s, Route 128 executives were more likely to consider job-hopping unacceptable and express a preference for professionals who were "in it for the long term."

The desired career path along Route 128 was to move up the corporate ladder of a large company with a good reputation. When managers or engineers changed jobs, they tended to move between established companies. The practice of leaving a large company to join a small firm or a promising new start-up was virtually unheard of. A long-term employee of Honeywell who finally left in the 1980s for an opportunity at a start-up noted:

> There is tremendous loyalty to the company and tremendous will to make things succeed within the company [on Route 128]. There were pockets of brilliance at Honeywell, but these individuals never took the leap to go off on their own or join another company. I stayed at Honeywell for more than twenty years. I had lots of opportunities to leave, but I never took them seriously because I had too many personal commitments and business ties. When I finally left it was like an 8.5 on the Richter scale. Everyone was shocked, they just couldn't believe it![7]

Another entrepreneur who worked along Route 128 during the early 1960s before moving to Silicon Valley and eventually starting his own firm noted the different attitudes of the two regions toward entrepreneurship:

> In Boston, if I said I was starting a company, people would look at me and say: "Are you sure you want to take the risk? You're so well established. Why would you give up a good job as vice president at a big company?" In California, I became a folk hero when I decided to start a company. It wasn't just my colleagues. My insurance man, my water deliverer—everyone was excited. It's a different culture out here.[8]

While New England boasts a long history of entrepreneurship dating to the early nineteenth century, by the 1970s there were fewer technology start-ups in Massachusetts than in Silicon Valley. A Boston-based investor and observer of technology start-ups on both coasts claims that there were two or three times as many entrepreneurs in Silicon Valley as along Route 128. He observed an important difference of style in the two places:

> On the East Coast people form a new business in a hush-hush way, working at their jobs during the day and putting together a business plan at night, which they circulate to the venture capital community hoping word does not get back to their employer. In California, entrepreneurs are more inclined to leave their employers and then go out and write a business plan and start raising money. Their attitude is "Even if I don't succeed I can always get another job."[9]

Risk-avoidance became self-reinforcing along Route 128. To start, there were only a handful of successful role models to inspire potential entrepreneurs, and those that did succeed, such as Ken Olsen and An Wang, were secretive and private individuals. In addition, most Route 128 entrepreneurs remained with the firms they started, rather than moving on to start new ventures, as was common in Silicon Valley. The exceptions, such as William Poduska and Philippe Villers, who started five and three different companies, respectively, were fairly well known. However, the region's best-known executives, such as Olsen, Wang, and Data General's Edson DeCastro, all remained firmly in charge of the firms they started for several decades.[10]

As a result, there were far fewer opportunities for entrepreneurial learning on Route 128 than in Silicon Valley. One study concluded that the typical Route 128 entrepreneur in this period had only one prior work experience before founding a start-up, and that a large percentage of the region's firms were direct MIT spin-offs whose founders lacked industrial experience altogether. In Silicon Valley, by contrast, most entrepreneurs had previously worked at several different firms.[11]

The Boston-based venture capital industry was largely responsible for the conservatism of the local electronics industry. While data are not available for the 1960s and 1970s, in 1981 venture capitalists backed only 17 early-stage start-ups in Massachusetts, compared to 37 in Silicon Valley. Despite a substantially greater pool of capital in the Northeast, more money was invested in the West from the beginning.[12]

Qualitative differences were at least as important. The Route 128 venture capital industry was established by old-line East Coast financiers and managed by professional bankers rather than entrepreneurs. The founders of American Research & Development, for example, included Ralph Flanders, former head of the Federal Reserve Bank of Boston, and Merrill Griswold of the Massachusetts Investors Trust. Russell Adams describes the persistence of traditional values among these members of a financial community that dates to the seventeenth and eighteenth centuries:

> Boston remained Boston, its prevailing spirit formed and jelled—not to say solidified—over many generations. The upper reaches of the city's financial establishment had opened of necessity to talented and ambitious men from other parts of the country, but the old traditions had been little disturbed. Prudence and integrity, qualities frequently honored elsewhere in their breach, were still scrupulously maintained in Boston, and if the

city's investment community was sometimes chided for an excess of caution, it was never charged with stinting on rectitude—or with losing sight of its past.[13]

Typically a generation older than their Silicon Valley counterparts, East Coast venture capitalists were more formal and conservative in their investment strategies. According to an engineer who worked for eleven years at DEC before moving to Silicon Valley to found a successful computer company:

> There is no way that I could have started Convergent [Technologies] in the Boston area. I am convinced that there are definite cultural differences in Silicon Valley compared with Route 128 . . . When I started Convergent, I got commitments for $2.5 million in 20 minutes from three people over lunch who saw me write the business plan on the back of a napkin. They believed in me. In Boston, you can't do that. It's much more formal. People in New England would rather invest in a tennis court than high technology.[14]

Unlike the entrepreneurs and engineers-turned-venture-capitalists of Silicon Valley, Boston investors rarely had the operating experience in the technology industry that would enable them to assist a business that ran into problems. In the straightforward words of Gordon Bell, who was DEC's vice president of engineering during the 1960s and 1970s and now serves as a consultant in Silicon Valley: "There is no real venture capital in Massachusetts. The venture capital community is a bunch of very conservative bankers. They are radically different from the venture capitalists in Silicon Valley who have all been operational people in companies. Unless you've proven yourself a hundred times over, you'll never get any money."[15]

Route 128 venture capital also lacked internal cohesion or strong ties to local industry. Studies of the venture capital industry document a greater degree of cross-fertilization and informal collaboration among West Coast venture capitalists than among those in Boston. And most local engineers attest to their greater prominence in the technical community of the West. According to a marketing manager who worked for more than twelve years on Route 128 before moving west: "In Silicon Valley, people are constantly talking about venture capital and start-ups: who they're funding for what and what's succeeded. In Boston, you have virtually no exposure to venture capital. As a result, everyone in Silicon Valley is motivated to do start-ups, while on the

East Coast nobody is." A former DEC executive, now based in Silicon Valley, reports: "We never talked about start-ups at DEC, and we never heard about them. Out here we're constantly talking about them."[16]

The relationship between MIT and Route 128 industry reflected the New England pattern of formal and hierarchical social relationships. Like Stanford and Berkeley, MIT graduated hundreds of engineers annually, provided faculty members as consultants and advisors to industry, and shared research findings in exchange for corporate funding and contributions. However, the initial differences in the relations between the universities and industry forged during the Second World War continued to shape the development of the two regions in the 1960s and 1970s.

MIT ignored Stanford's success in building programs that promoted interaction between the university and local technology firms. While Stanford's Honors Program granted advanced degrees to increasing numbers of local engineers, MIT refused to offer alternatives to its standard resident programs. According to executives in both regions, the opportunity to take courses through the instructional video network offered an important recruiting advantage for Silicon Valley firms.[17] Similarly, Stanford established a licensing office in 1969 to encourage the commercialization of technology developed at the university, while MIT did not set up such an office until the late 1980s.

This neglect of the region's emerging technology enterprises was partly the legacy of MIT's relations with established corporations such as DuPont, Eastman Kodak, and Standard Oil. The MIT Industrial Liaison Program reflects this orientation. Established in 1940, the program charges companies an average of $50,000 for access to university research findings and educational resources. Its structure and its fees reinforce a tendency toward arms-length relations and exclude most small and medium-sized companies.

The Stanford Industrial Affiliates program, in contrast, facilitates direct interaction between the university and firms of all sizes. For a modest $10,000 annual fee, companies can build a focused relationship with any one of the school's departmental laboratories. This affiliation offers the firm a special recruiting relationship and access to the lab's research projects. Company employees are entitled to attend research meetings on campus, visit faculty members and graduate students, and see university research publications and student résumés. A portion of the fees goes directly to the faculty in the lab to defer professional expenses such as equipment, travel, graduate student fellowships, and research materials. In return, Stanford invites managers of member firms to drop in on the labs casually, bring technical problems of a nonproprietary nature to faculty, and to help shape the direction of future research. By all accounts, this program builds closer relationships between faculty, graduate students, and local firms than MIT's more formal Industrial Liaison Program.[18]

Gordon Bell argues that during his twenty years at DEC, Stanford and Berkeley—despite their geographic distance—related to the company more extensively and more fruitfully than nearby MIT and Harvard:

> We were never able to get a good relationship with MIT. There was no cooperation or reciprocity. While I was at DEC we had better relationships with Stanford and Berkeley than we had with MIT. For example, we had more transfers of programs into the PDP-10 from Stanford than from MIT. The computer science department at MIT had an arrogance that made it very difficult to work with them; and nobody worked with Harvard. Every time I went to MIT I got sick because they wanted our money but we could never get joint projects going.[19]

A Xerox executive similarly suggests that faculty members from Stanford were more involved in the activities of local firms than those from MIT. He compared the seminars he gave at Xerox PARC in Palo Alto and at Xerox's Kurzweil Lab in Waltham, Massachusetts:

> The seminar at PARC was held in a large hall, and I noticed that about a third of the audience were not wearing Xerox employee badges, although they participated actively in the discussion. I learned afterwards that they were Stanford faculty, who have an open invitation to all PARC seminars. A couple of months later, I gave a similar seminar at the Kurzweil. No faculty from MIT or any other university were in attendance, nor had any evidently been invited.[20]

The public system of higher education and training in Massachusetts was no better organized to serve the region's emerging technology industry. The community and state colleges in Massachusetts were small, underfunded, and lacking in status, particularly compared with California's community and state college system, which had the funding and stature to establish large, high-quality programs. While some Massachusetts community colleges began offering courses in electronics technology and computer programming during the 1970s, most did little training in basic technology. Over time, some of the region's large firms began to offer employees training and education themselves. This posed an obvious problem for small and medium-sized firms, which could not afford the cost of training programs. Not surprisingly, the relations between local industry and the community colleges remained limited: local firms donated fewer resources (either equipment or personnel time) to community colleges, and the colleges, in turn, were less likely than those in Silicon Valley to provide on-site training or contract courses for companies.[21]

Other regional institutions also reproduced the formal and conservative practices of an earlier industrial era along Route 128. The region's public relations firms, for example, appeared lethargic by California standards. A Boston-based professional commented:

> Silicon Valley public relations is a much more vital, fast-moving, youthful practice than it is in New England. The average age of the PR decision-maker is at least 10 years less than his/her counterpart in the East . . . In northern California companies, the hierarchy seems compressed . . . everyone has your home telephone number, and uses it. One's personal life and one's business life seem borderless.

He went on to observe broader differences in the business culture of the two regions:

> Tactical decisions that take six weeks in Boston can take anywhere from six days to six nanoseconds in Cupertino. The protracted, sometimes agonized deliberation of the northeast is contrasted sharply with the more intuitive, quick-fire approach in northern California . . . In Silicon Valley, failure is an accepted way of life, unlike the East where failure is viewed as a death sentence . . . If you bomb in Palo Alto, you blame the advertising agency and start another company.[22]

Last, but not least, the Massachusetts High Technology Council (MHTC)—the business association that emerged in the 1970s to represent the interests of Route 128 firms—devoted most of its efforts to lobbying for tax cuts that further undermined the ability of the public sector to contribute to industrial development. The MHTC was formed in 1977 after Ray Stata, a Route 128 executive, visited Silicon Valley. Impressed by the way firms worked together to solve common problems, he formed the MHTC as Route 128's first association of technology companies. In Stata's words: "Before the Council got together, there was no interchange between the companies here. The presidents didn't know each other and there was no communication."[23] The MHTC did build closer relations among local CEOs, but its agenda and style differed completely from those of the Silicon Valley business community. From the beginning, the MHTC defined a deeply antagonistic relationship between existing industry and the public sector. Its agenda during the 1970s was dominated almost exclusively by efforts to reduce state and local taxes: it played a central role, for example, in the 1980 passage of Proposition $2\frac{1}{2}$, the property-tax-cutting initiative in Massachusetts. MHTC members were quick to remind local officials that their commitment to the region was conditional, repeatedly threatening investment strikes if the state did not improve the business climate. The MHTC differed fundamentally from the Santa Clara County Manufacturing Group (SCCMG), which worked to develop harmonious relations with the local public sector in order to work together to improve the region's transportation, housing, and environmental problems.[24]

Nor was there a parallel on Route 128 to Silicon Valley's integrative business associations. The MIT Enterprise Forum and the Route 128 Venture Group, which were founded to facilitate the formation of new businesses in the region, served primarily as one-time sources of information and/or contacts for managers, rather than as the basis for more enduring networks.[25] When the American Electronics Association established a branch in Route 128 in the 1970s, it too remained a traditional provider of business services rather than providing a basis for ongoing technical and social exchange among the local business community.

There was a business network in the Route 128 region: a small circle of senior technology executives who knew one another and shared ideas through the MHTC and other business forums. But it was confined to a traditional business elite that shared political and social views. It bore little resemblance to the far more inclusive networks that developed among managers, engineers, and entrepreneurs as well as executives at multiple levels of the Silicon Valley community.

THE SELF-SUFFICIENT FIRM

The industrial structure of Route 128 was defined by the search for corporate self-sufficiency or autarky. As they grew, local companies built self-contained and vertically integrated structures, just as Silicon Valley firms were experimenting with openness and specialization. The desire for self-sufficiency was largely a product of local executives' inherited ideas about how to organize production. The region's new technology start-ups drew most of their managers from the diversified electrical and consumer electronics producers of the Northeast such as Sylvania, General Electric, and RCA. Their notions of appropriate business strategies and structures were shaped by these models.[26]

The prolonged dominance of military production in Massachusetts reinforced corporate autarky. It was not until the 1970s that Route 128's electronics industry reduced its postwar dependence on defense spending, more than a decade after Silicon Valley did so, and the region remained more dependent on military markets than Northern California throughout the 1980s.[27] Serving military markets ensured the orientation of defense contractors like Raytheon toward the federal government rather than the region, and reinforced their emphasis on secrecy rather than collaboration.

Route 128's technology enterprises imitated the structure of the traditional mass production corporation. While Silicon Valley's entrepreneurs rejected the corporate practices of the large, established East Coast producers, the managers along Route 128 saw the same corporations as their models. One senior vice president at Data General (DG) commented: "I constantly study the way larger companies organize themselves, looking for ideas. I look at Texas Instruments, at IBM, at ITT, and at GE and GM." A twenty-year veteran of Route 128 noted: "The aim of all small companies out here is to become a big established company. They try to look like a big company, they put on the airs of being a big company. In fact, to satisfy the venture capitalists, your business plan has to make you look like a small DEC or Data General."[28]

These start-ups were quick to hire managers from the established corporations, seeing experienced personnel as important to their efforts to grow into mature corporations. In the early 1960s, for example, Ken Olsen called for "aggressive hired guns, people skilled in the ways of big companies" at DEC and brought in a team of senior managers from RCA, GE, and Honeywell. Similarly, when DG ran into difficulties in the late 1970s, the company hired a cadre of senior executives from larger computer companies, especially IBM.[29]

These hiring practices meant that the managers and executives of Route 128 firms were typically in their fifties and sixties and well equipped to implement the formal organizational structures and operating procedures of corporate America. The managers of Silicon Valley start-ups, by contrast, were often in their twenties and thirties and had little, if any, management experience. As late as 1980, Robert Noyce reported: "There's only one member of the board who has ever worked for a company larger than Intel is today." Rather than replicating an existing model, these novice Silicon Valley managers experimented openly with organizational alternatives.[30]

While the legend of Fairchild and its glorification of entrepreneurial risk-taking was one of the most powerful of the Silicon Valley founding myths, the story of the acrimonious split between DEC's Olsen and the founder of DG, Edson DeCastro, exerted a comparable influence on Route 128. When DeCastro and his partners left DEC in 1968 to start their own firm, Olsen was furious, convinced that they had designed their own machine on DEC time and with what he saw as proprietary DEC technology. Olsen let it be known throughout the company and the region that DG was an unethical enterprise that was doomed to fail. And while he never carried out his threat to sue DG, his consistent message was "Don't talk to Data General." Olsen's anger was so great that in 1979, eleven years after the split, he told reporters: "What they did was so bad, we're still upset about it."[31]

If the boundaries between firms and between firms and local society were blurring in Silicon Valley, the boundaries of Route 128 companies were being very strictly defined. DEC remained highly secretive and self-contained. By the late 1960s, the firm was the largest employer in the town of Maynard, yet none of its senior managers belonged to the local Chamber of Commerce and Olsen discouraged them from becoming involved in community affairs. Nor was this isolation diminished by subsequent decades of rapid growth. Twenty years later, Olsen's biographers Glenn Rifkin and George Harrar described the firm's location: "DEC, a multinational titan, is centered in the second smallest town in Massachusetts, a community with fewer than 10,000 people squeezed into 5.25 square miles an hour's drive west of Boston. The only access routes—Routes 27, 117, and 62—are two-lane country roads that wind lazily through the outlying rural communities. The only quick way into town is by helicopter—Digital helicopter." They concluded that the company was "a sociological unit, a world unto itself."[32]

Executives at the company were quick to point out that DEC did not see itself as part of Route 128 or even New England, but rather as an actor in the national and global economies. In the words of Gordon Bell: "DEC operated as an island. It was a large entity that operated as an island in the regional economy." This contrasts with DEC's West Coast counterpart, Hewlett-Packard, which identified deeply with Silicon Valley, frequently extended informal assistance to other local enterprises, and was at the center of much of the region's associational life.[33]

DEC's isolation was not the exception on Route 128. Its arch-rival, Data General, was also an insular organization. From its origins with DeCastro's acrimonious departure from DEC, the firm had an obsessive concern with corporate secrecy. DG was known for its reluctance to share information about future products with customers or suppliers. The company hired private detectives to trace security leaks and—at a time when lawsuits were still rare in Silicon Valley—repeatedly sued competitors and former employees to prevent the loss of proprietary corporate information.[34]

Tracy Kidder's *Soul of a New Machine*, an ethnographic account of the crash development of a new minicomputer at Data General in the 1970s, underscores the self-sufficiency of Route 128 firms. The book never mentions a broader technical community in the region.[35] Networking on Route 128 occurred almost exclusively within the large firms, not between them. As a result, information on markets and technologies remained trapped within the boundaries of individual corporations, rather than diffusing to other local firms and entrepreneurs as in Silicon Valley.

This defense of autonomy was reflected in differences in corporate structure. Silicon Valley's technology companies, surrounded by an increasingly diversified fabric of external relationships and supplier infrastructure, experimented with specialization. Route 128 producers, in contrast, lacking traditions of informal collaboration or integrative institutions, sought technological self-sufficiency. Following the model of the traditional vertically integrated corporation, the region's start-ups internalized as many operations as possible. They designed their computers or electronic systems, manufactured most of their own components, peripherals, and subsystems, wrote their own software, and performed final assembly. They also controlled all of their marketing, sales, and support services for their computer systems. According to a former DEC executive:

> DEC's business model was defined in 1961 and its structure was cast by 1965. The model dictated doing virtually everything internally. This did not extend only to custom components. Everything was to be planned,

designed, manufactured, and tested in-house. By the early 1980s, we made the memory chips, tape drives, disk drives, core memories, and operating system to fit our systems. We also assembled printed circuit boards and made power supplies, coils, cables, sheet metal, and machined components.[36]

This strategy of vertical integration remained unchallenged during the 1960s and 1970s; it was implicitly recognized as the appropriate corporate model. In the words of Data General's DeCastro: "Our discussions of vertical integration during the 1970s were mainly discussions of detail, of what particular parts we should begin producing and when; but there was *no* debate over the wisdom of the underlying concept that we should vertically integrate."[37]

Vertical integration was not unheard of in Silicon Valley at the time: Hewlett-Packard began manufacturing semiconductors and printed circuit boards during the 1970s, and several semiconductor firms tried, largely without success, to produce digital watches and computer systems. However, as the region's supplier infrastructure became more sophisticated, local producers questioned the need to perform certain operations internally. Horizontal and vertical specialization became increasingly common as the region's industrial base diversified.

The technical infrastructure of Route 128 was, to be sure, better developed than in most other parts of the nation. With the crucial exception of semiconductor design and manufacturing, which was ceded to Silicon Valley by the 1960s, suppliers of most technical components and services could be found on Route 128. But the increasingly integrated structures of the minicomputer manufacturers, combined with the inward focus of defense contractors such as Raytheon, slowed the growth, diversification, and upgrading of the regional infrastructure—particularly relative to its West Coast competitor. Autarky thus became self-reproducing along Route 128. The rate of start-ups slowed during the 1970s: 22 computer firms were started in Massachusetts between 1966 and 1970; the number dropped to 14 between 1971 and 1975, and to 9 between 1976 and 1980.[38]

HIERARCHY AND FORMALITY

The managers of Route 128 technology companies were also influenced by the bureaucratic structures of the established East Coast corporation. They created organizations characterized by formal decisionmaking procedures and management styles, loyal long-term employees, and conservative workplace procedures, dress, and work styles. A handful of companies consciously sought to avoid corporate hierarchies. DEC, in particular, pioneered a management model based on organizational decentralization and a participatory culture. These efforts, however, only partially departed from the traditional business model that dominated along Route 128.

From its origins, DEC's culture reflected the values of its engineering-oriented founder and workforce, and represented a departure from mainstream business culture of the era. One employee described the company in the early 1970s in terms that are reminiscent of Silicon Valley:

> DEC was a wild place, the Wild West . . . There we were in this cruddy old mill, with nineteen buildings and secret passageways. Some places you had to go downstairs in the middle because otherwise you couldn't connect to the bridge to another building. Ken used to say that the primary difference between the balance sheet of DEC and Honeywell was the cost of facilities. It was a company that captured an image and a spirit, a counterculture. We lived out in Maynard on the frontier, and we knew that we built the best computers. We knew we were going to win.[39]

This pioneering image was not simply a reflection of the company's physical facilities. DEC was known as "an engineer's sandbox" for its informality and almost chaotic openness.[40] Olsen believed that good ideas could come from anywhere in the organization, and—like Silicon Valley's founding fathers—consciously downplayed status and hierarchical authority. He eschewed status symbols such as reserved parking spaces or executive dining rooms that were common in the region's established firms, engineers worked in open cubicles rather than private offices, and dress was informal.

DEC innovated organizationally as well as technically. In the place of traditional bureaucratic controls, DEC management cultivated a strong corporate culture built on intense loyalty to the firm, "bottom-up" decisionmaking, and pride in the intrinsic technical value of the company's products. Olsen's role was that of a benevolent patriarch, the "brilliant, demanding, but supportive father figure." He cultivated a loyal and committed workforce by selecting only those who promised to become career employees and by treating them as members of a family. One long-time employee described the strong bonds of mutual support that developed: "Getting hired into DEC . . . is like getting married: you meet your wife's mother and father and her aunts, uncles and cousins. It is a bonding process to an extended group of peers, as well as executives higher up and workers lower down." According to Rifkin and Harrar: "The insular feeling of this unusual, but productive environment came from a work force uncommonly dedicated to the same goals as its leader." This culture of hard work was reinforced by an unwritten but widely acknowledged tradition of no layoffs.[41]

While this culture ensured that employee turnover was among the lowest in the computer industry, it also reinforced DEC's isolation from the region. Promotion came from building strong internal relations, not from success in dealing with the external world. Employees who left DEC were often treated as pariahs, rather than as potential resources. Once an employee left, there was no option of return. According to one executive who resigned: "If you're stupid enough to cut yourself off from the Mother Church, Digital's attitude is,'Don't bother to come back.'"[42] Whereas an engineer leaving a Silicon Valley company typically stayed in touch with former colleagues for the rest of his or her career, those who left DEC were often ostracized and completely cut off from the DEC community.

DEC's structure embodied the tension between Olsen's desire to maximize individual creativity and accountability and his deep commitment to group consensus. DEC employees were encouraged to think for themselves and challenge their superiors; yet they were also required to discuss all important matters widely within the organization, and to obtain consensus before moving forward. The resulting work organization was quite fluid. Employees worked in specialized product- or project-based work groups that provided autonomy and responsiveness; but these groups were required to compete with one another for resources and to defend themselves in a highly contentious, often adversarial environment.[43]

This combination of decentralized authority and continuous negotiation was formalized in a matrix, which overlaid a product-line structure on a strong functional organization. The product- or project-based work groups were linked horizontally to other groups, and then simultaneously linked vertically to centralized functional groups such as finance, engineering, manufacturing, and marketing. The aim of this complex—and often shifting—matrix structure was to preserve the creativity and entrepreneurial spirit of a start-up without sacrificing the stability and discipline of a functional organization.

DEC's matrix organization was widely imitated as a model for technology industries during the 1970s. In practice, however, it represented an ambiguous intermediate model—falling between the traditional corporate model and the more flexible Silicon Valley model. The elimination of direct hierarchical lines of authority and the creation of autonomous work groups stimulated informal communication and generated an immense reservoir of new technological ideas. However, the matrix also generated conflict. Employees were forced to report to at least two superiors, a functional manager and a project manager. Lacking traditional lines of authority, managers were forced to convince, cajole, or persuade subordinates. Moreover, Olsen required wide debate on important decisions, with group meetings to test an idea and sell it in the organization both vertically and laterally.

The matrix structure also masked extensive centralization: it allowed Olsen and a small number of powerful senior committees that survived the company's frequent reorganizations to retain final authority for all important decisions. Ed Schein, a long-time advisor to Olsen, reports that despite DEC's appearance of decentralization, the Operations Committee, a group of eight to ten senior managers, actually ran the company. This was not unique to DEC. Many Route 128 companies were characterized by a degree of centralization that was rare in Silicon Valley. A twenty-year employee of Honeywell observed: "The CEO ultimately makes all of the important decisions in a Route 128 company. Look at Olsen and DeCastro. Even though Honeywell was decentralized in many respects, there was a huge gap between the divisions and the corporate level. A small group of people at the corporate level made all the decisions that mattered." This contrasts with the pattern observed in Silicon Valley, where founders were more likely to either relinquish or share decisionmaking authority.[44]

Unlike DEC, the old-line electrical producers such as RCA, General Electric, and Sylvania, and the newer electronics producers along Route 128 such as Honeywell and Raytheon, reproduced a traditional—and far less flexible—organizational model. Theirs was a world governed by formal organizational charts, deliberate, analytical, and quantitative decisionmaking, and long-term strategic planning. Vertical lines of decisionmaking authority ensured that flows of information and communications were formal and hierarchically controlled. Corporate divisions were generally subject to the final authority of a central office.[45]

DG's traditional functional organization, for example, strictly separated research, engineering, manufacturing, and marketing. The traditional glass-protected "VP row" reinforced status divisions within the firm, and communication across functions or the sharing of information with employees was discouraged.

This management style contrasted greatly with the openness and informality of communications in Silicon Valley firms. As a public relations consultant describes it: "In Northern California, the hierarchy seems compressed. An account executive in Sunnyvale might be reporting directly to the president, the CEO, or the founder. In Cambridge, that person will speak to the communications manager, who works for the VP of you-name-it, who reports to an Executive VP, who whispers it to the Main Force."[46]

Employees in Route 128 firms tended to be loyal to the firm, and generally expected to stay for the long term, working their way up the corporate hierarchy and retiring with a comfortable pension. According to former Honeywell employee Paul DeLacey: "even people in their twenties worried about pensions and retirement plans." Stock options were typically reserved for top executives, if they were offered at all. DEC, for example, was "tight-fisted with stock options," with only vice presidents and top managers eligible.[47]

The traditional Route 128 corporation was also characterized by significant status differences. Formal lines of authority and procedures as well as salaries and benefits created barriers between functions and corporate ranks. A former employee of Prime Computers described it this way:

> The East Coast is locked into the number of years you've been out of school. If you don't have grey hairs then you can't be a vice president, even at a start-up. You'll never find anyone under fifty in the top ranks of the big Route 128 companies. Those companies hand out charts to all the employees showing number of years out of school and pay scales.
>
> That's the trouble with the parochial East Coast business environment, it's too rigid and conservative. There's no incentive for someone who's bright and energetic but has no degrees.[48]

Status differences were also reflected in the physical layout of the workplace, dress, and differing benefits. Not only were status and pay closely correlated with age, but dress, which tended to be formal, provided a quick indication of an individual's position in the organization. In addition, senior managers were likely to be isolated from the rest of the organization in executive suites, to eat in private dining rooms, and to park in reserved spaces.

Interviews with industry executives in Silicon Valley and Route 128 underscore the differences in the regions' management models. Notwithstanding the organizational innovations of firms like DEC and its imitators, most Route 128 firms continued to rely on a formal, vertical structure, more conservative and top-down management styles, and significantly greater formality in the workplace, dress, communication patterns, and attitudes toward authority than those located in Silicon Valley. In short, Route 128's technology firms remained stable, formal, and centralized organizations compared with the loosely linked confederations of engineering teams in emerging Silicon Valley.

REGIONAL REVERSAL

The Route 128 region was already a center of semiconductor production when William Shockley started his operation in Palo Alto in the mid-1950s. Several established electronics companies had receiving tube or transistor operations in the greater Boston area, including Sylvania, Clevite, CBS-Hytron, and Raytheon. The region also was home to start-ups such as Transitron, Crystal Onyx, and Solid State Devices. These firms together accounted for a third of the nation's transmitting and special-purpose receiving tubes and a quarter of all solid state devices.[49] Raytheon, for example, led the nation in transistor production in the early 1950s, while the local start-up Transitron ranked second by the end of the decade.[50]

Despite their initial advantage, Route 128 companies saw the locus of semiconductor innovation and production shift to Silicon Valley by the end of the 1960s. Employment data tell the story clearly: Route 128 firms employed more than twice as many workers in the electronic components sector as Silicon Valley firms in 1959. In 1975, these positions had reversed: employment in Silicon Valley had tripled to more than double that of Route 128, which had fallen to nearly half of its earlier level. By 1990, the gap had widened still further (see Figure 2).

This regional reversal illustrates the advantages of Silicon Valley's network-based system in a technologically volatile industry. There was every reason to expect that the older Route 128, with its established technical and financial infrastructure and its early lead in semiconductors, would continue to lead the industry. The region had the advantage of greater proximity to AT&T's Bell Labs in New Jersey, where the transistor was invented, facilitating informal communications and personnel exchange. In fact, Route 128's Transitron was one of the first

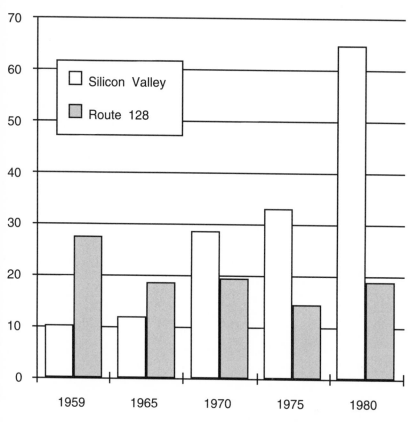

Figure 2. Employment in electronic components and semiconductor firms, Silicon Valley and Route 128, 1959–1980. Data from *County Business Patterns.*

and most successful Bell spin-offs. And when Shockley left Bell to start his own company, he located in Palo Alto only after being spurned by Massachusetts-based Raytheon.

Route 128 producers also enjoyed greater access to federal military and aerospace contracts for semiconductor research and production because of their longstanding ties to Washington. The Army Signal Corps contracts to Sylvania and Raytheon in 1952 and 1953 for pilot transistor production lines, for example, dwarfed those awarded to Silicon Valley companies. And while semiconductor start-ups on both coasts got started with military contracts, the absolute quantity going to Massachusetts was far greater during this period.[51]

It is therefore not surprising that Route 128 firms were among the earliest manufacturers of solid state components. Yet by the 1960s, both established firms like Raytheon and start-ups like Transitron had lost their lead in the industry.[52] Some Route 128 companies continued to produce semiconductors internally, but none could compete with the autonomously managed "merchant" firms that specialized in the business of manufacturing and selling microelectronic components. These independent producers, located primarily in Silicon Valley, dominated the semiconductor industry in the 1960s and 1970s.

The failure of Route 128 producers to maintain their initial lead in semiconductors offers insights into the limits of an independent firm–based industrial system in an environment of technological and market volatility. While the Route 128 system—with its emphasis on corporate secrecy, vertical integration, and formal hierarchies—provided the stability that is critical in an environment of volume markets and price-based competition, it was inadequate for the accelerating pace of technological and market change in semiconductors. As early as 1957, a *Fortune* magazine writer remarked on the pace of innovation in semiconductors in words that seem laughable today: "In the commercial market, product evaluation and timing were never more important . . . One component manufacturer which has been leading in its field—consisting of only 3–4 other firms—is constantly afraid that a brand new product will replace it. Two major changes in technology have already taken place in the eight years this firm has been in business." The rate of change only accelerated in subsequent decades: six thousand different types of transistor were introduced between 1956 and 1962, and the number of circuit components on a single chip jumped from one to about one thousand between 1959 and 1970. In addition, a multiplicity of new production techniques were developed based on oxide-masking, diffusion, planar, and epitaxial processes emerged in the early 1960s.[53]

In retrospect, the continued commitment of established electronics producers to their traditional receiving tube business was one source of rigidity. While receiving tube production grew rapidly until 1957, transistors did not become a real threat until the mid-1960s. Even as late as 1966, demand for receiving tubes strained the plant capacity of existing producers, and solid state devices had not been commercialized as fast as expected.[54] As a result, Route 128 companies did not turn their attention to semiconductors until a new generation of chipmakers—largely based in Silicon Valley—began to flourish.

There were also manufacturing obstacles rooted in their commitment to mass production. Receiving tube manufacturing was a stable, capital-intensive, and highly automated mass production process. By the mid-1950s most Route 128 producers were making receiving tubes in high volume on automated assembly lines that cost a minimum of $12 million to start and often required ongoing capital investment. Each variety of tube required a specialized set-up on the assembly line, typically necessitating runs of more than 10,000 units to break even, and economies of scale continued to increase even during the late 1950s and 1960s.[55]

Semiconductor production in this era, by contrast, was technologically unstable, flexible, and relatively easy to enter. Start-up costs remained below $1 million in the 1960s and early 1970s because production remained largely unautomated. Silicon Valley firms learned, for example, from the losses suffered by the old-line Philco Corporation, which in 1958 automated the manufacturing line for its state-of-the-art jet-etched transistor, only to be surpassed in 1963 by the more efficient planar technology. Philco, unable to recoup its investment, was forced to leave the business.[56]

The receiving tube companies suffered from organizational sources of rigidity as well. A former General Electric executive who later joined the semiconductor industry in Silicon Valley described the limits of the traditional American corporate model: "When it got into semiconductors, GE, like other large firms, attempted to build the business on old company traditions. Companies like RCA and Sylvania were the models . . . In semiconductors, it turned out that it was better to have a new industry filled with young people who didn't know much about how you were supposed to do business."[57]

Firms such as RCA and Sylvania were highly diversified, vertically integrated corporations. In addition to receiving tubes, they were engaged in the manufacture of television sets and radio receivers (which made up the primary market for tubes in the 1960s) as well as electrical equipment, consumer electronics products, and military and space apparatus. These companies had grown accustomed to competing in a mature and oligopolistic business environment, in which the emphasis was on reducing production costs rather than on bringing new product or process innovations rapidly to market. The semiconductor divisions were tightly controlled by higher levels of management and lacked the organizational autonomy or the incentives to respond rapidly to technological change. Most had erected functional barriers that weakened communications and interactions between R&D, manufacturing, and marketing.[58]

As a result, established receiving tube firms were unable to organize for innovation, or to retain their most talented engineers, who were often lured away by the more dynamic start-ups in California. One semiconductor industry executive noted: "a management style that permits geniuses to contribute is important. If you were to look at why GE and RCA have failed [in semiconductors], it is because their organization was too disciplined and unable to respond quickly to true innovation."[59]

Nor did the Route 128 semiconductor start-ups fare much better than the established electronics producers. Transitron's founders David Bakalar, an MIT Ph.D. who had worked briefly at Bell Labs, and his brother Leo, a former bakery manager, earned a reputation as arbitrary and unfair managers who cared more about cost-cutting than about providing an environment conducive to creativity and innovation. As a result, Transitron lost many of its best engineers during the first industry recession in 1961. In spite of early achievements in working out the problems associated with high-volume production of the gold-bonded diode, Transitron devoted little attention to research and development, and soon fell behind technologically. As one measure, the firm acquired only 26 semiconductor patents between 1952 and 1968, compared to industry leader Texas Instruments, which gathered 286, or Fairchild Semiconductor, with 52. Of course start-ups failed regularly in Silicon Valley as well. However, in a culture that encouraged risk-taking and exchange of information, failures contributed to a process of collective learning.[60]

The reversal of regional positions in electronic components foreshadowed the limits of autarkic strategies and structures in an environment of technological and market uncertainty. Yet neither the victors in Silicon Valley nor the vanquished along Route 128 assimilated the lessons of this initial confrontation. It would take severe economic dislocation in both regions to call these traditional industrial practices into question.

4

BETTING ON
A PRODUCT

The railroads did not stop growing because the need for passenger and freight
transport declined, but because it was not filled by the railroads themselves.

—Theodore Levitt

▶ Both Silicon Valley and Route 128 boomed in the late 1970s and
early 1980s. A handful of semiconductor firms in Silicon Valley and
minicomputer producers on Route 128 grew very large, dwarfing the
surrounding industry and accelerating regional growth. Despite differences in the organization of their local industrial systems, the leading
firms in each region flourished by adopting the high-volume strategies
and autarkic structures they saw as essential corollaries to industrial
maturation. Using the automobile industry as their model, major companies in each region competed by betting on a product and cutting
costs, rather than by innovating.

These firms fell into crisis in the mid-1980s. Producers in Silicon
Valley ceded the market for semiconductor memories to more efficient
Japanese manufacturers, while Route 128 minicomputer firms saw
their products displaced by personal computers and workstations.
Blinded by their initial successes, they failed to recognize the limits of
a business model that presumed stability in an environment of technological and market volatility. With their largest producers in crisis,
both regions faced the worst downturns in their histories.

Betting on a product was logical for firms in Route 128's firm-based
industrial system. The region's established electrical corporations had
prospered historically by building self-sufficient structures. For companies in Silicon Valley's decentralized, network-based system, however,
the turn to high-volume production marked an important departure.
Local semiconductor firms abandoned the social structure and institu-

tions they had pioneered and embraced the learning curves and scale economies of contemporary management models. Failing to recognize the importance of the region's networks to their dynamism, they also failed to foresee the costs of abandoning them.

From Custom to Commodity

The semiconductor industry of the 1970s was intensely competitive, technologically dynamic, and expansive. New competitors continued to emerge, and the rapid introduction of new products and processes remained a key source of advantage. As Robert Noyce put it: "A year's advantage in introducing a new product or new process can give a company a 25-percent cost advantage over competing companies; conversely, a year's lag puts a company at a significant disadvantage with respect to its competitors." Semiconductor sales grew an average of 25 percent annually, spurred in part by precipitous drops in the price of devices. And computer and industrial markets quickly replaced the military as the dominant consumers of integrated circuits.[1]

In spite of the appearance of instability, however, the structure of the semiconductor industry began to stabilize with the onset of the race to reduce the costs of semiconductor memories and microprocessors. A predictable trajectory of incremental refinements in technology, design, and production replaced the turbulence of continuous product and process innovation. The manufacture of vast quantities of standardized devices supplanted the customization of products for individual systems.

This marked a fundamental break from earlier decades. During the 1950s most semiconductor firms produced small quantities of specialized devices for military applications. By the 1960s, the industry consensus was that the future lay in custom integrated circuits, and that the role for standard products would be small. Despite the emergence of a commercial market, continuing innovation in product designs and production techniques confounded early efforts to automate production of general-purpose semiconductors. Moreover, customers resisted standard devices because they limited the company's ability to differentiate its products. According to the business press at the time: "Understandably, an innovative equipment maker does not expect to find his chips as standard items already on the supplier's shelf, nor does he want his own designs put in a catalogue for his competitors to use."[2]

Customizing semiconductors to optimize the performance of an individual system dominated during the 1960s. Industry analysts dubbed this period "the era of custom LSI." Engineers at firms like Texas Instruments and Fairchild actively developed computer-aided design (CAD) and test equipment to support the customization process. As late as 1971, the majority of large-scale integrated (LSI) circuit sales were custom devices.[3]

The drawback of custom circuits was that an individual design served a small market, and as devices became more complex, design costs rose and further narrowed the market. An alternative trajectory, based on high-volume production of standard devices, emerged during the 1970s. A few producers, such as Intel, avoided the custom business altogether and began producing memory circuits in the late 1960s. As it became increasingly apparent that these random access memories would replace the magnetic cores used in computers to store information, the expectation of a huge market spurred new entrants.

Competition to produce a low-cost semiconductor memory began in 1970, when Intel introduced a 1K (1,024-bit) dynamic random access memory (DRAM). By 1971 more than thirteen companies had introduced their own copies of the Intel chip, causing severe price-cutting, even on devices that were not produced in significant quantity. The downward pressure on prices intensified in 1974 after the emergence of a series of industry-standard 4K DRAMs permitted volume production. This pattern continued after Intel and others introduced the 16K DRAM a year later. By 1979 there were sixteen firms (including five Japanese firms) competing for the 16K DRAM market.

The "memory race" of the 1970s was defined by the standardization of products and processes, predictable increases in chip power and density, and precipitous declines in prices and profits. Memory producers lowered their costs by increasing product volumes and moving down the "learning curve," in which progressive increases in chip density led the industry in a virtuous cycle of higher production volume leading to lower costs leading to still higher production volumes. With this shift to high-volume production, incremental refinements in semiconductor technology, design, and production took the place of revolutions in underlying design concepts or production techniques.[4]

The microprocessor business followed a parallel trajectory, in spite of its greater design content. Intel introduced the first microprocessor, a programmable component that contains all the elements of a computer's central processing unit, in 1971. By 1973 the firm had introduced a second-generation 8-bit microprocessor (the 8080) that was twenty times faster than the original device. It became known as the "Model T" of the industry. By 1975 a swarm of new firms had entered the market. Some cross-licensed or second-sourced the 8080, while many simply imitated it with slight variations, initiating a round of severe price-cutting. The price of the Intel 8080A, for example, fell from $110 in 1975 to $20 in 1977. By 1980 a standard 8-bit microprocessor sold for between $5 and $8.

As in the memory market, falling prices opened up new markets and spurred longer production runs that further reduced costs. Intel remained market leader by aggressively designing newer, more powerful components that delivered premium prices and high margins, and by shifting out of older lines as they became commodities. Its competitors largely followed strategies of imitation and cost-cutting through scale economies in the successive generations of increasingly sophisticated 4-bit, 8-bit, 16-bit, and 32-bit devices.

Battered by an industry-wide recession in the early 1970s, semiconductor producers flocked to the emerging mass markets for memory, microprocessors, and the related peripheral devices—abandoning the custom business altogether. The microprocessor, in particular, appeared to render custom integrated circuits uneconomic because it offered a standard design that could be produced in volume and then programmed with software to meet customers' unique needs. As the industry pronounced the custom business a dead end, the pioneering work on customization at places like Fairchild was dismissed—and largely forgotten for nearly a decade.[5]

Semiconductor industry leaders concluded by the late 1970s that the challenge was no longer to advance technology but to mass manufacture standard devices. Intel cofounder Andy Grove coined the phrase "high technology jelly beans" to describe the millions of integrated circuits that Intel produced annually. He claimed the firm's goal was to "reduce the cost of solutions . . . to market pre-fabricated, mass produced solutions to users." Noyce similarly argued that "The industry has already achieved the complexity needed for today's mass markets— for example in the digital watch or calculator—and the profit potentia that motivates these developments can only be achieved by productior in high volume." Semiconductor firms increasingly produced only devices that would repay their development costs rapidly—devices with markets promising volumes of at least 100,000 units.[6]

The computer and equipment producers that still required custom devices were forced to set up their own in-house design and fabrication facilities, or to acquire small semiconductor firms, in order to get the limited quantities needed for their products.[7] Custom production was thus left almost exclusively to in-house captive suppliers such as IBM, DEC, and Bell Labs. Small systems companies that could not afford to enter the business themselves were left without a source of specialized circuits and forced—until the revival of semi-custom production in the 1980s—to rely on standard parts.

These changes were a response, in part, to the changing economics of semiconductor production. Chip design and manufacturing became far more complex and expensive with the transition from LSI to very large scale integration, or VLSI (the shift from 10,000 to at least 100,000 circuits per device). While fabrication facilities were built in the 1960s for less than $2 million, by 1980 the price for state-of-the-art fab—with an integrated, computer-controlled clean room and sophisticated, high-precision chip manufacturing equipment—surpassed $50 million.

Investments in new production capacity increased dramatically in the late 1970s. Fairchild, for example, built fab lines in five different cities and hired teams of corporate consultants from the oil, chemical, and optics industries to facilitate the shift to mass manufacturing. In just two years, from 1978 to 1980, the nation's semiconductor manufacturing capacity doubled and capital expenditures increased from 8 to 20 percent of sales. By 1980 the industry was seven times more capital-intensive than the U.S. average.[8]

Analysts and industry participants agreed that the industry was maturing. While small firms had dominated in the 1960s and 1970s by pushing the frontiers of technology, it appeared that only corporations with access to huge amounts of capital and the ability to amortize the costs of semiconductor design and production over large quantities of chips would be able to survive. One observer concluded: "The days when independent entrepreneurs could split off and start their own small companies manufacturing semiconductors is over."[9]

Drawing analogies to the American automobile industry, most managers agreed that the start-ups that had made Silicon Valley famous were a thing of the past. One executive articulated the consensus when he predicted that "By the mid-1980s, only half a dozen large semiconductor firms will remain independent and dominate the industry." This consolidation would be accompanied by fundamental changes in corporate organization. According to one Fairchild veteran, the industry's fragmented structure would not survive, and "vertical integration, from component design through system manufacture and sale, appears to be the prime requisite for the new order of business." A widely circulated analysis of the industry in *Science* magazine similarly concluded that "Microelectronics companies are changing in character from small, high technology ventures of the 1950s and 1960s to large, mature corporations as they struggle to compete in the upcoming VLSI era."[10]

ABANDONING THE NETWORKS

Silicon Valley's semiconductor firms transformed themselves and the regional economy as they shifted to mass manufacturing. A handful of local producers grew from small entrepreneurial firms into large-scale corporations. The rapid expansion of companies like Fairchild, Intel, National Semiconductor, and Advanced Micro Devices (AMD) contributed to the creation of more than 200,000 net new technology jobs in the region during the 1970s, more than quadrupling local technology employment.[11] At the same time, a wave of acquisitions by large computer and systems houses from outside the region eliminated nearly a dozen independent Silicon Valley firms.[12]

In their headlong race to serve fast-expanding markets for memories and microprocessors, Silicon Valley's semiconductor producers failed to recognize the impact of their break with the past. Embracing the management models of the time, they saw the shift to mass production as a natural and inevitable stage in their industry's maturation. The practices of open exchange and informal collaboration that had allowed them to design new products and develop innovative applications were of little value in manufacturing large volumes of standard products. As they standardized products and processes to increase output and move down the learning curve, they frequently abandoned the local culture and relationships that had been the source of their earlier dynamism. They distanced themselves from customers, antagonized equipment suppliers, adopted functional management hierarchies, and spatially segmented the production process, separating R&D from manufacturing and assembly.

Silicon Valley's chipmakers transformed their own structures—and abandoned the region and its networks—just as Japanese semiconductor companies were changing the rules of the game in high-volume production. They embraced the mass production strategies that had dominated in the United States during the postwar era at the precise moment when their Japanese competitors were developing a more flexible model of mass production.[13] Failing to understand either the sources of Japan's strength or their own regional resources, Silicon Valley firms abandoned their culture and institutions for an obsolete approach to high-volume production.

The incursion of Japanese manufacturers into the market for semiconductor memories was swift. U.S. firms securely controlled the memory business throughout the 1970s, yet in 1984 Japanese producers took an early lead and captured virtually all of the latest-generation 256K DRAM market. When U.S. producers began high-volume production of the device in 1985, price-cutting was so fierce that they suffered unprecedented financial losses. By 1986 Silicon Valley's producers had all dropped out of DRAM production, and only three U.S. firms remained in the market. Japanese firms quickly came to control high-volume markets for static RAMs and erasable programmable memories as well; and by the end of the decade they dominated world semiconductor memory markets.[14]

The loss of the memory business spurred the worst recession in Silicon Valley history. Observers concluded that Silicon Valley was "losing its edge"—that the semiconductor industry was going the way of the nation's auto and steel producers at the hands of Japanese competition. One in every five local semiconductor employees lost his or her job during the layoffs and plant closings of 1985 and 1986. As the downturn spread to related sectors in the region, more than 25,000 jobs were lost, three-quarters of them in high technology industries.[15]

The initial response of Silicon Valley semiconductor firms was to attribute Japanese successes in the memory business to lower wages and domestic market protection. As early as 1978, Silicon Valley executives traveled to Washington under the auspices of the newly formed Semiconductor Industry Association (SIA) to testify about unfair Japanese trade practices. These efforts culminated in the passage in 1986 of the U.S.–Japan Semiconductor Trade Agreement, which set floor prices on memory devices to prevent "dumping" and encouraged an opening of Japanese markets to U.S. products.[16]

The SIA's response to Japanese competition represented the classic response of a mass production sector in crisis, seeking to restore the conditions for profitable high-volume production by stabilizing prices and market shares. It also mirrored the autarkic strategies of its member firms and alienated both their customers, who were hurt by the higher prices for semiconductors negotiated into the agreement, and their competitors and suppliers, who saw it as an attempt to create an oligopoly.[17]

It became increasingly clear, however, that Japan's advantage in semiconductors lay neither in low labor costs nor in market protection but in a distinctive combination of domestic policies and institutions that promoted investment and innovation in high-volume manufacturing. Government policies during the 1960s established Japan as a center of semiconductor production by controlling competition, structuring markets, and providing a stable supply of cheap credit. By the late 1970s, however, Japanese competitive strength derived primarily from institutions that sustained continuous improvement of semiconductor manufacturing processes.[18]

This advantage was exposed in 1980, when Hewlett-Packard announced that a comparison of Japanese and American 16K DRAMs showed that Japanese chips were of consistently higher quality than those made in the United States. HP started buying Japanese memory devices when its American supplier had trouble producing them, but soon concluded that "At first glance the impression is that the Japanese are using low cost and domestic protection as levers to build a strong base for exports. On closer inspection, this premise does not hold up. The Japanese semiconductor companies are using superior product quality to gain competitive advantage of enormous magnitude." This claim was supported with data showing that Japanese yields—the proportion of total devices to emerge from manufacturing without defects—were substantially higher, and cost per device therefore substantially lower, than those in America.[19]

Other customers and industry analysts subsequently confirmed the superiority of Japan's semiconductor manufacturing processes. In 1986, for example, an American market research company concluded that Japanese production costs for the 256K DRAM were half those of their American competitors. Moreover, this efficiency was not achieved through automation: Japanese firms had consistently fewer defects and lower costs even when they used the same machines as U.S. firms.[20]

Japanese semiconductor firms were organized to continually rebuild their mass manufacturing capabilities. An integrated yet flexible industrial structure promoted collaboration among suppliers, subcontractors, and customers to incrementally improve the complex process of wafer fabrication. According to one analyst:

> Japanese semiconductor manufacturers work willingly with suppliers to perfect and modify equipment to suit their requirements . . . In Japan, comparable ties not only link groups within large Japanese electronics manufacturers, but also link those companies to their smaller equipment suppliers. This networking provides the Japanese manufacturers with an infrastructure that permits lower product costs and faster development times . . . These cooperative links . . . between product and process groups and with equipment and material suppliers are responsible in part for the superior processing yields achieved in Japanese plants.[21]

While equipment vendors were often partially owned by their customers, the structure of the Japanese electronics industry represented an important departure from then-dominant business models. Close but not exclusive relationships between suppliers and customers ensured a combination of competitive discipline and responsiveness to market pressure that was impossible in the traditional vertically integrated corporation. Semiconductor equipment and device makers, for example, never served exclusively captive markets, yet close, often familial, ties with customers facilitated mutual adjustment. Equally close ties with banks ensured supplies of patient capital for reinvestment in newer—and increasingly costly—generations of manufacturing equipment.[22]

Silicon Valley's semiconductor producers, failing to recognize these organizational innovations, adopted a more traditional model of mass production. They focused on designing increasingly sophisticated circuits which they then turned over to centralized manufacturing facilities, often at a distant location, to be produced in high volume. Engineering and design were thus isolated from manufacturing; and suppliers, subcontractors, and customers were frequently treated as distant entities or adversaries. As a result, these firms lacked the opportunities for interactive learning and improvement that were built into the structure of the Japanese system.

This autarkic pattern was new to the region. Relations between design and production engineers in Silicon Valley's early semiconductor firms were naturally close, as they experimented with new designs and processes. Their relations with equipment suppliers were likewise often cooperative. Most equipment makers were spin-offs of the chip companies, and while sometimes this created antagonism, it was equally common for their engineers, often former colleagues, to share information, technology, and data.[23] Yet they lacked preparation for mass manufacturing. In the words of one Intel vice president:

> Remember what Silicon Valley companies were good at to begin with: sensing new market opportunities, new market development, and product prototype development. The industry was pouring the bulk of its intellectual and marketing capabilities into those parts of the business . . . Until recently, the GNP of Silicon Valley was all new products. Silicon Valley simply hasn't been well positioned to handle the commodity market.[24]

As they geared up for high-volume production, Silicon Valley's chipmakers followed what they believed were the "dictates of business."[25] Faced with rapidly falling prices, they attempted to shift the burden of increasingly severe business cycles onto their equipment suppliers—which tended to be small, undercapitalized firms—by double ordering during boom times and canceling orders abruptly during downturns. They pitted key vendors against one another for price reductions in order to minimize costs, and they were unwilling to fund the development of new equipment, seeking rather to buy the lowest-cost equipment. Finally, the semiconductor makers refused to share proprietary product or process information with their vendors out of concern for the security of technical information in an increasingly competitive business.

This reinforced the tendency of the financially weak equipment vendors to ship products that were not fully debugged, and undermined the trust needed for joint refining of the manufacturing process. Recent research suggests that the inferior quality and lower yields of U.S. semiconductor producers relative to their Japanese competitors were a direct result of these arms-length relationships.[26]

The large chipmakers not only antagonized their suppliers, they also distanced themselves from customers. In shifting to standard products, they saw little need for the ongoing interaction with customers that had characterized custom production. They became preoccupied with rewriting the specs for successive generations of high-volume products, and gained a reputation for arrogant "take it or leave it" attitudes. Their largely unsuccessful attempts to compete with their customers by forward integrating into digital watches and calculators reinforced this distrust.[27]

This distancing from customers also meant that the leading Silicon Valley producers failed to do what they had done so well in the past: identify new trends and markets. As a result, they missed a series of key market and technical opportunities, including the return to semi-custom and application-specific integrated circuits (ASICs), the complementary metal-oxide semiconductor (CMOS) process, and chip sets (which integrate the functions of an entire computer system onto a small number of customized integrated circuits). It took a new generation of start-ups in the 1980s to commercialize these technologies.

The leading Silicon Valley firms also sacrificed organizational flexibility as they grew. In their efforts to become the "big three" of the semiconductor industry, National, Intel, and AMD built bureaucratic organizations that centralized authority and undermined the autonomy of formerly independent business units. They created functional groups that distanced engineering and design from manufacturing, and they adopted variants of popular matrix management models.[28] The matrix, which was pioneered by DEC, appeared to offer a compromise between the decentralization of their entrepreneurial origins and the traditional corporate hierarchies to which they increasingly aspired. In practice, however, these hybrid organizations often created confusion and conflict. They undermined informal communications and decision-making processes and distanced management from employees and customers.

Talented engineers began to leave many of the large Silicon Valley semiconductor firms in the early 1980s.[29] Frustrated with the bureaucratic sluggishness and technological conservatism of these once flexible companies, they pioneered a new wave of 1980s start-ups that would eventually challenge the established producers with design innovation and responsiveness as much as the Japanese did with high-volume production.

Finally, the region's semiconductor firms revealed their autarkic strategies in their location decisions. Driven by the pressures of commodity production to minimize costs, Silicon Valley's chipmakers shifted manufacturing out of the region to lower-cost locations, both in the United States and overseas. While they moved unskilled assembly and test operations to Asia during the 1960s to exploit substantial wage differentials, during the 1970s they relocated wafer fabrication to lower-cost areas in the United States. The organizational separation of design and development from manufacturing facilitated this shift. By the early 1980s it appeared that only research, design, and prototype production would remain in Silicon Valley.

The spatial separation of design, manufacturing, and assembly further undermined the ability of the region's firms to improve products or respond rapidly to market changes.[30] Although the problems created by distance can sometimes be overcome by active management, this geographic split appears to have exacerbated a growing gulf between design and manufacturing in many large Silicon Valley semiconductor firms. This contrasts with the Japanese pattern of maintaining design, engineering, wafer fabrication, and assembly in the same location. In fact, Japanese firms did not move semiconductor manufacturing or assembly offshore until the mid-1980s, when they were motivated as much by concerns about market access as by costs.

Although Silicon Valley's producers viewed self-sufficiency as the inevitable path to industrial maturity, two alternatives existed. The region's managers might have recognized that a more efficient model of mass production was emerging in Japan and created institutions that would allow them to competitively manufacture high-quality, low-cost components. This would have meant following the Japanese and building collaborative ties both internally, between product development and manufacturing, and externally, particularly with their equipment suppliers. It would also have meant creating institutions that supported long-term returns on the massive and continuous capital investments increasingly necessary for commodity semiconductor production.

This demanded leadership and self-understanding that did not exist in Silicon Valley at the time. The Japanese continued to perfect their mass production system during the late 1980s, dramatically increasing production volumes for standard devices such as memories through the use of dedicated, large-scale "monster" integrated circuit production lines.[31] As the logic of capital investment and scale economies became key to pricing strategies for aggressive market penetration, the Japanese conglomerates were joined by South Korean firms, which benefited from a similar mix of industry structure and government support.[32]

Alternatively, Silicon Valley's leading semiconductor producers could have exploited the strengths of the region's networks by focusing on the manufacture of high-value-added, differentiated devices. This would have required them to rebuild relations with their customers and suppliers and re-create flexible organizations that allowed for rapid responses to changing markets and technologies. Such a strategy of continuous innovation would have been a natural extension of the custom strategy of the 1960s. It would have fully utilized the local social networks, institutions, and shared understandings about production they had created in earlier decades.

By pursuing an autarkic production strategy just as competitive conditions were changing, however, Silicon Valley's leading chipmakers made themselves vulnerable both to the more efficient Japanese mass producers and to the region's innovative start-ups. As a result, they lost market share in commodity memories to Japanese firms throughout the 1980s, while ceding the highly profitable semi-custom and specialty markets to a new generation of more flexible Silicon Valley–based ventures.

THE "HOT BOX" DERBY

The explosive growth of the semiconductor business during the 1970s fueled, and was in turn fueled by, the equally dramatic expansion of the minicomputer industry. In the decade after the Digital Equipment Corporation (DEC) defined a market for small, low-cost, high-speed computers, these two industries expanded in tandem, with successive families of integrated circuit (IC) devices making possible newer generations of minicomputers and advances in minicomputers creating a market for the next generation of ICs.

The new minicomputer makers, most of which were located along Route 128, competed by increasing the computing power, speed, and reliability of standardized systems. The competitive race to produce smaller, more powerful memories and microprocessors in the West was thus paralleled by an equally intense race to introduce smaller, more powerful minicomputers in the East. The minicomputer firms, like their California-based counterparts, manufactured standardized systems in high volume in order to lower unit costs and benefit from the learning curve. Their increasingly autarkic structures, which built on the region's independent firm–based system, became a source of vulnerability in the 1980s as computer technology and markets shifted.

DEC single-handedly created the minicomputer industry in 1965 when it introduced the 12-bit Programmed Data Processor (PDP)-8. As the first small computer that could be reprogrammed for multiple applications, the PDP-8 was four times faster than any rival system and sold for an unheard-of $18,000. With the PDP-8, DEC created a market for low-cost, powerful machines among sophisticated scientific and industrial customers. It eventually sold more than 50,000 units, making the PDP-8 the first mass-produced computer.

The success of the PDP-8 catapulted DEC from a small, unknown technical company into the ranks of the major computer makers, and simultaneously attracted a wide range of new competitors into the emerging minicomputer industry. More than thirty-five computer firms were started in Massachusetts alone during the 1960s and 1970s, including future industry leaders Data General (DG), Prime Computer, and Wang Laboratories. Established producers such as Hewlett-Packard, IBM, Honeywell, and Varian Associates also entered the microcomputer business.

The media dubbed the race to increase number-crunching speeds for systems targeted at sophisticated scientific and industrial customers the "hot box" minicomputer derby. The derby began in earnest in 1969, when DG introduced the 16-bit NOVA and shipped more than 200 units in its first year. By the early 1970s, the 16-bit minicomputer, which offered a doubling of speed and memory capacity, replaced the 12-bit machines as the industry standard, and the price of DEC's PDP-8 fell below $2,000. In the mid-1970s, DEC's PDP-11 series and other imitators competed for market share with DG's low-cost, fast-selling NOVAs. DEC recaptured the industry lead in 1977 by introducing a powerful 32-bit super-minicomputer (the VAX-11/780) that began to approach the power of a mainframe at a fraction of the cost and size. This spurred another round of competition, as the industry's competitors sought to mass produce their own 32-bit machines.

The dominant strategy, churning out standard minicomputers in large volumes, came to be known as "pumping iron." Most firms adopted minor variants of this approach. DEC broadened its product line by introducing new products for sophisticated scientific and engineering users, while DG mass manufactured a single basic architecture at low cost, offering the same or more computing power as DEC for lower prices.[33] Others defined niches that protected them from direct competition. Wang, for example, pioneered office automation systems, while Computervision focused on computer-aided design and manufacturing (CAD/CAM) systems.

The overriding challenge for all minicomputer producers in the boom years of the 1970s—as for their counterparts in Silicon Valley—was to manage unprecedented rates of growth. The steady combination of technical advance and price decreases stimulated tremendous market expansion. Sales increased some 35 percent annually, as commercial applications such as business data processing and communications replaced the earlier, slower-growing scientific and industrial control markets, and as minicomputers increasingly supplemented or displaced mainframes in their own markets.[34]

Ignoring the lesson of their own origins—that innovation could displace existing technologies and revolutionize product markets—the minicomputer makers organized themselves on the assumption of stable markets and technologies. They adopted autarkic structures that supported their high-volume manufacturing strategies: they sought to stabilize supply by internalizing inputs through vertical integration, they sought to stabilize demand by locking their customers into proprietary technologies, and they built centralized organizations to coordinate the complex process of mass producing computer systems.

As they competed to catch up with the computer industry leader, IBM, the minicomputer makers mimicked its highly integrated structure. In the words of Data General CEO Edson DeCastro: "The minicomputer industry is like the auto industry in the late 1920s and early 1930s when a lot of companies made various bits and pieces. Now there are only a few fully integrated companies. The small computer business is going that way." Assuming that a small number of companies would control the entire process of minicomputer design and production—from manufacturing chips and other hardware to writing software to marketing and distribution—the minicomputer makers aggressively invested in vertical integration during the late 1970s. In contrast with the situation of the Silicon Valley chipmakers, however, this represented an extension of the region's industrial system rather than a break from it.[35]

DEC began designing and manufacturing its own integrated circuits in 1976. By 1979, after three years of heavy investment, its internal semiconductor operation had increased tenfold in size, making it one of the largest integrated circuit producers in the nation. By 1983 DEC was building its minicomputers from the bottom up, manufacturing everything from microprocessors, disk drives, and circuit boards to monitors, to floppy disks and power supplies. DEC even tooled the sheet metal and plastics for its components.

DG expanded its capacity to manufacture components such as semiconductor memories, peripherals, and printed circuit boards as well. By 1981, after five years and approximately $200 million of investment in vertical integration, a DG executive explained: "We've sacrificed short-term profit for long-term position. But this is the price that today's high flyers will have to pay for a real future in this business." He claimed that the investment allowed the firm to optimize the performance of its machines at the systems level and would significantly reduce manufacturing costs by ensuring economies of scale in component production.[36]

This autarkic business model was reinforced by the proprietary approach of the minicomputer companies. Emulating IBM, which derived substantial revenues in follow-on sales and service to its established customer base, they distinguished their products with proprietary architectures and software. In 1977, for example, DEC introduced the VAX line of minicomputers, which were optimized for its proprietary VMS operating system. The DG NOVA was likewise proprietary. Upgrades or add-on equipment for these systems could be purchased only from the original vendor. As a result, the initial purchase of a system typically tied customers tightly to the hardware vendor and created a long-term dependence on its technology.

Competition in computers intensified in the late 1970s with the introduction of the personal computer (PC). The PC, which was built around a simple microprocessor, changed the rules of the computer business by offering a small, flexible and very low-cost alternative to the minicomputer. The personal computer quickly invaded the low end of the minicomputer market after IBM introduced its PC in 1981. At the same time, established computer systems firms entered the high end of the market, reducing profit margins on high-performance products. As the market for minicomputers narrowed and the pressure to cut costs intensified, the industry began to consolidate.[37]

By 1980 DEC alone accounted for 40 percent of the market, and most observers predicted that only three or four firms would survive the inevitable shakeout in computers. In the words of DEC's Olsen:

> Massachusetts used to have several automobile manufacturers. It was before my time, but I was told that on Route 9 leaving Boston there were a number of people who made cars, and in the country once there were hundreds of car manufacturers. In time we got down to only two-and-a-half or three-and-a-half, and undoubtedly that's going to happen in the computer industry . . . That's a natural cycle in any industry.[38]

THE COSTS OF AUTARKY

The accelerated expansion of the minicomputer business during the 1970s fueled the revival of the Massachusetts economy popularly known as the "Massachusetts miracle." By 1980 Route 128's large minicomputer manufacturers—DEC, DG, Wang, Honeywell, and Prime—dominated the regional economy and together controlled more than two-thirds of the minicomputer market. Their growth spurred the creation of close to 100,000 net new technology jobs in the region between 1970 and 1985.[39]

Just as the industry's growth fueled the revitalization of the Route 128 economy, the crisis of the minicomputer business threw the region into prolonged decline. Faced with shrinking markets, the region's minicomputer producers all reported significant drops in earnings. More than 50,000 technology jobs were lost along Route 128 during the late 1980s; the region was so dominated by large minicomputer companies that, like Silicon Valley and its semiconductor firms, it followed its leading producers into crisis.[40] In this case, however, the competitive threat was not from Japan but rather from U.S. producers of personal computers and workstations, including many start-ups based in Silicon Valley.

The difficulties of the minicomputer firms are typically explained by their focus on a declining market. By this account, Route 128 producers simply bet on the wrong product. Investments in middle-sized minicomputers, rather than smaller machines, left them the victims of a maturing product cycle. This analysis begs the deeper questions of why these firms were so slow to respond to changes in computer markets and technologies, and why their belated efforts to adapt were unsuccessful. The computer business boomed throughout the 1980s, with the emergence of important new markets for microprocessor-based systems, but these markets were not served by Route 128 companies.

The difficulties of the Route 128 minicomputer firms lay in the autarkic business model they created in their drive to dominate the industry. Like Silicon Valley's semiconductor producers, they bet on a product and built organizations that assumed stable markets and technologies. Ironically, they had recently upstaged IBM's mainframe business by demonstrating to Big Blue precisely how quickly computer markets could be redefined. Yet ignoring the lesson of their own history—that they were in the computer business, not the minicomputer business—they clung to a single-product world view.

Building on the independent firm–based industrial system of Route 128, the large minicomputer firms achieved a far greater degree of autarky than did their counterparts in Silicon Valley. They became increasingly self-contained, inward-looking, and inflexible as they elaborated a business model that combined vertical integration, proprietary standards, and organizational centralization. While the costs of autarky remained largely hidden throughout the buoyant 1970s, when demand for minicomputers boomed, they became increasingly problematic once markets shifted.

Route 128 producers did not recognize that the nature of competition in computers was changing. No longer were their only competitors large, integrated minicomputer producers that periodically introduced new generations of existing systems. Both small start-ups and the relatively autonomous divisions of large firms were better organized to rapidly introduce innovative new products with state-of-the-art technology. Silicon Valley–based start-up Sun Microsystems, for example, introduced five new generations of workstations during its first four years of existence. Even IBM, in a rare departure from tradition, introduced its personal computer in only nine months by setting up an autonomous division and purchasing most of its components from outside suppliers.[41]

Initially, most Route 128 minicomputer firms did not recognize microprocessor-based technologies as a threat. They dismissed microcomputers as either irrelevant or silly, much as IBM had dismissed the threat of minicomputers two decades before. DEC's Ken Olsen claimed in the late 1970s that "the personal computer will fall flat on its face in business" and prohibited the use of the term "personal computer" within the company. Five years later he referred to workstations as "snake oil." DG, Wang, and Prime similarly regarded personal computers as toys, rather than as serious competition for their weightier systems. They continued to focus on "pumping iron" for existing customers and defending profitable installed bases, rather than developing products for new markets.[42]

The minicomputer makers also refused to abandon their proprietary architectures and operating systems, in spite of growing evidence that customers preferred the flexibility of open systems. Personal computers and workstations used publicly available operating systems such as MS-DOS or Unix, which allowed customers to run applications software produced by third-party vendors and allowed applications produced by different firms to work together. As a result, customers were no longer locked in to the proprietary standards of their hardware supplier—increasingly they were able to use hardware, peripherals, and software from different vendors. Having built organizations based on their highly profitable proprietary systems, however, the minicomputer makers were slow to offer lower-priced machines with standard operating systems.[43]

Even when producers like DEC and DG belatedly entered the personal computer and workstation markets, their autarkic structures subverted their efforts to develop competitive products in a timely fashion. Accustomed to the luxury of three-to-five-year product-development cycles in minicomputers and slowed by the need to develop all of the systems components internally, they introduced microcomputers that were often several years late. Their cumbersome organizations were unable to keep up with the rapid pace of new product introduction set by more flexible start-ups.

DEC's efforts to develop personal computers and other low-end machines foundered on its hybrid structure, which combined a decentralized, team-based organization with centralized functional groups. As company-wide employment surpassed 100,000, matrix management generated almost paralyzing conflict. While the business groups continued to generate innovative projects, these groups often became fiefdoms that fought over what to build and lobbied fiercely for support from the central engineering and manufacturing departments. Product managers faced a constant battle to marshal internal support for resources, manpower, and influence to develop new products. They fought over pricing, volume, and design, and they fought not only with one another but also with Olsen and the powerful Operations Committee.[44]

By the mid-1980s DEC insiders acknowledged that their biggest adversaries were internal DEC divisions and groups, not other companies. In the early 1980s, for example, Olsen established three groups to develop personal computers. Rather than the healthy competition that he envisioned, however, the groups fought continuously over resources. Avram Miller, who directed the top-of-the-line Professional Group, complained: "It was a total disaster. Nothing worse could have happened. We managed to split all the engineering activities, all the third-party software activities, manufacturing, everything. I ended up without any word processing software, for instance. I couldn't go outside to get it, and I couldn't get the DEC group to do it because they were busy doing it for the DECMate."[45]

DEC's functional groups also grew increasingly insulated from changing market demands. The engineering group, still oriented toward highly engineered mid-sized time-sharing systems for price-insensitive markets, built costly features into new products that consumers were unwilling to pay for. Marketing continued to devote most of its efforts to the company's profitable mid-sized computers rather than promoting personal computers. As a result, DEC's early PCs were overengineered, overpriced, and undermarketed. It is not surprising that they attracted few customers.[46]

Vertical integration further narrowed the possibilities for innovation in Route 128 firms. DEC's commitment to controlling all of the internal components of its systems became a major constraint on its efforts to build personal computers. DEC designed and built every piece of its Professional personal computer, except for the hard disk drive and the line cord. This created problems of timing and coordination. One observer recounts how a group manager scaled back the original production and sales estimates for the personal computer from 250,000 to 100,000 units. But when he visited the assembly lines that produced the keyboards and power supplies, managers reported that they were still building 250,000 units of each component because they had orders from higher up in the organization—the powerful Operations Committee—to supply the original volumes.[47]

More important, the reliance on captive sources of supply locked the company into its existing technologies and skills and eliminated competitive pressure to innovate or control costs. Vertical integration may have permitted important cost savings during the long and proprietary product cycles of the 1960s and 1970s. As the pace of innovation accelerated, however, it became impossible for any firm to remain at the leading edge of every system component or to quickly reorient narrowly specialized technological capabilities toward entirely new products. By the early 1980s many of DEC's internally manufactured products were technologically obsolete. The emergence of laser printers, for example, undercut DEC's market leadership in impact printing technology, and its disk drives were two years behind those of the leading-edge Silicon Valley suppliers.[48]

Other Route 128 minicomputer firms struggled with still less flexible structures. DG, Prime, and Wang, for example, all combined centralized functional hierarchies and vertical integration—lacking even the partial decentralization that DEC had pioneered. They failed to recognize the importance of personal computers, they remained committed to proprietary operating systems long after customers had rejected them; and they faced mounting difficulties as a result. Despite a wave of corporate reorganizations in the early and mid-1980s, none of the Route 128 minicomputer firms managed to capture a significant share of the growing personal computer or workstation markets.[49]

As a result, the minicomputer makers began losing their most talented employees: DG lost eight vice presidents and several dozen middle managers during an eighteen-month period in 1983 and 1984, and DEC lost some thirty senior executives in 1983 alone.[50] These defectors left both for other firms in the region, such as start-up Apollo, and for opportunities on the West Coast with competitors such as Sun Microsystems. Others, like Jeff Kalb, started their own firms, many in Silicon Valley. And in 1985 DEC set up a research lab in Palo Alto—acknowledging that the state of the art in computer systems had shifted from Route 128 to Silicon Valley.

The experience of the Route 128 minicomputer companies during the 1970s and 1980s—like that of the commodity semiconductor producers of Silicon Valley—illustrates the danger of betting on a product in an era of rapid technological and market change. Strategies and structures dedicated to incremental refinements within a single, established trajectory undermined the ability of these companies to respond rapidly to product and process innovations. Blinded by their own success, producers in both regions focused primarily on local competitors and failed to see the transformations that had not only changed the rules but indeed had redefined the game.

By the end of the 1980s Route 128 had ceded its position as the locus of computer innovation to the West Coast just as Silicon Valley had lost the commodity memory business to more efficient Japanese manufacturers. The leading producers in each region struggled unsuccessfully for the remainder of the decade to regain their former dominance. Of the minicomputer makers, only DEC remained profitable during the late 1980s. By 1992 Prime had been acquired and its computer operations discontinued, Wang had filed for Chapter 11 bankruptcy protection, and Data General had undertaken a major reorganization in the face of a bleak future. In Silicon Valley, both National Semiconductor and AMD continued to lose money and lay off workers through the end of the decade. Only Intel recovered quickly from the loss of the memory markets, largely because of its control of the lucrative microprocessor market.

But important differences continued to distinguish the two regions. Route 128's minicomputer makers continued to invest in the independent firm–based system from which they had emerged. DEC, which was far more dominant in the Route 128 economy than any single company was in Silicon Valley, remained a model of corporate autonomy and self-reliance throughout the 1980s. While its downfall came later than that of its local competitors, DEC's autarkic structure would have far-reaching consequences for the region's ability to adjust.

Silicon Valley's large semiconductor producers, in contrast, were shaped by their origins in a more decentralized network-based industrial system. As a result, these firms never achieved the scale or vertical integration of other domestic chipmakers such as Texas Instruments or Motorola. Nor did they completely withdraw from the region's informal networks and relationships. They continued to rely on local patterns of interfirm mobility, new firm formation, and informal exchange. These relationships would ultimately facilitate the recovery of the large chipmakers and, more immediately, the turnaround of the regional economy.

5

RUNNING WITH TECHNOLOGY

Somehow, companies in California get things done faster, deals go down faster
. . . they seem to run with technology faster; each year we're spending money
faster there.
—Howard Anderson, Yankee Group and Battery Ventures

▶ Silicon Valley recovered rapidly from the collapse of the semiconductor memory business. A wave of start-ups and the restructuring of
several large firms fueled industrial diversification and renewed regional growth. By the end of the 1980s Silicon Valley had surpassed
Route 128 as the national center of computer systems innovation. The
strengths of Silicon Valley's producers helped account for America's
continued dominance of the markets for specialty semiconductors and
microprocessors as well as for small computers and software—in spite
of the loss of consumer electronics and commodity semiconductors to
Japan.

The prospects for industrial recovery along Route 128, in contrast,
appeared increasingly bleak. The difficulties of the big four minicomputer firms continued to worsen. Even DEC, which survived the 1980s
intact, faced the worst losses of its history in the early 1990s. The
performance of the Route 128 start-ups was equally disappointing. Well
before cuts in defense spending dealt a second blow to the regional
economy, the "Massachusetts Miracle" seemed no more than a cam-
paign slogan and a distant memory.

It was not Japan, Inc., but Silicon Valley that overwhelmed Route
128. Silicon Valley firms introduced a continuing stream of high-value-
added semiconductors, computers, components, and software-related
products, while the Route 128 producers remained shackled by institutional and cultural rigidities and fell further behind technologically.

By the end of the decade, Silicon Valley producers even dominated the market for workstations that had been invented by Route 128's Apollo Computer.

The new firms formed in the two regions during the 1980s fared very differently, reflecting their locations in contrasting industrial systems. The entrepreneurs in Silicon Valley rejected the corporate models of their predecessors and returned to the strengths of the Valley's network-based system, pioneering a more flexible business model that contributed to the region's revitalization. Route 128 start-ups, in contrast, were isolated from sources of essential market information, technology, and skill. Lacking forums for experimentation or learning, they repeated the mistakes of the minicomputer makers, and foundered or grew only slowly.

DIVERGING ECONOMIES

While both Route 128 and Silicon Valley experienced employment downturns in the middle of the 1980s, Route 128 continued to lose technology jobs while technology employment in Silicon Valley recovered rapidly, surpassing its prerecession levels by 1988. Technology firms based in Silicon Valley added more than 65,000 net new jobs during the decade compared to only 18,000 added along Route 128.

Data on corporate performance, which paint only a partial picture of regional economic activity, reinforce this story. By the end of the 1980s, in spite of Silicon Valley's inferior starting position, there were 50 percent more public technology companies headquartered there, and they recorded greater total sales and faster rates of growth than those located in Route 128. Most striking was the performance of public technology firms started after 1980. By the end of the 1980s public companies started in Silicon Valley during the decade collectively accounted for more than $22 billion in sales, while their Route 128 counterparts had generated only $2 billion.[1]

Investment decisions reflected this divergence as well. Annual venture capital investments in Northern California were double or triple those in Massachusetts throughout the 1980s (Figure 3). Over the course of the decade, Massachusetts-based companies received $3 billion in venture capital, or 75 percent of the total raised in the region, while firms in Northern California received $9 billion, or 130 percent of the total capital raised locally. Silicon Valley companies were consis-

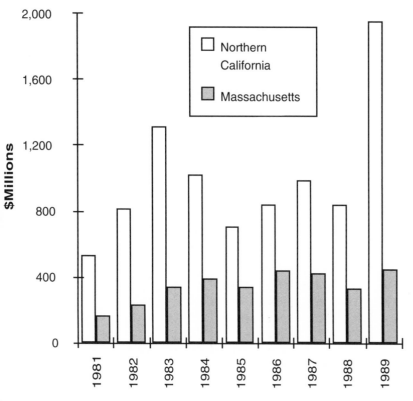

Figure 3. Venture capital investment, Northern California and Massachusetts, 1981–1989. Data from *Venture Capital Journal*.

tently awarded at least one-third of the nation's total pool of venture capital.[2]

Silicon Valley companies also grew faster than those along Route 128. By 1990, 39 of the top 100 fastest-growing electronics companies in the nation were based in Silicon Valley and only 4 were based on Route 128 (Figure 4). These rankings are based on five-year sales growth rates, but the list is not limited to small firms. Multi-billion-dollar companies such as Sun Microsystems, Apple Computer, Intel Semiconductor, and Hewlett-Packard all ranked among the fastest-growing enterprises in 1990.

Nothing in the Route 128 experience matched the spectacular successes of the 1980s generation of Silicon Valley start-ups such as Sun

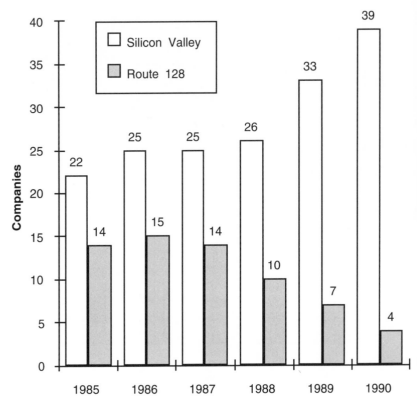

Figure 4. Number of fast-growing electronics firms, Silicon Valley and Route 128, 1985–1990. Data from *Electronic Business*.

Microsystems, Conner Peripherals, and Silicon Graphics. By 1992, 74 Route 128 technology establishments enjoyed annual revenues of $100 million. Almost half of these were units of firms headquartered outside of the region, and most had been founded before 1970. Silicon Valley, in contrast, had 113 technology companies reporting 1992 revenues in excess of $100 million. The great majority were headquartered in the region and had been started during the 1970s and 1980s (Figure 5).

The divergent performance of the Route 128 and Silicon Valley economies during the 1980s cannot be attributed to regional differentials in real estate costs, wages, or tax levels. Land and office space costs were significantly higher in Silicon Valley than in the Route 128 region, as were the wages and salaries of production workers, engineers, and

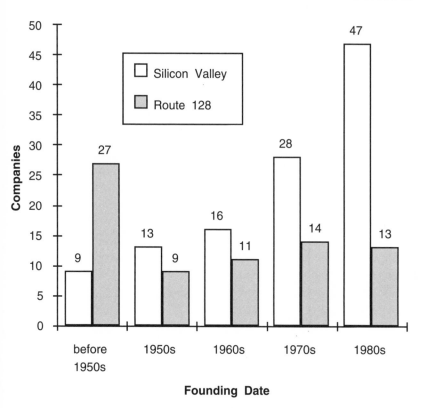

Figure 5. High technology firms and business units with revenues over $100 million in 1992, by date of founding and region. Data from Corporate Technology Information Service, 1993.

managers. Similarly, there were no significant differences in tax rates between California and Massachusetts. It is ironic, in light of traditional theories of industrial location, that a relatively high-cost location like Silicon Valley was the more attractive location for both start-ups and the business units of technology companies headquartered elsewhere.[3]

Nor can the differences in regional performance be traced to patterns of defense spending. Route 128 has historically relied more heavily on military spending than Silicon Valley, and hence is more vulnerable to defense cutbacks. However, the downturn in the Route 128 electronics industry began in 1984, at a time when the value of prime contracts to the region was still increasing (Figure 6). While defense spending cannot account for the timing of the downturn in the region's technol-

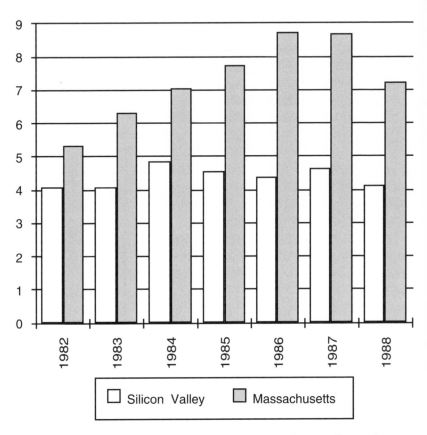

Figure 6. Department of Defense prime contracts, Silicon Valley and Massachusetts, 1982–1988. Data from *Washington HQ Services Directorate*, U.S. Department of Defense.

ogy industry, the military spending cutbacks that began in the late 1980s exacerbated the difficulties of an already troubled regional economy.

Finally, Route 128's failure to maintain its lead in state-of-the-art computing—particularly its failure to shift from minicomputers to personal computers and workstations—is sometimes attributed to the absence of a local semiconductor industry. There is a clear technological trajectory from microprocessors to the third generation of smaller computers, and Silicon Valley computer companies surely benefited from proximity to leading-edge chipmakers. But Route 128 did not lack for semiconductor capacity: DEC's captive semiconductor operations in Massachusetts were state of the art; Raytheon and DG also had in-house chip facilities. The problem lay instead in the organization of the region's industrial system. Many of Route 128's technological capabilities were internalized within large firms and thus not available to start-ups or to other local producers.

LEARNING FROM FAILURE

By the 1980s Silicon Valley was no longer the tightly knit community of technological pioneers that it had been in earlier decades. No longer did everyone in the region "know everyone else," and the semiconductor downturn had forced engineers to recognize the limits of the feverish pace of innovation and wealth generation of the 1960s and 1970s. There was a newfound willingness among some Silicon Valley firms to initiate lawsuits against former employees, cross-licensees, or suspected imitators. The pace of job-hopping slowed and the days of overnight venture capital funding waned. But the culture of relative openness, the fast pace of business activity, and the cooperative practices that distinguished the region remained intact.

Repeat entrepreneurs were increasingly common in Silicon Valley during the 1980s. When John Gifford founded Maxim Integrated Products in 1983, for example, he had already been involved in six different start-ups in a twenty-five-year career. This pattern was not atypical. As the Apple Computer CEO, John Sculley, put it: "In Silicon Valley, if someone fails, we know they're in all likelihood going to reappear in some other company in a matter of months."[4]

Some outsiders viewed the intensification of competition and the frenzy of entrepreneurial activity as "pathological," criticizing the formation of multiple start-ups in the same technology and the proliferation of small firms as a wasteful drain of resources. But the competitive rivalries among Silicon Valley firms forced new firms to define and defend their markets, while the complex mix of competition and collaboration spurred innovation. Although many individual firms did not survive these competitive struggles, the region as a whole thrived.[5]

There were many failures in Silicon Valley in the 1980s. Some, such as Gavilan and Trident, were spectacular. But failure was viewed as an opportunity for learning. One executive recruiter noted: "Everybody knows that some of the best presidents in the Valley are people that have stumbled." These entrepreneurs learned both from their own experiences and from those of their colleagues and predecessors. An accumulation of local knowledge allowed them to experiment with new strategies and organizational forms as well as new technologies. George Gilder describes how this phenomenon of succeeding by learning from failure enhanced the region's competitiveness:

> Unless failure is possible, no learning is possible . . . in the realm of ideas, unless falsification is possible, learning isn't possible. As a matter of fact, in information theory, no information is transmitted unless negation is possible, and so the tolerance of failure is absolutely critical to the success of Silicon Valley. If you don't tolerate failure, you can't permit success. The successful people have a lot more failures than the failures do.[6]

The continuous recombination of differently specialized resources in turn strengthened the region's industrial fabric. According to one semiconductor executive:

> There is a unique atmosphere here that continually revitalizes itself by virtue of the fact that today's collective understandings are informed by yesterday's frustrations and modified by tomorrow's recombinations . . . Learning occurs through these recombinations. No other geographic area creates recombination so effectively with so little disruption. The entire industrial fabric is strengthened by this process.[7]

The ease of new firm formation meant that many more technical paths were pursued in Silicon Valley than would have been possible in either a traditional large firm or a region with less fluid social and industrial structures. Most companies or stable regions pursue a single technical option and, over time, become increasingly committed to a single technological trajectory. A network-based regional economy like Silicon Valley, alternatively, generates and pursues a rich array of technological and organizational alternatives.

The Silicon Valley entrepreneurs of the 1980s, like those of earlier decades, were typically engineers who were frustrated by unsuccessful attempts to pursue new ideas within the region's established companies. The local venture capitalist Don Valentine claimed that this frustration was more important than the promise of financial gain:

> The presumption is that employees of the big companies leave and go to venture companies to found start-ups to make more money. That's not the way. Andy Grove, Bob Noyce and others left Fairchild to found Intel, not to make more money. They left to make a product that Fairchild was either unable or unwilling to make or, for whatever reason, didn't get

around to making. That's why ventures are started: from lack of responsiveness in big companies . . . The only reason good people leave is because
they become frustrated. They want to do something they can't do in their
present environment.[8]

The entrepreneurial process was nourished by the region's networks
of social relations and technical infrastructure. The case of Silicon
Graphics is illustrative. In the early 1980s two Stanford University
engineering professors defined an approach to producing high-performance 3-D graphics workstations that exploited powerful new semiconductor technologies being developed in the region. Several local
venture capital funds, including the Mayfield Fund, provided seed
funding and helped identify and hire an experienced manager from
Hewlett-Packard to serve as CEO. After Silicon Graphics was started in
1985, its founders encouraged Mayfield to finance MIPS Computer
Systems, a venture founded by a Stanford colleague who was working
on the technology that would eventually provide the central processor
for their systems. Silicon Graphics purchased many of the specialized
inputs for its systems, including semi-custom integrated circuits and
software, from local producers. In some cases, as with its microprocessor vendor, MIPS, these relations were extremely close and collaborative.[9]

In this string of decentralized relationships—among Silicon Graphics,
Stanford, venture capitalists, MIPS, and other local suppliers and service
providers—the boundaries between the inside of the firm and its external environment were blurred. It was difficult to define where Silicon Graphics ended and Silicon Valley began. The founders of Silicon
Graphics insist that the firm could not have been started elsewhere in
the country and that proximity to the region's sophisticated infrastructure was key to their ability to continue innovating.

Similar entrepreneurial histories were common in Silicon Valley in
the 1980s. A 1988 study commissioned by Digital Equipment Corporation assessing Silicon Valley's engineering and technical strengths
concluded:

the region possesses a special kind of infrastructure that has in effect
institutionalized innovation in technical fields across the board . . . The
Bay Area is unrivaled in sheer variety of companies and level of formal
and informal networking among companies in technical fields. Hardware
and software are closely aligned. Prototype development and engineering
is particularly strong. It is this cross cutting strength—and an economic
infrastructure comprising strong technology, human resource, capital in-

puts, and numerous industrial synergies—that makes Northern California a magnet for top engineering talent, innovative start-ups, and major breakthroughs in technical fields across the board.[10]

An executive at 3Com, a producer of computer networks, explained the advantages of this infrastructure in terms of reduced time-to-market:

> One of the things that Silicon Valley lets you do is minimize the costs associated with getting from idea to product. Vendors here can handle everything. If you specify something—or, as is often the case, if the vendor helps you specify it—you can get hardware back so fast that your time-to-market is incredibly short. This means that the majority of our vendors are here. Silicon Valley has an incredibly deep vendor base, and it is intensely competitive. You can build relations with vendors here that are not replicable elsewhere.[11]

Geographic proximity to a wide range of sophisticated customers and potential customers also enhanced and accelerated product development. One study concluded that Silicon Valley semiconductor firms founded in the early 1980s could prototype products 60 percent faster and ship them 40 percent faster than firms in other parts of the United States.[12]

A venture capitalist with experience in both regions described the competitive advantage that close relationships with state-of-the-art suppliers provided: "In Silicon Valley, I learn that my buddy is designing a new chip, so I develop a system to use it and have a big lead on the competition. Likewise, I can design a new Conner Peripherals disk drive into my product before my competitors elsewhere have even heard of Conner."[13]

An executive at a semiconductor firm founded in the 1980s described why the presence of a local customer base was critical to his firm's success:

> When we come out with the specs for a new product, we take them to a series of companies that we have relations with and that have good technical horsepower, and they'll give us feedback on the features they like and don't like. It's an iterative process: we define a product, we get feedback and improve it, we refine it and develop associated products. The process feeds on itself. And the fact that these customers are nearby means that the iterations are faster; rapid communication is absolutely critical to ensuring fast time-to-market.[14]

The region's networks of personal relationships and culture of open exchange facilitated this process of adjustment and learning. An executive of another semiconductor company described it this way: "It's not necessary that our customers are geographically close, but the fact that the Valley has some of the leaders in systems and computers is a vital part of the cross-pollination process. We use others' existence to create our own existence: our form is vitally affected by their presence. We change and so do they."[15]

Silicon Valley's venture capital community promoted these interactions by encouraging the companies in their portfolios to work together. Kleiner Perkins Caufield and Byers imitated Japanese corporate models and created a *zaibatsu* fund that allowed them to remain intimately involved with the older firms in their portfolio and to promote cross-investment by member firms. The idea was to create a network that would strengthen each individual venture as well as the collective. As MasPar Computer Corporation's Jeff Kalb noted: "My venture capitalists are always pushing me to work with or at least talk with other members of their portfolio about my business problems; and the zaibatsu fund allows us all to invest in each other's companies."[16]

Stifled Opportunities

Although the autarkic structures of Route 128's independent firm–based system had provided economic scale and organizational stability that were valuable in an earlier era, by the 1980s they served primarily to discourage adaptation. The commitment of local companies to vertical integration meant that technical capabilities and know-how in the region remained locked up within large firms. The paucity of horizontal communications stifled opportunities for experimentation and learning, while traditional corporate structures limited the development of managerial initiative and skill. As a result, while Route 128's skill base and supplier infrastructure were advanced by comparison with those of most other regions, by the mid-1980s they were neither as technologically sophisticated nor as diversified as Silicon Valley's.

This may have posed a minor inconvenience to large firms, but it became a significant disadvantage for start-ups and small firms that were unable to learn about or acquire state-of-the art components or services as rapidly as their West Coast counterparts. In Kalb's words:

> It's hard for a small company to start in Massachusetts because you can't get stuff like ICs and disk drives fast. Route 128 is dominated by large, vertically integrated firms that do everything themselves. In Silicon Valley, you can get anything you want on the market. You can get all those things in Route 128 sooner or later, but the decisions are much faster if you're in Silicon Valley. From the East Coast, interacting with the West Coast is only possible for three to four hours a day because of the time difference, and you spend lots of time on the phone. It's no one thing, but if you get a 20–30 percent time-to-market advantage by being in Silicon Valley, that's really significant.[17]

Another transplanted engineer, who was hired by Sun Microsystems after fifteen years in Massachusetts, described the limits of the Route 128 infrastructure: "In Silicon Valley, I feel like I'm much more in touch, like my hand is on the pulse of the industry. When you're at a Route 128 company, the vendors with the leading-edge technologies who come and talk to you are all either from Silicon Valley or Japan, they're not from Norwood."[18]

The legacy of corporate secrecy further inhibited entrepreneurship in the region. The gossip about new start-ups that was continuous in Silicon Valley was rare along Route 128. Former DEC employees report that they rarely knew about local start-ups and that there were few forums at which to develop role models or to learn from the experiences of other local entrepreneurs. Moreover, there were few places in the region to develop general management skills. While Silicon Valley management models accorded extensive autonomy and responsibility to individuals, the organizational structures of the large Route 128 minicomputer companies were far less conducive to the development of broad management capabilities. Hewlett-Packard's semi-autonomous divisional structure and participatory management style, for example, offered ideal training in the general management skills needed for a start-up. HP executives alone were responsible for starting more than eighteen firms between 1974 and 1984, including notable successes such as Rolm, Tandem, and Pyramid Technology.[19]

DEC's styles of management and decisionmaking, for example, limited opportunities to develop general management skills. With the exception of Data General, it is difficult to identify successful DEC spin-offs. Even Data General's hard-edged environment, which regularly drove employees to quit, was so centralized and hierarchical that it stunted managerial development. A local venture capitalist described the problem:

the bigger companies in Massachusetts all are poor development ground for managers of new companies . . . We do a lot of research on senior people, and in Massachusetts some large companies aren't as attractive as the Intels and HPs on the West Coast. Digital is famous for its somewhat elaborate consensus decisionmaking, but venture capital people have concluded it's not a good place to find entrepreneurs for running a start-up . . . The matrix management and decision by consensus means that a manager who's been at DEC for a long time is going to be indecisive.[20]

DEC's inward-looking, familial culture, which tended to ostracize departed employees, further discouraged entrepreneurship in the region.

Not surprisingly, when large numbers of engineers ultimately left Route 128's large minicomputer firms during the 1980s, many of the most talented relocated to Silicon Valley. As one Route 128 consultant and venture capitalist noted: "We always worked on the theory that there were good people in the old traditional companies and that they were ready to come out if we had the money. Now we wake up to find that half of them moved to California and started companies like MIPS."[21]

The decline of Route 128 accelerated as the region's most experienced and ambitious engineers recognized that opportunities to join or start technologically exciting new ventures lay not in New England but along the increasingly crowded freeways of Northern California. In 1983 the San Jose metropolitan area had the densest concentration of highly skilled manufacturing workers in the country, while the Boston area ranked sixth. Migration flows were largely responsible for this difference: Silicon Valley was the largest net recipient of skilled manufacturing workers in the country, while the Boston area showed a net loss.[22]

The New Chip Companies

The largest wave of start-ups in Silicon Valley's history began in the late 1970s and accelerated during the 1980s. The region's new ventures included not only semiconductor firms but also scores of computer, disk drive, software, networking, and computer-aided engineering and design companies. These firms diversified the regional economy and created markets for a range of new technologies including reduced instruction set computing (RISC), application-specific integrated circuits (ASICs), workstations, small disk drives, flash memory, pen-based and hand-held personal computers, multimedia, and virtual reality.[23]

Perhaps the defining feature of Silicon Valley's 1980s-vintage start-ups is the extent to which they explicitly rejected the corporate models of their predecessors. They pioneered not only products but also corporate strategies and structures, revitalizing the traditions of innovation and responsiveness that had characterized Silicon Valley in its early decades. In so doing, they constructed a more flexible local industrial system, one that was remarkably well suited to the competitive conditions of the 1980s. By creating new markets and defining new applications, these firms flourished in a competitive environment characterized by shorter product cycles and accelerating technological change.

The semiconductor industry led the revitalization of Silicon Valley. Although observers had predicted consolidation and the demise of the U.S. semiconductor industry, an unprecedented wave of semiconductor start-ups began in the late 1970s.[24] The majority of these new ventures were located in Silicon Valley, and they quickly became the most profitable and innovative segment of the industry. Realizing that they were no match for low-margin Japanese commodity producers, Silicon Valley firms soon dominated world markets for design-intensive, high-value-added specialty and semi-custom semiconductors.[25]

These 1980s start-ups represented a collective revolt by Silicon Valley engineers against the region's established chipmakers. Entrepreneurs like T. J. Rodgers of Cypress Semiconductors and Gordon Campbell of Chips and Technologies quit jobs at large semiconductor firms in frustration with their employers' growing isolation from customers and unwillingness to pursue promising technologies. Complaining that the big firms had lost the agility that had made Silicon Valley famous, these engineers "voted with their feet" and exposed the rigidities of the established semiconductor firms even before Japan did so.[26]

These start-ups pioneered a model of semiconductor production that built on the region's social and technical networks. They introduced specialized, design-intensive devices that allowed them to define new markets and avoid the price wars that plague commodity producers. Many focused on product development and design, subcontracting manufacturing in order to avoid the costs and risks of semiconductor fabrication. And most created flexible, decentralized organizations that allowed them to respond rapidly to market changes.

While the region's established firms manufactured large volumes of general-purpose devices such as DRAMs and other commodity memories, the newcomers produced small batches of complex, high-value-added components. Rather than attempting to achieve scale economies to reduce unit manufacturing costs, Silicon Valley's new chipmakers introduced a continuing stream of differentiated products. These design-intensive chips were often custom or semi-custom devices designed for a particular customer or specialized for a particular application. They were typically developed in collaboration with customers and designed to improve the performance of everything from cameras, cars, machine tools, missiles, and microwave ovens to industrial robots, telecommunications networks, fax machines, disk drives, printers, and ultrasound machines. In computers, the largest single market for semiconductors, they were used to increase processing speed and power, to improve computational and graphics capabilities, and to reduce size—often at a significant price premium over standard products.[27]

While producers of standard memories manufactured millions of copies of a single design at low cost, start-ups such as Cypress Semiconductor, Cirrus Logic, and Maxim Integrated Products designed smaller lots of specialized devices that added distinctive value to their customers' products. Cirrus, for example, designs chips that improve the performance of hard disk drives and other PC-related applications such as display graphics, audiovisuals, and data fax modems. Cypress introduced 56 new chips and chip subsystems in 1989 alone; Maxim developed an average of 67 new products each year between 1983 and 1989.[28]

These firms consciously rejected the strategies of their predecessors. In the words of one Cypress founder: "We don't want to be a high-volume, low-cost producer, cranking out millions of standard parts on rigid, capital-intensive fab lines." Rather, according to the founder of Performance Semiconductor: "Small companies like Performance will grow at the expense of the established firms by fragmenting their markets. The only way that the United States will beat Japan in semiconductors is by fragmenting mass markets." By 1987 Cypress was able to manufacture more than 75 different products on a single manufacturing line. While few of these individual products were large or stable enough to attract a major competitor, they collectively represented a $1.4 billion market—comparable to the market for 256K DRAMs.[29]

This strategy built on Silicon Valley's longstanding strengths, particularly the ability to identify new markets and applications and rapidly introduce differentiated designs. Recent advances in computer-aided design, engineering, and testing that allowed chip and system designers to implement their ideas directly onto silicon supported this strategy. By the late 1980s engineers could design complex semi-custom logic circuits in weeks rather than months and specialty VLSI products were developed in months rather than years.[30]

The semiconductor start-ups also increased their flexibility by unbundling semiconductor production. Whereas established firms had designed, manufactured, and assembled integrated circuits in-house, the new firms typically focused on either chip design, manufacturing, or marketing. A few, including Cypress and Integrated Device Technology, specialized in leading-edge process technologies and design-process integration. Others, such as Chips and Technologies, Xilinx, and Weitek, specialized in speedy design and subcontracted manufacturing to outside fabs. Some two-thirds of the new Silicon Valley semiconductor firms were "fabless."[31] Producers of ASICS, such as LSI Logic and VLSI Technology, assisted systems firms in designing semi-custom chips that they manufactured. Others, such as Orbit Semiconductor, served as flexible, quick-turnaround manufacturing foundries for a variety of chip and system houses.

Reliance on external manufacturers allowed small semiconductor makers to avoid the cost and risk of a fabrication facility and to use multiple foundries to optimize their designs. The use of external fabs often increased responsiveness as well. An executive at start-up Altera compared the service of an outside vendor with that of an internal manufacturing facility: "As an Advanced Micro Devices (AMD) division without a fab, we got less service from other AMD divisions than I now get as an outsider from the Intel fab." The new strategies also led to collaboration among local start-ups, as when Altera agreed to invest in a state-of-the-art fab run by Cypress to ensure manufacturing capacity for its chips.[32]

The new semiconductor firms that chose to manufacture pioneered the use of low-cost, low-volume, flexible "mini-fabs" that could quickly process short runs of different designs on a single line. These modular fab lines represented an important departure from the traditional, dedicated production lines that were optimized for very high throughput of a single design. The traditional "mega-fab" cost more than $250 million and took two to three years to build, while a "mini-fab" could be built in six months for $20–50 million. By 1985, Silicon Valley start-ups produced an average of 100 to 200 different types of chips on the same line with production runs ranging from 10 to 10,000 units.

U.S. commodity memory or logic producers, by contrast, produced 10 to 20 different devices on a line, with runs of millions of units.[33] Finally, Silicon Valley's new semiconductor firms consciously attempted to avoid the cumbersome organizations of their predecessors. Seeking to create structures that rewarded individual initiative and preserved the focus and responsiveness of start-ups, these firms experimented with highly decentralized organizations. Once Cypress reached $100 million in sales, for example, it adopted a venture capital model. The firm invested $65 million between 1987 and 1990 to spin off four satellite companies in closely related lines of business, including a chip fabrication facility and a design group to develop a second-generation microprocessor.[34] Other firms, such as IDT and Chips and Technologies, decentralized internally, constructing product-based business units that retained significant autonomy yet shared a common corporate vision.

These organizational innovations allowed Silicon Valley's new chipmakers to introduce state-of-the-art products faster than their more integrated competitors. While new-product lead times in the industry had traditionally exceeded two years, by the end of the decade firms like Cirrus Logic and Chips and Technologies had shortened their development times to nine months.[35]

By 1990 the semiconductor industry consisted of two businesses with distinct technical and economic requirements.[36] The production of memory and other commodity devices was the province of a small number of very large companies that could afford the massive investment required to become high-volume, low-cost manufacturers. This business was increasingly dominated by Japanese companies that had committed to making the long-term investments and continuous improvements in quality and yield essential for efficient high-volume manufacturing.

A radically different semiconductor business flourished in Silicon Valley during the 1980s alongside the crisis-ridden established producers. These new companies successfully captured the unique strengths of Silicon Valley, including access to leading-edge customers, sophisticated design talent, specialized suppliers, and up-to-date information. In the words of the founder and CEO of Weitek: "Contrast commodity products which have no engineering content and are priced at cost with Weitek chips which have high engineering content, small output, and high value-added. This is a talent-leveraged business which is highly competitive but not capital intensive. The key to winning is [not cost or price, but] getting close to the customer." The new firms were highly profitable and fast-growing. While traditional firms such as AMD and National Semiconductor struggled to stay in business, many of the start-ups boasted growth rates of 45–50 percent a year, and only a handful failed.[37]

The balance between these two segments of the semiconductor business reversed during the 1980s. Commodity chips generated 80 percent of worldwide semiconductor industry revenues in 1983, but by 1990 their share had fallen to 33 percent. This change, referred to by one investment analyst as a "structural shift in the semiconductor industry away from a commodity-driven business," forced even the established Silicon Valley producers to become more flexible. Intel, which abandoned memory production in 1985, dramatically increased its pace of new product introduction and by the end of the decade had revitalized its microprocessor business. National Semiconductor and AMD both began replacing standard, off-the-shelf parts with more specialized, design-intensive devices. And while the attention of policymakers focused on the declining U.S. share of the commodity memory market, Silicon Valley's specialist chipmakers continued to dominate in high-performance, high-value-added, and customized semiconductors.[38]

The commodity semiconductor business was large and continued to expand, but its markets were increasingly eroded by the strategies of the fast-growing specialty companies. In the words of Weitek's vice president of marketing, John Rizzo: "You've got to keep subdividing the market and making the niches smaller and smaller. A $1.5 billion market is not one product, it's one hundred products." As demand for semi-custom products such as gate arrays turned them into commodities, firms like LSI Logic responded by designing higher-performance products for ever narrower, more specialized niches. Even the prototypical commodity market, standard memories, by the late 1980s was being segmented by a proliferation of products that were more tightly coupled to particular applications or systems. There were half a dozen basic memory designs in 1985, and by 1988 there were more than a hundred standard memory architectures and options.[39]

SPECIALIZING AND DIVERSIFYING

Silicon Valley outgrew its origins as a center of semiconductor production during the 1980s to become a complex of computer-related specialists. The new semiconductor firms allied themselves with computer start-ups in order both to influence and to respond to changing systems requirements. The computer companies in turn designed specialty or semi-custom chips into smaller, more differentiated systems. Similar interactions across the production chain contributed to a significant diversification of the regional economy.

The dramatic expansion of computer-related employment in Silicon Valley reflected these changes. Electronic components, computing, and computer and data processing services (including software) were the region's largest and fastest-growing sectors during the 1980s. By 1990 computer manufacturing businesses alone employed close to 60,000 workers in Silicon Valley, four times as many as on Route 128, where computing employment had fallen to under 15,000.[40]

The new generation of computer start-ups that emerged in Silicon Valley during the 1980s adopted strategies similar to those of their semiconductor counterparts. Firms such as Sun Microsystems, Silicon Graphics, MIPS Computer Systems, MasPar, and Pyramid Technology created new markets and developed differentiated services and applications rather than simply lowering manufacturing costs on standardized systems. As they did so, they fragmented computer systems markets and uprooted the industry's dominant producers.[41]

The computer market of the 1970s was a relatively stable business with two segments, mainframes and the smaller and less expensive minicomputers. During the 1980s new firms—in Silicon Valley and elsewhere—introduced a continuing stream of more specialized products. In the decade following IBM's introduction of the personal computer, the computer business splintered into scores of market segments, including supercomputers, super-minicomputers, fault-tolerant computers, workstations, and pen-based and hand-held computers. By 1987 41 percent of the world's data-processing revenues were from the sale of minicomputers and workstations, 35 percent were from personal computers, and only 24 percent were from mainframes.[42]

The systems designers at the new computer companies collaborated closely with Silicon Valley's new crop of chipmakers. They substituted semi-custom and specialized chips for commodity devices in order to differentiate their products, improve performance, and reduce development times. Sun Microsystems, for example, replaced the 70 standard chips in its Sun 3 workstation with 5 ASICs from LSI Logic. This not only saved space, improved performance, and lowered price, but the custom-designed circuits could not be used anywhere else—even in comparable workstations made by a competitor, Apollo.[43]

The geographic proximity to the new semiconductor companies afforded by a location in Silicon Valley was particularly important to firms like Silicon Graphics:

> The fact that the semiconductor companies are right nearby is really critical to us, and has been since we started (it's even reflected in our name). Our hardware strategy coincided with the chip companies getting booted out of the commodity business and shifting to serve our needs of increasing miniaturization and specialization. This coincidence of supply and demand created a whole new breed of computer companies.
>
> In the past year, we've designed 50 different ASIC chips, and they all tend to work the first time. This allows our technical ideas and architectures to be implemented in silicon in very short time periods, which is essential since product cycles in this industry used to be three to five years long, but now they are closer to eighteen months.[44]

By the end of the 1980s Silicon Valley was the home of increasingly diversified networks of specialized equipment, component, subsystem, and software producers, including firms that specialized in disk drives (such as Conner Peripherals, Maxtor, and Quantum), networking and communications products (such as 3Com, Excelan, Cisco, and Bridge Communications), computer-aided design and engineering systems (Daisy Systems, Cadence Design, and Valid Logic Systems), and color displays (SuperMac, Radius, and RasterOps). Like the new wave of semiconductor and computer firms, these specialist producers often defined the state of the art in their respective fields. They competed by rapidly introducing differentiated, high-value-added products; and they relied on the active involvement of nearby customers and suppliers to continue innovating.

The efforts of a new generation of Silicon Valley disk drive makers, for example, ensured that the United States controlled more than 75 percent of the world market for fixed disk drives in 1988. Some have even suggested that the region should have been called "Disk Drive Valley," since the evolution of the disk drive industry bears striking similarities to that of the semiconductor industry. An early IBM disk drive facility located in San Jose became the spawning ground for successive waves of disk drive start-ups in the region. The largest, Seagate, followed the traditional model of vertical integration and high-volume manufacturing of low-cost, standard products in the 1970s. By the 1980s it lost market share to a wave of spin-offs that were more flexible and innovative. The new firms pioneered small, high-performance drives by avoiding vertical integration and collaborating with customers to design and introduce new products rapidly.[45]

These new firms in turn spawned a further diversification of the supplier infrastructure. During the 1980s a new crop of manufacturers of semiconductor equipment and materials (such as Novellus Systems, Lam Research, and Genus), makers of disk drive equipment and components (such as Read-Rite, Komag, and Helios), and providers of contract manufacturing services (such as Solectron, Flextronics, and Logistix) emerged in Silicon Valley. As in the past, many were spin-offs of the established companies. These firms remained highly focused and often replicated the strategies adopted in the computer and semiconductor industries. Robert Graham, the CEO of the start-up Novellus Systems, advised other equipment manufacturers: "Avoid vertical integration like the plague. Vertical integration forces a company to build in a high fixed cost, which assures loss of profitability when volume drops. It can also assure that the design of components and assemblies which are a product of vertical integration will likely be inferior to those which can be obtained from a vendor that specializes in particular designs."[46]

Silicon Valley's computer systems complex continued to grow and diversify during the 1980s, confounding the predictions of industrial consolidation that had prevailed a decade earlier. One industry expert estimated that the computer industry in 1965 consisted of some 2,500 firms, and that by 1990 it included 50,000—most of which had entered the industry during the 1980s.[47]

False Starts

Many viewed entrepreneurs as the salvation of the recession-battered Route 128 economy of the 1980s, but new technology firms failed to compensate for the crisis of the region's minicomputer producers. In contrast with the upsurge of entrepreneurial activity in Silicon Valley, the rate of start-ups along Route 128 actually declined during the 1980s. Massachusetts thus experienced lower rates of formation of new high tech firms between 1976 and 1986 than either New England or the United States as a whole.[48]

The performance of the few companies founded during the 1980s was disappointing. By the end of the decade, only three of the region's 1980s start-ups had surpassed $100 million in revenues: Apollo Computer, Stratus Computer, and Lotus Development Corporation. Of the three, only Stratus could be regarded as an unqualified success. Apollo floundered and was ultimately acquired by Hewlett-Packard, while Lotus struggled to follow its best-selling 1–2–3 spreadsheet with new products.

The paucity and poor performance of Route 128 start-ups was a direct legacy of the region's independent firm–based industrial system. Not only were the region's skill base and technical infrastructure largely internalized within firms like DEC, Data General, and Raytheon; Route 128 start-ups also lacked the social networks or institutional forums to experiment and learn about new markets, technologies, and organizational forms. While Silicon Valley's entrepreneurs rejected the experience of their crisis-ridden predecessors, Route 128 entrepreneurs tended to model their companies after the region's large minicomputer firms. Many of these new firms created inward-looking organizations that were as out of touch with customers and market trends as those of their predecessors.

While many of the region's start-ups pioneered innovative products and technologies, they failed to keep pace with the rapid technological and market changes in computing. As one Route 128–based venture capitalist noted: "In 1988, Silicon Valley received . . . 50% of the nation's total seed investment; only 10% went into Massachusetts/Route 128. So we are doing 10 percent, and northern California is doing half. It's pretty clear that a lot more innovation is going on there than here."[49]

The contrasting experiences of Apollo Computer and Sun Microsystems—start-ups competing in the same market but located in different regions—demonstrate the limits of the autarkic structures and practices of Route 128's firm-based system in a technologically fast-paced industry. Apollo pioneered the engineering workstation in 1980 and initially was enormously successful. By most accounts, the firm had a product that was superior to that of its Silicon Valley counterpart, Sun Microsystems (which was started two years after Apollo, in 1982). The two firms competed neck-and-neck during the mid-1980s, but in 1987 Apollo fell behind the faster-moving, more responsive Sun, and it never regained its lead. By the time it was purchased by Hewlett-Packard in 1989, Apollo had fallen to fourth place in the industry.[50]

Apollo's founder, William Poduska, one of Route 128's few repeat entrepreneurs, had worked for Honeywell and helped to found Prime

Computer before starting Apollo at age 46. Not only was Poduska himself well steeped in the culture and organizational practices of the region's large minicomputer firms, but the entire Apollo management team moved with him from Prime. This contrasts with the typical Silicon Valley start-up, in which talent was typically drawn from a variety of different firms and even different industries, representing a mix of corporate and technical experience.[51]

Not surprisingly, Apollo's initial strategy and structure reflected the model of the established minicomputer companies. In spite of its pioneering workstation design, for example, the firm adopted proprietary standards and designed and fabricated its own central processor and specialized integrated circuits.[52] Though it purchased disk drives, monitors, and power supplies from outside suppliers, Apollo's commitment to a proprietary operating system and hardware made its products incompatible with other machines.

Sun, by contrast, pioneered open systems. The firm's youthful founders, all in their twenties, adopted the Unix operating system developed by AT&T because they felt that the market would never accept a workstation custom designed by four graduate students. They used standard, readily available components—relying on outside suppliers even for the design and manufacture of their reduced instruction set computing (RISC) microprocessor, and encouraging them to market the chip to Sun competitors.[53] As a result, the Sun workstations, while vulnerable to imitation by competitors, were also significantly cheaper to produce and lower priced than the proprietary Apollo systems. In the words of Sun founder and CEO Scott McNealy:

> We were totally open with them and said, "We won't lock you into anything. You can build it yourself if we fail," whereas our competition was too locked up in this very East Coast minicomputer world, which has always been proprietary, so that encouraging cloning or giving someone access to your source code was considered like letting the corporate jewels out or something. But customers want it.[54]

It quickly became apparent that customers preferred the cheaper, Unix-based Sun workstations. However, Apollo, like its minicomputer predecessors, was slow to abandon its proprietary operating system and hardware. As late as 1985 Apollo management still refused to acknowledge the growing demand for open standards, and the company turned down the offer of a RISC chip from Silicon Valley–based MIPS. In 1986

Apollo finally committed 30 percent of its R&D budget to RISC development, but the effort became an economic burden and the chip they ultimately developed internally was no faster than the chip they could have bought two years earlier from MIPS.[55]

Apollo's second major misstep was in its 1984 choice of a president and CEO to replace Poduska. Following Route 128 tradition, they hired an established East Coast corporate executive who had worked his way up through the ranks at General Electric and then had become the president of GTE Corporation. The 53-year-old Thomas Vanderslice was asked to bring "big-company organizational skills" to fast-growing Apollo and help the firm to "grow up." His background couldn't have been more different from those of the twenty-something graduate students and computer whizzes who had founded Sun Microsystems two years earlier.[56]

The media played up the superficial differences between Apollo and Sun: the buttoned-down, conservative Apollo executives alongside the casually attired, laid-back founders of Sun. It made for great journalism: while Vanderslice enforced a dress code and discouraged beards and mustaches at Apollo, Sun threw monthly beer bashes and employees showed up in gorilla suits on Halloween. While Vanderslice was chauffeured to work daily in a limousine, an April Fool's Day prank at Sun involved placing founder Bill Joy's Ferrari in the middle of the company's decorative pond.[57]

But the important differences between the two firms lay in their management styles and organization: Vanderslice brought in a traditional, risk-averse management team that focused on imposing financial and quality controls, cutting costs, and diversifying the firm's customer base. Former Apollo employees describe him as an archetypical "bean counter" who established formal decisionmaking procedures and systems in the firm at a time when flexibility and innovation were most needed. In the late 1980s, as Sun surpassed Apollo in sales and profitability, more than a dozen Apollo managers defected to their West Coast rival.

Other 1980s start-ups on Route 128 like Stellar Computer and Symbolics failed to match even Apollo's short-lived success. Stellar was William Poduska's third start-up. It repeated many of Apollo's problems, and it also suffered from its distance from the technological leading edge in semiconductors. Poduska chose to design most of the components for Stellar's high-priced, high-performance graphics workstations internally. In spite of strong objections from his engineers, he insisted on designing a proprietary processor at a time when most Silicon Valley firms were purchasing microprocessors from specialist producers. Stellar rapidly lost ground to Silicon Graphics and ultimately merged with Silicon Valley–based Ardent to create Stardent.[58]

Symbolics was a pioneer in artificial intelligence (AI) and was seen as one of the region's most promising start-ups. The firm was founded in 1980 by a group of engineers from MIT's Artificial Intelligence Lab and grew rapidly on the basis of the technological excellence of its special-purpose AI computers. In 1985 Symbolics had reached $75 million in sales and was highly profitable. Within two years, however, sales stalled, losses mounted, and layoffs began. Symbolics, like Stellar and Apollo, failed to learn from the experience of the minicomputer makers. It was slow to recognize customers' preferences for standard operating systems and it underestimated the threat to its expensive AI systems posed by general-purpose workstations and personal computers. While Symbolics systems were faster than Sun and Apollo workstations they were also several times more expensive and designed to run only one language, LISP (symbolic processing language). Once its traditional customer base of high-end research labs, universities, and other sophisticated users was saturated, Symbolics had nothing to offer customers who demanded less specialized, and less expensive, systems.

Stratus Computer, the most successful of Route 128's 1980s start-ups, is the exception that confirms the general rule. Stratus was started in 1980 by a former Hewlett-Packard executive, William Foster, to produce fault-tolerant minicomputers. Foster worked as a software engineer in Silicon Valley for a decade during the 1970s and 1980s before leaving to join Route 128's Data General. Four years later, angered by DG's closed and hierarchical management style, he left to start his own firm. Foster transplanted lessons from a decade in Silicon Valley, as well as from his time at Data General, to his new East Coast start-up.[59]

Stratus was organized like a Silicon Valley computer company. Its products were, from the start, based on the Unix operating system. Foster also chose to purchase most components externally in order to avoid the burden of vertical integration. He built collaborative relations with subcontractors and suppliers and sought to reproduce what he described as "the great openness of the West Coast management style" at Stratus.[60] Seeking to avoid the secretive and distrustful relations he had experienced at Data General, he created a flat organization with few status differentials and consciously emphasized open communications with employees at all levels. Foster also distributed stock options widely and prohibited the trappings of rank such as reserved parking, management suites, and executive dining rooms that were still common in many Route 128 companies.[61]

The success of Stratus was due at least in part to a strategy and organization more like its Silicon Valley counterparts than its Route 128 neighbors. Yet even Stratus achieved only modest success relative to Silicon Valley firms of the same generation. Silicon Valley–based Tandem Computer, for example, the market leader in fault-tolerant computing, was four times the size of Stratus in 1992, with sales of $1.9 billion compared to Stratus's $449 million. Although many factors contributed to the differential performance of the two firms, the lack of a supportive local culture, institutions, and industrial structure restricted the prospects of Route 128 start-ups. Without forums for learning and information exchange and a diversified technical infrastructure, the weight of inherited practices and institutions limited the possibilities for regional adaptation.

The difficulties of the Route 128 economy in the late 1980s are typically attributed to maturation of the minicomputer. This argument, based on the product life cycle model, suggests that regions follow their leading products, or industries, in a predictable pattern of innovation and growth, maturation and scale production, and ultimate decline. A new industry is expected to cluster geographically during its early, innovative and growth phases to take advantage of the concentration of specialized skill and suppliers. As the product, whether autos or semiconductors, matures and is standardized, however, production is inexorably shifted to lower-cost regions to take advantage of low factor costs and scale economies. Route 128 flourished, according to this interpretation, when the minicomputer emerged and its markets grew, but as demand for the product stabilized, the region's economy declined.[62]

Product cycle theory cannot explain why Silicon Valley did not decline, but rather adapted, when the semiconductor industry matured. In addition, it cannot explain why the locus of computer innovation shifted decisively to the West in the late 1980s, despite Route 128's longstanding concentration of technology, skill, and expertise in computer systems architecture and design. According to the product cycle model, innovation would have continued to concentrate in Route 128 rather than migrating to Silicon Valley.

The product cycle model describes the logic of industrial evolution and location in mass production industries that compete on the basis of minimizing manufacturing costs. Route 128's minicomputer firms and Silicon Valley's commodity semiconductor firms—both of which were organized to produce standard products in high volumes—followed its organizational and locational logic closely during the 1980s. Competition based on continuous innovation, however, undermines the logic of industrial maturity implicit in the life cycle model. As firms in the computer and semiconductor industries rejected the model of stable cost-based competition for a strategy of creating new markets by constantly introducing new products and applications, they dramatically shortened product cycles. This new competitive environment privileged Silicon Valley's regional network–based system, with its capacity to promote experimentation, learning, and the pursuit of multiple technological trajectories. As firms in this decentralized industrial system successfully fragmented mass markets, they continued to undermine the advantages of Route 128's independent firm–based industrial system.

6

INSIDE OUT: BLURRING
FIRMS' BOUNDARIES

High technology obeys the iron law of revolution . . . the more you change, the more you have to change . . . you have to be willing to accept the fact that in this game the rules keep changing.

—Bill Joy, Sun Microsystems

► The surge of start-ups was the most visible sign that Silicon Valley was adapting successfully, but deeper changes were also under way. As established computer systems producers such as Hewlett-Packard decentralized their operations and as new firms such as Sun Microsystems grew, they created interfirm production networks that formalized the region's interdependencies and strengthened its industrial system. By institutionalizing longstanding practices of informal cooperation and exchange, they formalized the process of collective learning in the region. Not only did individual firms redefine themselves by participating in production networks, but the region as a whole was organized to continuously create new markets and sectors.

During the 1980s Silicon Valley turned itself inside out, rendering almost useless the categories by which businesses traditionally defined themselves. Intense competitors became partners, sectoral lines merged and faded as technology advanced, and, perhaps most telling of all, the distinctions between large and small firms all but collapsed.

Adaptation in the Route 128 economy, in contrast, depended increasingly on the reorganization of its large firms. Constrained by autarkic structures and lacking dynamic start-ups from which to draw innovative technologies or organizational models, Digital Equipment Corporation and the other minicomputer firms adjusted very slowly to new market conditions.

RETHINKING THE LARGE FIRM

The contrasting responses of Digital Equipment Corporation and Hewlett-Packard to changing competitive conditions in computing illustrate the relative strengths of network- and firm-based industrial systems. By 1990 DEC and HP were $13 billion companies and the largest and oldest civilian employers in their respective regions.[1] Both were vertically integrated producers of proprietary minicomputers, and they shared origins in an earlier era of computing. Both faced comparable competitive challenges, but they responded to these quite differently. HP adjusted by gradually opening itself up, building a network of local alliances and subcontracting relationships while maintaining global operations. DEC, in spite of its formal commitment to decentralization, retained a substantially more insular organizational structure and corporate mind-set.

The transformations in the computer industry during the 1980s placed a premium on speed and focus. The pace of product introduction accelerated and the cost of bringing new products to market increased. HP vice president of corporate manufacturing Harold Edmondson claimed in 1988 that half of the firm's orders in any year came from products introduced in the preceding three years: "In the past, we had a ten-year lead in technology. We could put out a product that was not perfectly worked out, but by the time the competition had caught up, we'd have our product in shape. Today we still have competitive technology, but the margin for catch-up is much shorter—often under a year." Computer makers were forced to develop new products and bring them to market faster than ever before, often in a matter of months.[2]

At the same time, the cost of developing new products increased as they became more technologically complex. Innovation was occurring in all segments of the industry, from microprocessors and logic chips to system and applications software to disk drives, screens, input-output devices, and networking devices. It became increasingly difficult for a single firm to produce all of these components, let alone stay at the forefront of each of the underlying technologies.

These changes drove the shift away from proprietary standards in computing. When Sun Microsystems pioneered open systems in the mid-1980s, it was largely making a competitive virtue out of an economic necessity. As a start-up, Sun lacked the financial resources to develop the broad range of new technologies needed for a computer system. The firm published the specifications for its RISC microprocessor, SPARC, in order to enlist outside engineering and manufacturing resources. It forged partnerships with several suppliers of components who in turn shared Sun's efforts to improve the SPARC design and rapidly introduce new generations to market. Although competitors as well as suppliers had access to its specs, this open model allowed Sun to grow in ten years from a start-up to a $3 billion company that dominated the workstation market.

Open systems marked a radical break from the proprietary approach of the established computer industry leaders. Proprietary systems promoted stable competition by locking customers in to a single vendor of hardware and software services. Open systems, by contrast, encouraged new entrants and experimentation by forcing vendors to differentiate their products while competing within a common industry standard. This allowed systems firms to focus on only those elements of the product in which they had specialized skills, purchasing all other components externally.[3]

This increasingly fast-paced and competitive environment posed a challenge for established industry leaders like DEC and HP. By 1990, however, HP had successfully managed the transition from proprietary minicomputers to workstations with open systems, while DEC remained dependent on its proprietary VAX line of minicomputers and showed only limited progress in the shift to an open architecture. As a result, even though both enjoyed 1990 revenues from electronics products of $13 billion, HP earned $771 million, while DEC lost $95 million.[4]

Although variations in corporate performance always have multiple causes, the two firms' organizational structures and their relationships to their respective regions help explain the differences in their performance. As a classic large firm in an independent firm–based industrial system, DEC maintained clear boundaries between itself and other companies or institutions in the region. By the late 1980s DEC dominated the Route 128 economy as neither HP nor any other single firm ever dominated Silicon Valley. In the words of a computer executive who had worked in both regions: "When you work in Route 128, you see DEC as the center of the universe. Silicon Valley isn't like that; it isn't dominated by any big company or companies."[5]

HP was both less dominant in Silicon Valley and more open to the surrounding regional economy. The firm's participation in local labor markets and in the associational life of the region allowed its engineers to learn about new computing technologies and market trends more rapidly than those at DEC. HP's semi-autonomous business units and growing reliance on external suppliers allowed it to bring products to market faster than DEC, which continued to rely upon its conflict-ridden matrix organization and extensive vertical integration.

Both DEC and HP began the decade of the 1980s with bureaucratic decisionmaking processes and internal conflicts typical of large firms. Both missed opportunities and made false starts in workstation and reduced instruction set computing (RISC) markets, and both had difficulty keeping up with newer, more agile competitors. Yet HP quickly became the leading producer in the fastest-growing segments of the market, including RISC and Unix-based computer systems, and had a strong position in desktop computing, particularly workstations and nonimpact printers. By 1990 HP controlled 31 percent of the $8 billion RISC computer systems market—a market in which DEC still had no presence. HP also boasted a 21 percent share of the $7.2 billion workstation market and 13 percent of the $33 million Unix computer systems market, compared to DEC's 16 percent and 8 percent respectively. HP also controlled 66 percent of the market for desktop laser printers and 70 percent of the market for ink-jet printers.[6]

HP invested heavily in RISC microprocessor technology and the Unix operating system in the early 1980s, well before most established computer companies recognized the importance of open standards. By developing an early strategy for personal computers, workstations, and networks, it quickly became one of the world's biggest sellers of Unix-based systems. A financial analyst for Salomon Brothers assessed the situation in 1990: "Over the past four or five years, they [HP] have done an excellent job of identifying trends in the computer market such as Unix, RISC, and PCs. No other major computer company has done a better job of positioning . . . They are the one company I can count on surviving. Hewlett-Packard has a better base today than IBM or DEC."[7]

HP's ability to identify these market trends early reflected the firm's openness to external changes in technology and markets and a location that gave it easy access to state-of-the-art technology. This contrasts sharply with DEC's prolonged denial of the growing demand for personal computers and Unix-based systems. According to a former DEC marketing manager: "DEC had its head in the sand. They didn't believe that the world would really change . . . They got focused on the internal evolution of the company rather than on the customer or markets."[8] HP responded decisively to these changes. In 1990 the firm created an independent team to develop a RISC-based workstation. The ultimate product, the Series 700 workstation, was far ahead of the rest of the industry. By betting the future of the computer division (which accounted for 53 percent of HP revenues) on RISC-based systems in 1985 and by undertaking internal reorganizations that unified and rationalized the firm's disparate computer divisions and component technologies, HP positioned itself advantageously for emerging markets.[9]

DEC, in contrast, was plagued by continuing internal conflicts and a series of costly course reversals in its efforts to enter the workstation and open systems markets. The firm's strategy remained confused and inconsistent even after large DEC customers such as GE and AT&T forced CEO Ken Olsen to authorize a shift to open systems and away from DEC's proprietary VAX minicomputer architecture and VMS operating system.[10]

DEC's research lab in Silicon Valley developed state-of-the-art RISC and Unix technologies in the early 1980s, but its discoveries were virtually ignored by headquarters, which continued to favor the highly profitable VAX-VMS system. Company insiders claim that DEC's Palo Alto lab contributed more to other Silicon Valley firms such as Sun and MIPS than it did to DEC because its findings quickly diffused to other Silicon Valley firms through technical papers and local industry forums. They compare the Palo Alto lab to Xerox PARC, which is well known for inventions that were ultimately commercialized by other firms.[11]

DEC finally decided to build its own RISC-based workstation in late 1986. The conventional wisdom within the firm was that the RISC microprocessor should be designed and built in-house. An internal team, generously financed and based in the state of Washington, was assigned to develop Prism, DEC's first commercial RISC computer. Two years later this 100-person group still had very little to show for their efforts.[12]

DEC's Palo Alto workstation group—watching the impressive technical and commercial advances being made in RISC technology by Silicon Valley firms—offered to develop a workstation based on non-DEC chips. The resulting conflict, predictably, was over the wisdom of turning to outside suppliers for a key technology. One faction was of the opinion that DEC had invented small computers and didn't need Silicon Valley "twerps" to design for it; another group feared the loss of control over DEC systems; still others remained reluctant to give up the VAX vision of a single architecture for the entire product line.

In an unprecedented victory, Palo Alto eventually overcame the deep internal resistance at DEC to purchasing the microprocessor from outside the firm. For the first time in DEC history, the senior executive committee approved the development of a workstation based on an externally created architecture. The Prism project was canceled, and DEC invested heavily in Silicon Valley's MIPS Computer Systems to develop a RISC chip. This appeared to be evidence that DEC was, at last, opening its doors to the outside world.

Four years later, however, DEC reversed course once again and announced an internal RISC design named Alpha that could run under either Unix or VMS. Abandoning its relationship with MIPS, DEC transferred the Palo Alto workstation group back to Maynard. The result of this inconsistent strategy left the firm with only 13 percent of the workstation market. When it was announced in 1992, the Alpha chip was the fastest RISC processor available, although it was a very late entrant and left DEC's long-term prospects uncertain.[13]

The contrast between DEC's Palo Alto lab and its East Coast operations is instructive. Engineers who worked at both emphasize how different the two were: DEC East was internally focused, while DEC Palo Alto was well integrated into Silicon Valley's social and technical networks. According to Joe DeNucci, a former employee:

> DEC is the largest employer on Route 128 and you come to think that the center of the universe is north of the Mass Pike and west of Route 128. The thinking is totally DEC-centric: all the adversaries are within the company. Even the non-DEC guys compete only with DEC.
>
> DEC Palo Alto is a completely different world. DEC is just another face in the crowd in Silicon Valley; the adversaries are external, firms like Intel and Sun. It forces a far more aggressive and "prove-it" mind set.

DeNucci described his years with the DEC engineering and development group in Palo Alto:

> We had an immense amount of autonomy, and we cherished the distance from home base, from the "puzzle palace," and from the "corridor war-

riors" and all the endless meetings. It was an idyllic situation, a group of exceptionally talented people who were well connected to Stanford and to the Silicon Valley networks. People would come out from Maynard and say "this feels like a different company." The longer they stayed, the more astounded they were.[14]

Tom Furlong, who headed a DEC workstation division in Maynard for five years before moving to Palo Alto in 1985 to run the newly formed workstation group, described the growth of the Palo Alto workstation group in the late 1980s as a typical Silicon Valley start-up. The group's autonomy from headquarters allowed members to take full advantage of the local knowledge available within Silicon Valley. At the same time, the group benefited from the financial backing and reputation of a large, well-established corporation. By 1990 Furlong was the manager of a 275-person group. He compared his experience working in the two locations:

> It would be very difficult for me to do what I'm doing here within DEC on the East Coast. I'm a fairly autonomous business manager out here, with all the functions necessary to success reporting to me and the freedom to use outside suppliers. Back East, I would have to rely on DEC's internal suppliers and functional groups for everything.

Furlong explained the consequences of these organizational differences for new product development:

> The same job of bringing a new workstation to market takes two times as long on the East Coast and many more people than it does here. In Maynard, I had to do everything inside the company. Here I can rely on the other companies in Silicon Valley. It's easier and cheaper for me to rely on the little companies in Silicon Valley to take care of the things I need, and it forces them to compete and be more efficient. At DEC, the commitment to internal supply and the familial environment means that bad people don't get cut off. I had to depend on all sorts of inefficient people back at DEC East.

The workstation group did not achieve this independent position without resistance: "It was a huge embarrassment to them that we had to rely on external suppliers such as MIPS. DEC takes great pride in being vertically integrated, in having control over its entire system."[15] DEC was ultimately unable to assimilate the lessons of its geographically distant Palo Alto group, in spite of their technical advances, and in 1992 transferred the group back to Maynard headquarters. Furlong and other members of the Workstation team left DEC to work for MIPS.

Hewlett-Packard began the decade with a level of vertical integration comparable to DEC's but soon recognized that it could not continue to produce everything in-house. In the late 1980s HP began to subcontract most of the sheet metal fabrication, plastics, and machining for its computer systems. It also consolidated the management of some fifty disparate circuit technology units into two autonomous divisions, Integrated Circuit Fabrication and Printed Circuit Board Fabrication. These divisions were organized as internal subcontractors for the company's computer systems and instrument divisions. They were forced to compete with external vendors for HP's business and were expected to remain competitive in technology, service, and cost in order to sell successfully to outside customers.

HP also built alliances with local companies that offered complementary technologies. During the 1980s the firm created partnerships with Octel Communications for voice-data integration, with 3Com for local-area network-manager servers, with Weitek for semiconductor design, and with Informix for database software. An HP manager explained the acquisition of a 10 percent stake in Octel: "In the business and office processing environment, no one company can develop everything on its own, so we're increasingly looking at forming alliances of various sorts to meet our customers' needs."[16]

As HP opened itself to outside influences during the 1980s, it created a new model of the decentralized large firm. The firm's divisions gained autonomy and began collaborating with other specialist producers, many of which were local. DEC's dominant and isolated position in the Route 128 region, in contrast, hindered its efforts to shift to new technologies or a new corporate form. Saddled with an autarkic organizational structure and located in a region that offered little social or technical support for a more flexible business model, DEC found its difficulties worsening.

In 1992 Ken Olsen, DEC's founder and CEO, was forced to resign after the company reported a $2.8 billion quarterly loss—the biggest in computer industry history. One year later HP surpassed DEC in sales to take its place as the nation's second-largest computer company, after IBM.

As a final irony, in 1993 DEC moved a design team for its new Alpha microprocessor from the East Coast to Palo Alto in order to immerse Alpha engineers in the Silicon Valley chip community. According to industry analyst Ron Bowen of Dataquest: "Digital is finding the support network of other companies is very very limited back East. In effect, what's been happening is the people who work on the East Coast spend a lot of time flying to San Jose anyway."[17]

FORMALIZING PRODUCTION NETWORKS

The new generation of Silicon Valley computer systems firms such as Sun Microsystems and Silicon Graphics responded to rising development costs, shrinking product cycles, and rapid technological change by building production networks from the bottom up. By focusing on what they did best and purchasing the remainder from specialist suppliers, they created a network system that spread the costs of developing new technologies, reduced product-development times, and fostered reciprocal innovation.

When Sun Microsystems was established in 1982, for example, its founders chose to focus on designing hardware and software for workstations and to limit manufacturing to prototypes, final assembly, and testing. Sun purchased application-specific integrated circuits (ASICs), disk drives, and power supplies as well as memory chips, boxes, keyboards, mice, cables, printers, and monitors from external suppliers. Even the SPARC microprocessor and printed circuit boards at the heart of its workstations were manufactured by outsiders.[18]

While specialization is essential for a start-up, Sun did not abandon this strategy even as it grew into a multi-billion-dollar company. Why, asked Sun's vice president of manufacturing Jim Bean in the late 1980s, should Sun vertically integrate when hundreds of Silicon Valley companies invest heavily in staying at the leading edge in the design and manufacture of microprocessors, ASICs, disk drives, and most other computer components and subsystems? Relying on outside suppliers greatly reduced Sun's overhead while ensuring that the firm's workstations contained state-of-the-art hardware.

This focus also allowed Sun to introduce complex new products rapidly and to alter their product mix continually. According to Bean: "If we were making a stable set of products, I could make a solid case for vertical integration." Relying on external suppliers allowed Sun to introduce an unprecedented four major new product generations during its first five years of operation and to double the price-performance ratio each successive year. Sun eluded clone-makers through the sheer pace of its introduction of new products. By the time a competitor could reverse engineer a Sun workstation and develop the manufacturing capability to imitate it, Sun had introduced a successive generation.[19]

Most of the new Silicon Valley computer systems firms, like Sun, concentrated their resources on the design and assembly of a final system and the advance of technologies at the core of their firm's capabilities. Continuing to operate like start-ups, they shared the costs and risks of the development of new products with partners and suppliers. The computer producers Tandem, Silicon Graphics, Pyramid, and MIPS all relied heavily on networks of external suppliers. Apple CEO John Sculley described the importance of these networks:

> The old paradigm was that you had as much self-sufficiency as possible
> . . . When you do everything yourself, in the short term you may get better margins, but you also lose tremendous flexibility to change. And as hard as we work to define what the information technology industry might look like in the beginning of the next century, we still can't do it with much accuracy. We want to retain the flexibility of being able to change as circumstances change.[20]

Intel cofounder Andy Grove reached a similar conclusion: "I wouldn't categorically say that companies structured the old way can't survive, but it's hard to see them thriving. Anything that can be done in the vertical way can be done more cheaply by collections of specialist companies organized horizontally."[21]

While it is difficult to develop accurate measures of vertical integration, the higher sales per employee for representative Silicon Valley firms than for their Route 128 counterparts shown in the following table are an indication of the Westerners' greater reliance on outside suppliers.

Sales per employee, 1990 ($ thousands)[22]

Silicon Valley		Route 128	
Apple	$382.6	Prime	$128.0
Sun	214.6	Wang	123.0
Silicon Graphics	200.0	Data General	114.0
HP	143.8	DEC	104.4

The 1980s-generation computer firms also experimented with flexible organizations. Learning from the experience of their predecessors, they avoided hierarchy and created flat organizations that significantly dispersed decisionmaking and authority. Silicon Graphics CEO Ed McCracken explained:

> There is no steady state in this business. We have to reinvent our company continuously because our product line changes every eighteen months. If you ever slip a cycle, it's hell to catch up. It takes ten times as much effort to leapfrog. [Because] we have to reinvent our company every two years, we are set up for change. We are careful that there are no major structures in place that will resist change: we hire people who are change junkies and we have an extremely fluid organizational chart based on small, interdisciplinary teams that focus on bringing new products to market fast.[23]

When Sun became a $3.5 billion company in 1990, the workstation maker pioneered a radical reorganization, breaking itself into five quasi-independent companies under a single corporate umbrella. The de-centralization sought to bring the market "inside the company." The managers of each of the five Sun companies—known as the "planets"—were given full responsibility for profit and loss and their own independent sales force. The planets were encouraged to exploit business opportunities even when they might harm another Sun unit. So, for example, the SunSoft group provided the Solaris operating system for Sun workstations built by Sun Microsystems Computer Corporation (SMCC) but also sold it to SMCC competitors such as HP, Intel, and Next Computer Co. The notion was that customers—not managers—would best identify where Sun was and was not competitive. This radically open structure forced the company continually to redefine where it added value and where it should rely on external partners for critical innovations.[24]

Silicon Valley's networked industrial system was built on two paradoxes. First, the success of the region's specialized companies depended critically upon commonly accepted technical standards. Second, as supplier networks grew in richness and complexity, they reduced the favored market access enjoyed by large firms and so tended to reward smaller ones disproportionately.

The promulgation of standards was essential to the promotion of flexibility, specialization, and diversity in Silicon Valley. In McCracken's words: "Silicon Valley is the center of the new trend toward standardization and modularization that allows companies to specialize and get products out very fast. In Silicon Valley, you can pick up modules of software and hardware easily, and then focus on specializing. This allows you to get new products out very, very fast. It would be much harder to do this elsewhere in the world."[25]

Hardware standards allowed Silicon Graphics to develop the three-dimensional graphics for its high-performance workstations. According to McCracken: "Silicon Graphics would not be the company that it is without standards. We could develop a highly capable computer with a very low investment in hardware. This allowed us to take the risks of a very deep investment in graphics and a new systems architecture to integrate the graphics. We were only able to do this because we didn't have to worry about standards."[26]

Networks also reduced the differences between large and small firms in Silicon Valley. As the value of a clear technology focus grew, the ability of any single firm to dominate all the segments of the production chain diminished. Size no longer conferred the cost or market advantages that it had in the past. Sun and Silicon Graphics collaborated both with industry giants such as AT&T and HP and with other start-ups—often depending as much on the technological expertise of the start-ups as on the resources of established firms. Even the powerful marketing organizations and name recognition of large producers like DEC or IBM did not ensure competitive advantage.

Competition in computing was increasingly based on the ability to add value—to identify new applications and improvements in performance, quality, and service—rather than simply on lower cost. Silicon Valley computer firms became known during the 1980s for creating new products for specialized new markets such as Tandem's fault-tolerant computers, Silicon Graphics's high-performance-graphics workstations, and MasPar's parallel-processing systems, as well as new applications such as Apple's desktop publishing. As specialist producers continued to advance the technologies critical to their own products, they reproduced the technological instabilities that allowed this decentralized system to flourish.

Systems makers in Silicon Valley thus came to depend on suppliers for their own success. They relied on suppliers not only to deliver reliable products on time but also to continue designing and producing high-quality, state-of-the-art components and software. While many systems firms began as Sun did, integrating standard off-the-shelf components and distinguishing their products with proprietary software, over time many sought more specialized inputs to differentiate their products further. They replaced commodity semiconductors with ASICs and designed customized disk drives, power supplies, and communication devices into their systems.[27]

Sun differentiated its workstations by replacing standard Intel or Motorola microprocessors with the RISC-based SPARC microprocessor that it designed in collaboration with Cypress Semiconductor. Rather than manufacturing the new chip itself, or subcontracting it to a single producer, Sun established partnerships with five semiconductor manufacturers. Each partner used its own process technology to produce specialized versions of SPARC. The resulting chips had a common design but differed in speed and price. After supplying Sun, these vendors were encouraged to market the chips to Sun competitors or to develop SPARC-based clones of Sun workstations. In this way Sun extended acceptance of its architecture while its suppliers gained a new product.[28]

Similarly, when Sun asked Weitek to develop its floating-point chip, it lent two engineers and two of its expensive workstations to the nearby Weitek facility to assist in the development process.[29] In these relationships it was difficult and somewhat pointless to determine where Sun ended and Weitek or Cypress began. It is more meaningful to describe Sun's workstations as the product of a series of projects performed by a network of specialized firms.

These interfirm networks were not confined to computer systems producers and chipmakers. Silicon Graphics, for example, worked closely with local software developers because the three-dimensional graphics capabilities that differentiate its products required specialized software. Conner Peripherals, a maker of disk drives, worked with Cirrus Logic to develop a specialized controller chip for its state-of-the-art disk drives. Acuson, a manufacturer of medical imaging equipment, joined Xilinx in designing semi-custom logic devices to improve the performance of its ultrasound apparatus.

SUPPLIERS AS PARTNERS

Silicon Valley computer firms redefined relations with their most important suppliers during the 1980s. Recognizing that their success was tied irretrievably to that of their suppliers, they began treating them as partners in a joint process of designing, developing, and manufacturing innovative systems. These collaborative relationships allowed both customer and supplier to become more specialized and more technologically advanced. A network of long-term partnerships with specialist suppliers also gave a computer company a formidable competitive advantage that was difficult for competitors to replicate.

These new partnerships marked a decisive break with the adversarial supplier relations of traditional mass-production companies, in which subcontractors manufactured parts according to standard specifications, competed viciously to lower price, and often served as buffers against fluctuations in demand. Suppliers in the traditional system were subordinate producers, often dependent on a single large customer. IBM was notorious for managing its Silicon Valley suppliers in this fashion during the 1970s and early 1980s, controlling and exploiting its vendors.[30]

The new Silicon Valley systems firms sought to avoid making their suppliers dependent, explicitly rejecting IBM's model for more reciprocal relationships. They came to view their relations with suppliers as long-term partnerships rather than short-term procurement arrangements. They saw collaboration as a way to speed the pace of introduction of new products and to improve product quality and performance. They recognized that close interaction with suppliers created opportunities for valuable feedback while avoiding the cost and risk of vertical integration. As one HP purchasing manager put it: "Manufacturing talks about integrating suppliers into our manufacturing process. Each supplier is viewed as an extension of our factory."[31]

These partnerships evolved out of shared recognition of the need to ensure the success of a final product. They represented an important departure from the traditional practice of sending out precise design specifications to multiple sources for competitive bids. Many firms designated a group of "privileged" suppliers with whom they built close relationships. These suppliers were selected on the basis of product quality, responsiveness, and service. Although price was never irrelevant, it was seldom the determining factor that it had often been in the past. Most firms were willing to pay a premium for components of consistently superior quality, for reliable and timely delivery, and for a commitment from a supplier to develop state-of-the-art technologies.[32]

Companies often initiated this transformation by exchanging long-term business plans with suppliers and sharing confidential sales forecasts and cost information. This allowed suppliers to plan investment levels and encouraged them to set prices that would guarantee a satisfactory return without making their customer uncompetitive. In some cases these relationships originated with adoption of just-in-time (JIT) inventory control systems, which focused attention on jointly improving product delivery times and quality, often with a reduced number of suppliers.[33]

Most of these relationships moved quickly beyond the inventory and quality control objectives of JIT to encompass a shared commitment to a long-term partnership. Loyalty grew out of reciprocal decisions to honor unwritten obligations as well as contracts and not to take advantage of one another when market conditions changed. Some firms even supported key suppliers through tough times by extending credit, providing technical assistance, equipment, or manpower, or helping them find new customers. Businesses freely acknowledged this mutual dependence. Statements like "our success is their success" or "we want them to feel like part of an extended family" were repeated regularly by purchasing managers in Silicon Valley systems firms, whose roles changed during the 1980s from market intermediaries to builders of long-term relationships.

Suppliers were increasingly drawn into the design and development of new systems and components at a very early stage, and they often became integrated into the customer's organization in the process. Steve Kitrosser, vice president of operations at the disk drive producer Maxtor, explained that the firm's vendors had "become an extension of our internal manufacturing system." A key supplier would often be consulted during the initial phases of a new product's conception—between two and five years prior to actual production—and remain closely involved throughout design and development. According to Kitrosser: "In the really good relationships, we're sharing process technology and knowledge back and forth with our suppliers, just like we try to share information across functional groups within the company."[34]

Early cooperation with customers allowed suppliers to adapt their products to meet new systems requirements, and simultaneously exposed the systems engineers to changing component technologies. In the words of HP manufacturing VP Harold Edmondson: "We share our new product aspirations with them and they tell us the technological direction in which they are heading . . . We would never have done it this way 10 years ago." Another HP executive reported sharing proprietary product designs with suppliers as much as five years in advance in order to ensure access to state-of-the-art components: "A lot of our products are pushing the edge of technological barriers: we need the fastest, highest-density SRAMs or the most powerful disk drives, and we need them early. If we collaborate, we share the risk of developing high-performance products fast."[35]

In many cases, the flow of information between the two firms was continuous, occurring across different levels of the organization and different functional specializations. According to Tandem's director of materials John Sims: "It is essential that many levels of the companies involved interact face to face, and fairly frequently, for these relationships to develop." Maxtor's Kitrosser similarly stressed the importance of close, personal ties at the highest levels of the organization: "I personally spend a lot of time with the executives of the supplier companies, not specifically to negotiate things, but more to have a personal relationship with the people we deal with."[36]

As these relationships matured, firms became less bounded by their immediate employees. When Adaptec, a Silicon Valley–based maker of input-output controller devices, was formed in 1981, management chose to focus on product design and development and to subcontract both semiconductor fabrication and circuit-board assembly. The firm invested heavily in partnerships with key suppliers, including the local start-up International Microelectronic Products (IMP), old-line Texas Instruments (TI), and the local division of the contract manufacturer SCI. Adaptec's vice president of manufacturing, Jeffrey Miller, described the high degree of trust fostered by continuing interaction between the engineers in these organizations, and claimed:

> Our relations with our vendors are not much different than my relationship was at Intel with our corporate foundry—except now I get treated as a customer, not as corporate overhead . . . It really is very hard to define where we end and where our subcontractors begin: Adaptec includes a portion of IMP, of TI, and of SCI. We absolutely *have* extended the boundaries of this company.[37]

This blurring of firm boundaries transcended distinctions of corporate size, age, or sector. While many Silicon Valley start-ups allied with one another and "grew up" together, others benefited from relationships with established firms, both in the region and elsewhere. A materials manager at Tandem Computers reported that some of the firm's strongest alliances were those it had developed in the mid-1970s when it was founded. Seventeen of Tandem's twenty-two key suppliers in 1990 had been with the firm for at least eight years. Tandem also strongly encouraged its closest suppliers to establish similar long-term relationships with their own suppliers and subcontractors, thereby extending the chain of interdependencies.[38]

While nondisclosure agreements and contracts were normally signed in these alliances, few believed that they really mattered, especially in an environment of high employee turnover like that in Silicon Valley. Firms recognized that they had a mutual interest in one another's success and that their relationships generally defied legal enforcement. According to one Apple purchasing manager: "We have found you don't always need a formal contract . . . If you develop trust with your suppliers, you don't need armies of attorneys." As an industry consultant described it: "Company lawyers are trained to write 90 paragraphs to protect their client, but in the end, the relationship is based on mutual trust. If you don't have that mutual trust, then you probably shouldn't have the marriage in the first place."[39]

Although these relationships were often remarkably close, both parties were careful to preserve their autonomy. Many Silicon Valley firms prevented their business from accounting for more than 20 percent of a supplier's revenues and preferred that no customer account for more than 20 percent of their own revenues either. One local executive suggested that the ideal situation was to hold a preferred position with suppliers but not have an exclusive relationship. "Dependence," he noted, "makes both firms vulnerable." Suppliers were therefore encouraged to find outside customers, which ensured that the loss of a single account would not put them out of business. This avoidance of dependence protected both supplier and customer and promoted the diffusion of technology across firms and industries.[40]

To be sure, the openness of these partnerships entailed the risk of sharing technical advances with competitors. In the words of a Maxtor executive: "There is no doubt that, over the years, we have indirectly helped our competitors through our suppliers because of the expertise we have provided to those suppliers."[41]

However, most Silicon Valley executives grew comfortable with the complex balance of cooperation and competition that had long characterized the region. They believed that the process of technological upgrading benefited everyone over time, and that the new competitive environment simply did not permit defensive strategies. According to Silicon Graphics CEO McCracken:

> Our engineers jointly design products with other companies. We don't worry if they go and sell them to our competitors. Our whole style is not to compete defensively, but to take the offensive. The world is changing too fast to just try to defend your position. In order to keep up with change, you have to be on the offensive all the time . . . The key is to have products that are good.[42]

Certainly Silicon Valley systems firms did not collaborate closely with all of their suppliers. More traditional arms-length relations persisted, for example, with suppliers of commodity products such as semiconductor memories, disk drives, and power supplies, many of which were located in Asia. And these partnerships rarely extended to the manufacturers of fungible inputs such as raw materials, process materials, sheet metal, and cables.

Nor did collaborative relations emerge overnight or function flawlessly. There was a constant tension in these relationships between cooperation and control. Sometimes it took years before a supplier was trusted with increased responsibility, and as with any close relationship, misunderstandings arose. Some arrangements were terminated—in industry lingo, they resulted in "divorce"—while others languished temporarily, to be revitalized later. What is striking, however, is how frequently these relationships not only survived but appeared to flourish in Silicon Valley.

Networks and Learning

By 1990 Silicon Valley was far more than an agglomeration of individual firms, skilled workers, capital, and technology. Complex interfirm and interindustry networks of producers were increasingly organized to innovate and grow together.

Two cases demonstrate how this network system promoted technological advance. The first illustrates how computer systems firms redefined their relationships to contract manufacturers, which evolved rapidly from labor-intensive sweatshops into sophisticated, capital-intensive businesses that assumed substantial responsibility for product design and process innovation. The second case involves a relationship between a large systems firm and a small design specialist in which each contributed distinctive, state-of-the-art expertise to a process of complementary innovation. Taken together, these cases demonstrate how collaboration in a network system encouraged joint problem-solving between systems firms and their suppliers and how Silicon Valley's firms learned to respond collectively to fast-changing markets and technology.

The assembly of printed circuit boards (PCBs) has, until recently, been among the most labor-intensive and technically backward phases of electronics manufacturing. Contract assembly was traditionally used by systems firms in Silicon Valley to augment in-house manufacturing capacity during periods of peak demand. Commonly referred to as "board stuffing," it was the province of small, undercapitalized, and marginal firms that paid unskilled workers low wages to work in sweat-shops or at home. Many of these assemblers moved to low-wage regions of Asia and Latin America during the 1960s and early 1970s.

This profile changed dramatically during the 1980s. Systems firms like IBM, HP, and Apple expanded their business with local contract manufacturers in order to reduce fixed costs and respond to shorter product cycles, while start-ups like Sun relied on contract manufacturers so that they could focus on new product development. The contract manufacturing business expanded by 20–40 percent annually during the decade, enabling many of the contract assemblers in Silicon Valley to expand and to upgrade their technology. As small shops received contracts and assistance from larger systems firms, they invested in state-of-the-art manufacturing automation and assumed more and more responsibility for the design and development of new products.

Flextronics, Inc., was one of Silicon Valley's earliest board-stuffing shops. During the 1970s it was a small, low-value-added, "rent-a-body" operation that provided quick turnaround board assembly for local merchant semiconductor firms. By the late 1980s Flextronics was the largest contract manufacturer in the region and offered state-of-the-art engineering services and automated manufacturing.

This transformation began in 1980 when Flextronics was purchased by new management. The company expanded rapidly in subsequent years, shifting the bulk of its services from consignment manufacturing, in which the customer provides components which the contract manufacturer assembles according to the customer's designs, to turnkey manufacturing, in which the contract manufacturer selects and procures electronic components as well as assembling and testing the boards.

The shift from consignment to turnkey manufacturing represented a change from a low-value-added, low-loyalty subcontracting strategy to a high-value-added, high-trust approach because the contract manufacturer took responsibility for the quality and functioning of a complete subassembly. This greatly increased the systems firm's dependence on its contract manufacturer's process and components. Flextronics CEO Robert Todd described the change: "With turnkey, they're putting their product on the line, and it requires a great deal of trust. This kind of relationship takes years to develop and a major investment of people time."[43]

Todd claimed that whereas a competitor could replicate a consignment relationship in weeks, it would not find it easy to duplicate the trust required for a mature turnkey relationship. He found that it often took years to build the required trust before a company would share the design details of its new product. As a result, while firms that consigned their manufacturing typically had six or seven suppliers that competed on the basis of cost, those relying on turnkey contractors built close relations with only one or two firms, selected primarily for quality and responsiveness.

These relationships demanded extensive interaction and a surprising amount of organizational integration. According to one Flextronics executive: "In the early stages of any project, we live with our customers and they live with us. Excellent communication is needed between [their] design engineers and marketing people, and [our] production people."[44]

Once production began, the relationship between the two firms continued at many different levels. Not only did the customer firm's purchasing staff work with the supplier, but managers, engineers, and production staff at all levels of both firms met regularly to redefine specifications and to solve design or manufacturing problems. The Flextronics CEO met with Sun's senior vice president of operations for breakfast once a month to ensure that trust was maintained at the top and high-level problems were addressed. Planning, engineering, purchasing, and marketing personnel from the two firms met still more frequently—often weekly, and in some cases daily—to solve problems and plan for the future. This involved an immense amount of sharing and typically resulted in highly personalized relationships between the two firms.[45] The shift to turnkey manufacturing had clear implications for a contract manufacturer's location. Todd said about Flextronics: "We've never been successful for any length of time outside of a local area. We might get a contract initially, but the relationship erodes without constant interaction. Sophisticated customers know that you must be close because these relationships can't be built over long distances." This explains why the contract manufacturing business is highly regionalized. During the 1980s Flextronics expanded into Massachusetts, South Carolina, and Southern California as well as Hong Kong, Taiwan, and Singapore. SCI Systems, the largest U.S. contract manufacturer, is based in Alabama where costs are very low, but operates a major facility in high-cost Silicon Valley in order to build the relationships needed to serve the local market.[46]

Whereas Flextronics had been entirely a consignment business in 1980, by 1988 over 85 percent of its revenue was from turnkey customers. Flextronics initially benefited from a close relationship with rapidly expanding Sun Microsystems, which by 1988 accounted for 24 percent of its business. The two firms explicitly decided at that time to limit Sun's share in order to avoid dependency. Flextronics diversified its customer base significantly during the late 1980s, developing customers in varied industries including disk drives, tape drives, printers, and medical instruments as well as computer systems.

Two trends in contract manufacturing illustrate how specialization and collaboration bred complementary innovation. The first is that Silicon Valley systems companies began to rely on contract manufacturers for the earliest phases of board design. Flextronics developed internal engineering services and gradually took responsibility for the initial design and layout of Sun's printed circuit boards as well as the pre-screening of its electronic components. This implied a radical extension of interdependence because systems firms began to entrust their subcontractors with the proprietary designs that are the essence of their products. When successful, such a relationship increases the agility of systems firms while enhancing the capabilities of contract manufacturers.

The second trend, the use of surface mount technology (SMT), transformed the process of assembly of printed circuit boards. Traditional through-hole assembly involved soldering individual leads from an integrated circuit through the holes in circuit boards. SMT uses epoxy to glue electronic components onto the board. The new process is attractive for two reasons: it produces smaller boards because components can be mounted on both sides of the board, and it is cheaper in high-volume production than the through-hole process.

SMT is, however, far more complex and capital-intensive than through-hole assembly. It requires tight design rules, high densities, and a soldering process that takes years of experience to perfect. Industry analysts describe SMT as five to ten times more difficult a process than through-hole. Moreover, a single high-speed SMT production line costs more than $1 million.

The contract manufacturer Solectron Corporation led Silicon Valley in the adoption of SMT. Solectron was started in 1977 as a repair house for Atari video games and quickly moved into "board stuffing." It captured the business of IBM, Sun, Apple, and HP, as well as many smaller Silicon Valley firms, by investing heavily in SMT technology and emphasizing customer service, quality, and fast turnaround of high-value-added products. By the end of the decade, Solectron's manufacturing quality was reputedly superior to that found in any systems firm in Silicon Valley, and in 1991 the firm received the Malcolm Baldrige National Quality Award.[47]

This manufacturing excellence was due in part to Solectron's investment in state-of-the-art equipment. It was also the result of the firm's accumulated expertise. All of Solectron's customers benefited from learning that would formerly have been captured only by individual firms. Moreover, lessons learned in manufacturing for firms in one sector were spread to customers in other sectors, stimulating the diffusion of process innovation from industry to industry.

The use of contract manufacturers produced a mutually beneficial process of technological upgrading. While many of Silicon Valley's contract assemblers remained small and labor-intensive, by the late 1980s some, such as Flextronics and Solectron, were no longer subordinate or peripheral units in a hierarchical production system. Rather they had transformed themselves into sophisticated specialists that contributed as equals to the vitality of the region's production networks.

The second illustrative case concerns silicon foundries, the facilities used for manufacturing semiconductors. The use of external foundries, or fabs, grew rapidly during the 1980s as computer and other systems firms began to design their own integrated circuits but chose—like the fabless chipmakers—to avoid the enormous investment required for an up-to-date foundry. Silicon foundries are comparable to contract manufacturers because they offer their customers the cumulative experience and expertise of specialists. Unlike contract manufacturers, however, foundries have long been capital-intensive and technologically sophisticated, relating to customers as relative equals offering complementary strengths.

The partnership between Hewlett-Packard and the design specialist firm Weitek illustrates the potential for complementary innovation. Weitek, which had no manufacturing capacity of its own, was the leading designer of ultra-high-speed "number crunching" semiconductors for complex engineering problems. In 1987, hoping to improve the performance of the Weitek chips, HP opened up its state-of-the-art fabrication facility—which had historically been closed to outside firms—to Weitek for use as a foundry.

The alliance grew out of a problem that HP engineers were having with the development of a new model workstation. They preferred to use Weitek designs for the new product, but Weitek (which had supplied chip sets to HP for several years) could not produce chips that were fast enough to meet HP's needs. Realizing that the manufacturing process at the foundry Weitek used slowed the chips down, the HP engineers suggested fully optimizing the Weitek designs by manufacturing them with HP's more advanced fabrication process. This culminated in a three-year agreement that allowed the two firms to benefit directly from each other's technical expertise. The agreement guaranteed that HP would manufacture in its foundry and purchase at least $10 million worth of the Weitek chip sets, and it gave Weitek the option to purchase an additional $20 million of the chip sets from the foundry to sell to outside customers.

The arrangement assured HP of a steady supply of Weitek's sophisticated chips and allowed it to introduce its new workstation faster than if it had designed the chip in-house. It provided Weitek with a market and the legitimacy of a close association with HP as well as access to a state-of-the-art foundry. Moreover, the final product itself represented a significant advance over what either firm could have produced independently.

Both firms saw the real payoff from this partnership in expected future exchanges of technology. According to an HP program manager who helped negotiate the deal: "We wanted to form a long-term contact with Weitek—to set a framework in place for a succession of business opportunities." This relationship allowed each to draw on the other's distinctive and complementary expertise to devise novel solutions to shared problems. HP enjoyed greater access to Weitek's design talent and could influence the direction of the designs. Weitek acquired first-hand access to the needs and future plans of a key customer as well as assured access to HP's manufacturing capabilities.[48]

In spite of this increased interdependence, HP and Weitek were careful to preserve their autonomy. Weitek sold the chip sets it produced on HP's fab to third parties, including many HP competitors, and continued to build alliances and collect input from its many other customers (in fact Weitek deliberately limited each of its customers to less than 10 percent of its business). HP meanwhile considered opening its foundry to other chip-design firms and still maintained its own in-house design team. The openness of this partnership ensured that the design and manufacturing innovations that it produced would diffuse rapidly throughout the region and the industry.

Both firms saw this partnership as a model for the future. While HP did not intend to become a dedicated foundry, it sought other relationships that would leverage its manufacturing technology using external design expertise. Weitek in turn depended upon a strategy of alliances with firms that could provide manufacturing capacity as well as insights into fast-evolving systems architectures and markets.

Regional Networks in a Global Economy

The elaboration of interfirm supplier networks reinforced the advantages of locating in Silicon Valley, even as production was becoming globally footloose. Firms located or expanded in the region—in spite of relatively high costs—in order to become part of its social and technical networks. Geographic proximity allowed firms to monitor emerging technologies closely and avoid being caught off guard by unanticipated breakthroughs. It provided the advantage of speed, as local firms learned about market changes before others did. And it facilitated the frequent face-to-face communications needed for successful collaboration, while also intensifying competitive rivalries.[49]

Executives at Silicon Valley firms came to understand the value of proximity. According to Tom Furlong, former manager of DEC's workstation group in Palo Alto:

Physical proximity is important to just about everything we do. I have better relationships with Silicon Valley companies than I have even with my own company [DEC] because I can just get in the car and go see them. The level of communication is much higher when you can see each other regularly. You never work on the same level if you do it by telephone and airplane. It's very hard to work together long distance. You don't have a feel for who the people are, they are just a disembodied voice.

Furlong pointed out the difficulties of collaborating over long distances on the complex engineering problems that computer companies and their suppliers typically face: "An engineering team simply cannot work with another engineering team that is three thousand miles away, unless the task is incredibly explicit and well defined—which they rarely are. If you're not tripping over the guy, you're not working with him, or not working at the level that you optimally could if you co-located."[50]

Other executives noted that proximity was essential for the detailed and often continuous engineering adjustments required in making complex electronics products. In the words of the president of a power supply manufacturer that moved part of its manufacturing from Hong Kong to Silicon Valley in the late 1980s to be closer to a major customer: "I don't care how well the specifications are written on paper, they are always subject to misinterpretation. The only way to solve this is to have a customer's engineers right here. There is no good way to do it if you are more than fifty miles away."[51]

Silicon Valley–based computer makers often preferred local suppliers, particularly for technologically complex or customized parts. This desire for geographic proximity was not reducible to cost considerations. Most saw the advantages of timely delivery but also recognized that it was difficult to create over long distances the trust and teamwork needed for collaborative supplier relations. When the computer maker Ncube moved its headquarters from Beaverton, Oregon, to Silicon Valley in 1991, for example, it did so to be closer to Oracle, its supplier of database management software.[52]

Obviously not all suppliers were located within the region. Some products and services were not available locally, others were available but at higher cost. Most Silicon Valley computer firms purchased components such as memory chips and flat panel displays from Asian vendors. Many also relied on offshore fabrication facilities or contract manufacturers to reduce costs when they shifted into high-volume production. However, even this reliance on low-cost labor lessened in the late 1980s because automation increasingly allowed firms to manufacture cost-effectively in Silicon Valley while taking advantage of proximity to customers and suppliers.

Moreover, Silicon Valley firms demonstrated a clear preference for local suppliers in relationships that involved technically complex and fast-changing products. An Apple Computer materials manager reported: "Our purchasing strategy is that our vendor base is close to where we're doing business . . . We like them to be next door. If they can't, they need to be able to project an image like they are next door." Sun's director of materials put it this way: "In the ideal world, we'd draw a 100-mile radius and have all our suppliers locate plants, or at least supply depots, in the area." Several medium-sized Silicon Valley firms such as Pyramid, 3Com, and Silicon Graphics reported that the majority of their suppliers were located within the Bay Area and Southern California.[53]

As large Silicon Valley producers expanded their operations to other parts of the world, they replicated this pattern of geographic localization. Firms such as HP, Sun, and Apple increasingly rejected the traditional model of internationalization, which called for developing products at home and purchasing low-cost inputs from cheap-labor sites, in favor of a strategy that involved building, and even designing, products in the markets in which they were sold. These firms invested in local ties that allowed them to accumulate the local knowledge needed to respond more rapidly to the subtle differences between countries and even regions in the ways a product is used and what customers expect of it. HP established a strong position in the German mechanical computer-aided-design market by locating a facility in Böblingen and building partnerships with local machine tool companies that allowed HP to adjust its products quickly to meet their requirements. The firm also established ties with universities in the region, thereby developing loyalties among students who trained on HP systems.[54]

Even locations that had once been attractive simply for low-cost labor, such as Singapore and Malaysia, began to upgrade their technology infrastructures during the 1980s, and increasingly offered skilled labor and sophisticated suppliers and customers. When Conner Peripherals moved its high-volume production to Singapore, the firm encouraged its suppliers to locate facilities in the region as well in order to replicate the cross-fertilization found in Silicon Valley. HP similarly transformed its assembly plant in Singapore into a research and development center with a state-of-the-art chip fabrication facility in response to increasing local capabilities. And the contract manufacturer Solectron built a plant in Penang, Malaysia, to take advantage of the area's burgeoning technical infrastructure and to better service local customers.[55]

Apple Computer's "multi-local" strategy was based on a similar vision of localized clusters of suppliers and customers expanding together by promoting reciprocal innovation.[56] Apple established design centers in its main production sites in Europe and Asia that allowed it to differentiate its products for those markets, while simultaneously promoting the development of a local technical infrastructure. By decentralizing product development and marketing, as well as manufacturing, companies like Apple and HP positioned themselves to respond more rapidly to local needs. Their challenges became how to balance these local activities with the broader framework of a corporate whole and how to transfer learning effectively between locations.

As Silicon Valley firms extended their local production networks, they reinforced the technological dynamism of the regional economy. In the early 1990s the region's computer firms collaborated with media and publishing companies and consumer electronics firms to create innovative multimedia and interactive entertainment and education products, and they built on telecommunications technologies to introduce new generations of video conferencing, electronic mail, and hand-held communications devices. The boundaries of the computer industry thus continued to dissolve as local producers continued to define new products, markets, and industries.

Expanding in distant locations, Silicon Valley firms simultaneously enhanced the capabilities of these independent, but linked, regional economies. The lessons of Silicon Valley's network system thus began to diffuse to other regions, reinforcing the importance of geographic proximity even in an era of market globalization. The greatest challenge would be to transfer these lessons back to places like Route 128, with industrial systems that favored stability, self-sufficiency, and market control rather than flexibility, openness, and continuous innovation.

CONCLUSION:
PROTEAN PLACES

We know from Greek mythology that Proteus was able to change his shape with relative ease—from wild boar to wild dragon to fire to flood. But what he did find difficult, and would not do unless seized and chained, was to commit himself to a single form.

—Robert Jay Lifton, "Protean Man"

▶ The contrasting experiences of Silicon Valley and Route 128 suggest that industrial systems built on regional networks are more flexible and technologically dynamic than those in which experimentation and learning are confined to individual firms. Silicon Valley continues to reinvent itself as its specialized producers learn collectively and adjust to one another's needs through shifting patterns of competition and collaboration. The separate and self-sufficient organizational structures of Route 128, in contrast, hinder adaptation by isolating the process of technological change within corporate boundaries.

Paradoxically, regions offer an important source of competitive advantage even as production and markets become increasingly global. Geographic proximity promotes the repeated interaction and mutual trust needed to sustain collaboration and to speed the continual recombination of technology and skill. When production is embedded in these regional social structures and institutions, firms compete by translating local knowledge and relationships into innovative products and services; and industrial specialization becomes a source of flexibility rather than of atomism and fragmentation.

Spatial clustering alone does not create mutually beneficial interdependencies. An industrial system may be geographically agglomerated and yet have limited capacity for adaptation. This is overwhelmingly a function of organizational structure, not of technology or firm size. Route 128's industrial system generated countless new firms and technologies, but its producers failed to adapt or commercialize them rapidly or consistently enough to sustain the regional economy.

The current difficulties of Route 128 are to a great extent the product of its history. The region's technology firms inherited a business model and a social and institutional setting from an earlier industrial era. When technology remained relatively stable over time, vertical integration and corporate centralization offered needed scale economies and market control. In an age of volatile technologies and markets, however, the horizontal coordination provided by interfirm networks enables firms to retain the focus and flexibility needed for continuous innovation.

To be sure, regional institutions and culture are difficult to change. An industrial system is the product of historical processes that are not easily imitated or altered. However, the first step toward the regeneration of the Route 128 economy is self-understanding. The challenge facing the Route 128 region today is to learn from Silicon Valley's success. Managers and policymakers need to overcome their outdated conception of the firm as a separate and self-sufficient entity; they need to recognize that innovation is a collective process as well as an individual one. Adopting a business model that breaks down the institutional and social boundaries that divide firms represents a major challenge for Route 128, but it is decidedly less daunting than the challenges faced by regions with less sophisticated industrial infrastructures.

The reorganization of the Digital Equipment Corporation offers an important opportunity. Not only will a leaner, more decentralized DEC be better positioned to integrate itself into the regional economy, but the firm has laid off thousands of experienced engineers who can contribute to the growth of the cluster of software, networking, and supercomputer enterprises that emerged in the region in the early 1990s.[1] The continuing impact of defense cuts and the legacy of autarky suggest that regenerating the region will be neither easy nor fast, but the depth of the region's technical skill certainly makes the task achievable.

Silicon Valley, meanwhile, must not assume that the greater flexibility of its industrial system guarantees its continued success. The regional economy continues to flourish. In 1992 the sales of the region's largest 100 public companies grew more than 15 percent, to over $77 billion, dwarfing the 4 percent sales growth recorded by the companies in the nation's Fortune 500.[2]

But if Silicon Valley's social networks and technical infrastructure are unparalleled, the semiconductor crisis of the mid-1980s underscores potential weaknesses of its decentralized system. Network systems, like all forms of productive organization, are fragile constructs that must be continually renewed and redefined to meet new economic challenges. The individualistic world views of Silicon Valley entrepreneurs have—for most of the region's history—limited their ability to respond collectively to challenges or to build cross-cutting institutions that would sustain regional interdependencies.[3]

This has left the region vulnerable to the adoption of autarkic strategies or to a deterioration of its skill base and infrastructure. The difficulties of Apple Computer—which failed to open up the proprietary architecture for its Macintosh personal computers—are a reminder that even once-innovative companies can succumb to betting on a product. Apple, in the words of one analyst, "built a fortress to protect themselves, but found out they are isolated from the rest of the industry," and began losing share in a market they had helped to create.[4]

This danger is particularly great in recessionary times, when firms are often tempted to compete by simply cutting costs rather than differentiating their products and services or creating new markets. Firms may also be tempted to resort to litigation rather than negotiation and innovation to solve their problems. Similarly, cuts in public funding for education, research, and training, tax policies that discourage venture capital, or transportation congestion and soaring housing prices may undermine the institutions and infrastructure that support the region's network-based system.

There are, however, signs of change in Silicon Valley. Intensifying competition from other American technology regions such as Austin, Texas, as much as from Japan, spurred an unprecedented mobilization of the region's industrial community in the early 1990s. A broad-based consortium of local businesses, governments, and educational institutions called Joint Venture: Silicon Valley was formed to address shared regional problems. A kick-off luncheon in 1992 attracted more than one thousand of the region's business and community leaders; within six months the group had raised $700,000 in private contributions. Today hundreds of local people are part of working groups seeking to identify common industrial, infrastructural, and regional problems and to construct both detailed strategies and an overall blueprint for "re-inventing" the Silicon Valley economy.

Although Silicon Valley's success has been based on collaborative practices, the region has long been dominated by the language of individual achievement. For the first time, that language is being replaced by a vocabulary that recognizes the value of community as well as competition. In the words of Tom Hayes, a founder of Joint Venture: Silicon Valley and an executive at Applied Materials, a manufacturer of semiconductor equipment: "Our aim is to build a comparative advantage for Silicon Valley by building a collaborative advantage . . . to transform Silicon Valley from a valley of entrepreneurs into an entrepreneurial valley." This reflects the growing recognition that the region owes as much to its rich social, technical, and commercial relationships as to competitive rivalries and the initiative of individual entrepreneurs.[5]

For example, competitors in the region's semiconductor and disk drive industries have forged pathbreaking agreements to avoid costly patent infringement litigation. Eight semiconductor specialists (Cypress, IDT, LSI Logic, VLSI Technology, Altera, Sierra Semiconductor, Linear Technology, and Seeq) agreed in 1990 to pool information and legal strategies in lawsuits brought by their larger rivals, as well as to cross-license their own patents. The disk drive makers Seagate and Quantum signed a similar cross-licensing agreement in 1992 that let each use technologies covered by the others' patents. Seagate CEO Alan Shugart called for the entire industry to join the pact to avoid costly litigation and to focus competition on technological advance and manufacturing practices.[6]

Joint Venture: Silicon Valley is still rife with internal political conflict—as is to be expected in such a wide-ranging and inclusionary effort—and its ultimate contribution remains uncertain. Some see its activities as no more than a public relations effort or a 1990s version of traditional corporate bids for public funds and environmental leniency. Others criticize its membership, which consists primarily of white professional men in a region with a diverse ethnic population. But the consortium has the potential to construct a broad-based community of interests in the region and to mobilize the business community to respond collectively to a wide range of shared problems. The process of organizational experimentation and innovation is now shifting to the regional level in Silicon Valley.[7]

CREATING COLLABORATIVE ADVANTAGE

Regional policy is likely to be as important as macroeconomic or sectoral policies to ensuring industrial competitiveness in the 1990s. The challenges facing Route 128 and Silicon Valley mirror the challenges facing American regions and industry more broadly. Large parts of American industry need to overcome the autarkic mind-sets and structures of an outmoded model of mass production. For these older industrial regions, the task will be to construct more decentralized industrial systems that encourage collaboration as well as competition. But even the newer industrial regions that boast elements of network systems will need to promote the local relationships needed to sustain collaborative—and competitive—advantage.

Regional policymakers will face the challenge of creating institutions that promote a decentralized process of industrial self-organization without sacrificing individual autonomy and flexibility. Unlike either traditional top-down intervention or laissez-faire approaches, regional policy can be organized locally and designed to catalyze and coordinate—rather than directly manage—relations among the myriad public and private actors that populate a regional economy.

Debates over industrial policy in the United States tend to polarize rapidly between those who advocate national efforts to promote particular technologies or industries and those who believe that market forces will guarantee successful economic adjustment. For market liberals, the pressures of unfettered market competition automatically ensure flexible industrial adaptation. The entrepreneurs and small and medium-sized enterprises of Silicon Valley, in this view, are evidence of the intrinsic vitality of free markets; any constraints on flows of resources, or any government interference in the entrepreneurial process, threatens to stifle this dynamism.[8]

Proponents of national industrial policy, alternatively, argue that competitiveness depends on carefully targeted national economic promotion and guidance. In this view, the enterprises of Silicon Valley and Route 128 cannot match the scale or resources of Japan's integrated, government-supported producers. National policy is therefore needed to coordinate industrial adjustment.[9]

Neither of these approaches alone offers a convincing agenda for policymakers. The widespread failure of science parks and other efforts by localities around the world to "grow the next Silicon Valley" underscores the limits of an approach that focuses solely on ensuring the free flows of capital, labor, and technology needed for market adjustment.[10] However, Silicon Valley's sustained technological dynamism in the early 1990s undercuts the urgency of simplistic calls for national industrial policy. Indeed, American producers—many based in Silicon Valley—have regained their former strength in semiconductors and semiconductor equipment and continue to dominate world markets for personal computers, workstations, and software.[11]

National policies that direct public resources toward particular technologies or sectors are seldom effective mechanisms for industrial adaptation. It is notoriously difficult for public officials, with or without the collaboration of business, to "pick winners" and effectively concentrate national resources on future technologies.[12] While particular sectors, such as semiconductors, may provide critical linkages and spillovers of technology and knowledge, efforts either to protect or to promote such "strategic" sectors in an era of rapid technological and market change rarely succeed.[13] Policies to increase national competitiveness through the promotion of vertical integration or scale economies are similarly flawed. The recent experiences of IBM and DEC should confirm that large firms are not inherently more stable or successful than small producers.

As markets fragment and traditional industry boundaries blur, efforts to improve competitiveness by promoting particular technologies or industries are further confounded. Technological advance in Silicon Valley depends on shifting patterns of collaboration and competition among networks of specialist producers. The dynamism of the region's industrial system lies not in any single technology or product but in the competence of each of its constituent parts and their multiple interconnections. As a result, efforts to protect an individual sector, such as memory chips, often have perverse and unintended consequences upon linked sectors. Ultimately, regions are best served by policies that help companies to learn and respond quickly to changing conditions—rather than policies that either protect or isolate them from competition or external change.

Policies to support network-based industrial systems are most effectively achieved at the regional rather than the national or sectoral level. Regional policy serves best as a catalyst—stimulating and coordinating cooperation among firms and between firms and the public sector. Rather than being orchestrated as top-down intervention or bureaucratic guidance, policy initiatives should evolve as interested local parties exchange information, negotiate, and collaborate.[14]

The starting point for a regional industrial strategy is fostering the collective identities and trust to support the formation and elaboration of local networks. By providing public forums for exchange and debate, policymakers can encourage the development of shared understandings and promote collaboration among local producers.

The creation of such a community of interests is an important first step, but it is not sufficient in an environment of intense international competition. Industrial fragmentation, the source of flexibility in network systems, is also the source of its greatest vulnerability. The dynamism of an industrial system based on regional networks depends equally on institutions that transcend the interests of individual firms, industries, and political jurisdictions and allow companies to respond jointly to shared challenges.

The decentralized industrial structures and strong territorial linkages of regional network–based systems demand collective action at two levels. First, the specialist producers in network systems rely on the external provision of a wide range of collective services that spread risk and pool technological expertise. Institutions that provide capital, research, managerial and technical education, training, assistance to entrepreneurs, and market information are vital to the firms in a decentralized industrial system. Yet the firms have little incentive to provide such services individually—or to ensure their continuation during downturns—because of their inability to capture the benefits of their investments.[15]

These services can be provided by private actors, by the public sector, or by a combination of the two. Their particular form and content will vary according to the nature of the regional economy. The small-firm networks of crafts producers in north-central Italy, for example, have institutional needs that differ from those of the technology firms of Silicon Valley and Route 128. This means that while the institutions in other regional network–based systems may offer broad templates for policymakers, a regional industrial strategy will work only if it is tailored to the specific problems and conditions of the particular locality and its industrial community.

Second, the intense localization of economic activity in a network-based system places unusual demands on a region's physical infrastructure. Transportation congestion, housing price inflation, land scarcity, and environmental degradation are all direct outgrowths of the geographic interdependencies of a highly localized industrial system. These problems can be addressed only at a regional level, as individual localities lack the resources or the capacity to solve them without the cooperation of neighboring jurisdictions.[16]

Regional planners and policymakers thus have an important leadership role to play in promoting collaboration among fragmented and often jealous city and local governments. Just as individual entrepreneurs must recognize and institutionalize their interdependencies, so too must individual political jurisdictions overcome narrow self-interest in order to define and advance a common interest. The creation of such institutions is an intensely political process—one that requires continuing debate and compromise, but that offers the possibility of sustained industrial and regional prosperity.

NOTES

HISTORICAL DATA

DEFINITIONS AND DATA SOURCES

ACKNOWLEDGMENTS

INDEX

NOTES

INTRODUCTION: LOCAL INDUSTRIAL SYSTEMS

1. "The Upside 100: Ranking the Top 100 Technology Companies by Wealth Created," *Upside*, Dec. 1990, 23–30.
2. "Electronic Business Top 100 Exporters," *Electronic Business*, March 16, 1992, 40–42.
3. Fastest-growing companies are ranked according to five-year average annual sales growth rates. "Electronic Business Fastest-Growing Companies," *Electronic Business*, April 22, 1991, 38–40.
4. For the classic description of the vertically integrated mass production corporation, see Alfred D. Chandler, Jr., *The Visible Hand: The Managerial Revolution in American Business* (Cambridge, Mass.: Harvard University Press, 1977), and *Scale and Scope: The Dynamics of Industrial Capitalism* (Cambridge, Mass.: Harvard University Press, 1990); see also David A. Hounshell, *From the American System to Mass Production, 1800–1932* (Baltimore: Johns Hopkins University Press, 1984); Michael Storper, "Oligopoly and the Product Cycle: Essentialism in Economic Geography," *Economic Geography* 61, no. 3 (1985), 260–282.
5. See Michael Best, *The New Competition: Institutions of Industrial Restructuring* (Cambridge, Mass.: Harvard University Press, 1990); Charles Sabel, "Flexible Specialization and the Reemergence of Regional Economies," in *Reversing Industrial Decline? Industrial Structure and Policy in Britain and Her Competitors*, ed. Paul Hirst and Jonathan Zeitlin (Oxford: Berg, 1988); Charles Sabel and Jonathan Zeitlin, "Historical Alternatives to Mass Production: Politics, Markets and Technology in Nineteenth Century Industrialization," *Past and Present* 108 (1985), 133–176; Michael Piore and Charles Sabel, *The Second Industrial Divide: Possibilities for Prosperity* (New York: Basic Books, 1984); Philip Scranton, *Proprietary Capitalism: The Textile Manufacture at Philadelphia, 1800–1885* (Cambridge: Cambridge University Press, 1983), and *Figured Tapestry: Production, Markets and Power in Philadelphia Textiles, 1885–1941* (Cambridge: Cambridge University Press, 1989).
6. See Nitin Nohria and Robert G. Eccles, eds., *Networks and Organizations: Structure, Form, and Action* (Boston: Harvard Business School Press, 1992);

Chris DeBresson and Richard Walker, eds., "Networks of Innovators," *Research Policy* 20, no. 5 (Oct. 1991); Walter W. Powell, "Neither Market nor Hierarchy: Network Forms of Organization," *Research in Organizational Behavior* 12 (1990), 295–336.

7. See Frank Pyke, Giacomo Becattini, and Werner Sengenberger, *Industrial Districts and Inter-Firm Cooperation in Italy* (Geneva: International Institute for Labour Studies, 1990); Richard Locke, *Rebuilding the Economy: Local Politics and Industrial Change in Contemporary Italy* (Ithaca, N.Y.: Cornell University Press, 1994); Gary Herrigel, *Reconceptualizing the Sources of German Industrial Power* (New York: Cambridge University Press, forthcoming); Frank Pyke and Werner Sengenberger, *Industrial Districts and Local Economic Regeneration* (Geneva: International Institute for Labour Studies, 1992); Allen J. Scott, *New Industrial Spaces: Flexible Production Organization and Regional Development in North America and Western Europe* (London: Pion, 1988); Sabel, "Reemergence."

8. See Masahiko Aoki, "Toward an Economic Model of the Japanese Firm," *Journal of Economic Literature* 28 (March 1990): 1–27; Ken-ichi Imai, "Evolution of Japan's Corporate and Industrial Networks," in Bo Carlsson, ed., *Industrial Dynamics* (Boston: Kluwer, 1989); Ken-ichi Imai, Ikujiro Nonaka, and Hirotaka Takeuchi, "Managing the New Product Development Process: How Japanese Companies Learn and Unlearn," in Kim Clark et al., eds., *The Uneasy Alliance* (Boston: Harvard Business School Press, 1985); David Friedman, *The Misunderstood Miracle: Industrial Development and Political Change in Japan* (Ithaca, N.Y.: Cornell University Press, 1988); Toshihiro Nishiguchi, "Strategic Dualism: An Alternative in Industrial Societies" (Ph.D. diss., Nuffield College, Oxford University, 1989); Richard Child Hill and Kuniko Fujita, eds., *Japanese Cities in the World Economy* (Philadelphia: Temple University Press, 1992).

9. For the case of Japan's aircraft industry, see David Friedman and Richard Samuels, "How to Succeed without Flying: The Japanese Aircraft Industry and Japan's Technology Ideology," in Jeffrey Frankel and Miles Kahler, eds., *Regionalism and Rivalry* (Chicago: University of Chicago Press, 1993). On the reorganization of large firms, see Sabel, "Reemergence."

10. Scholars who seek to explain the process of adaptation to intensifying international competition have largely focused on the nation-state or the industrial sector. Those who analyze the former identify national economic practices and institutions to account for the superior competitive performance of nations such as Germany and Japan. See, for example, Richard R. Nelson, *National Innovation Systems: A Comparative Analysis* (New York: Oxford University Press, 1993); Chalmers Johnson, *MITI and the Japanese Miracle: The Growth of Industrial Policy, 1925–1975* (Stanford, Calif.: Stanford University Press, 1982); John Zysman, *Governments, Markets, and Growth: Financial Systems and the Politics of Industrial Change* (Ithaca, N.Y.: Cornell University Press, 1983). Students of the latter focus on the micro-level

organization of production to show why certain firms or sectors have been more successful than others in adapting to market or technological change. See, for example, Michael Cusumano, *The Japanese Automobile Industry: Technology and Management at Nissan and Toyota* (Cambridge, Mass.: Council on East Asian Studies, Harvard University, 1985); James Womack, Daniel Jones, and Daniel Roos, *The Machine That Changed the World* (New York: Rawson Associates, 1990). A handful of studies have combined the national and sectoral approaches. See, for example, Michael Dertouzos et al., *Made in America: Regaining the Productive Edge* (Cambridge, Mass.: MIT Press, 1989); Ronald Dore, *Flexible Rigidities: Industrial Policy and Structural Adjustment in the Japanese Economy, 1970–80* (Stanford, Calif.: Stanford University Press, 1986).

11. See, for example, Steven Cobrin, "Two Paths of Industrial Adjustment to Shifting Patterns of International Competition: The Political Economy of Flexible Specialization and Mass Production in British Textiles" (Ph.D. diss., Harvard University, 1990); Scranton, *Proprietary Capitalism* and *Figured Tapestry*; Sabel and Zeitlin, "Historical Alternatives"; Herrigel, *German Industrial Power*; Locke, *Rebuilding the Economy*.

12. The notion of external economies is simply that producers benefit from sharing the costs of common external resources such as infrastructure and services, skilled labor pools, specialized suppliers, and a common knowledge base. When these factors of production are geographically concentrated, firms gain the additional benefits of spatial proximity, or "economies of agglomeration." Once such an advantage is established in a particular industry or locality, the presence of external economies ensures that the advantage becomes self-reinforcing. For the original statement, see Alfred Marshall, *The Principles of Economics* (London: Macmillan, 1920).

13. See Paul Krugman, *Geography and Trade* (Cambridge, Mass.: MIT Press, 1991); Michael E. Porter, *The Competitive Advantage of Nations* (New York: Free Press, 1990). Geographers and regional scientists first developed these themes. See, for example, Peter Hall and Ann Markusen, eds., *Silicon Landscapes* (Boston: Allen and Unwin, 1985); Manuel Castells, *The Informational City: Information Technology, Economic Restructuring and the Urban-Regional Process* (Oxford: Basil Blackwell, 1989); Scott, *New Industrial Spaces*.

14. These theories account for the stagnation or relative decline of a regional economy through imprecise references to "diseconomies" of agglomeration or the accumulation of negative externalities. But if such diseconomies are related to the overall size of a regional cluster, the degree of congestion, or the costs of production, growth should have slowed in the more densely populated Silicon Valley long before it did so along Route 128. Thanks to Bennett Harrison for pointing this out.

15. See Richard Florida and Martin Kenney, "Silicon Valley and Route 128 Won't Save Us," *California Management Review*, Fall 1990, 68–88; Charles Ferguson, "From the People Who Brought You Voodoo Economics," *Har-*

vard *Business Review,* May–June·1988, 55–62; AnnaLee Saxenian, "A Response to Richard Florida and Martin Kenney," *California Management Review,* Spring 1991, 136–142.

16. Marshall's references in *Principles of Economics* to the atmosphere of industrial districts, for example, where "the mysteries of the industry are in the air," imply a blurring of the boundaries between firms and between firms and the environment. For a sophisticated treatment of external economies that completely blurs these boundaries, see Michael Storper, "The Transition to Flexible Specialization in the U.S. Film Industry: External Economies, the Division of Labor, and the Crossing of Industrial Divides," *Cambridge Journal of Economics* 13 (1989), 273–305. See also Bennett Harrison, "Industrial Districts—Old Wine in New Bottles," *Regional Studies* 26, no. 5 (1992), 469–510.

17. Mark Granovetter, "Economic Action and Social Structures: the Problem of 'Embeddedness,'" *American Journal of Sociology* 91, no. 3 (1985), 481–510.

18. The notion of an industrial system is adapted from Herrigel's concept of "industrial order." It avoids the term "industrial organization," which assumes a strict boundary between the economy and society and politics. Herrigel defines industrial order as "the sum of practices, rules and institutions that constitute and shape the way that the production of goods and its administration takes place." Gary Herrigel, "Industrial Order and the Politics of Industrial Change: Mechanical Engineering," in *Industry and Politics in West Germany: Toward a Third Republic,* ed. Peter J. Katzenstein (Ithaca, N.Y.: Cornell University Press, 1989), 185–220.

19. While these dimensions are normally treated in isolation, recent research has revealed their interrelations. Economists now recognize, for example, that innovation is a product of interactions among customers and suppliers, a firm's internal operating units, and the wider social and institutional environment. See Giovanni Dosi, "Sources, Procedures, and Microeconomic Effects of Innovation," *Journal of Economic Literature* 26 (Sept. 1988), 1120–1171; Stephen J. Kline and Nathan Rosenberg, "An Overview of Innovation," in *The Positive Sum Strategy,* ed. R. Landau and N. Rosenberg (Washington, D.C.: National Academy Press, 1986). Sociologists and political scientists similarly have identified the importance of shared identities and local culture as sources of the trust needed to foster collaboration and industrial adaptation. See Robert D. Putnam, *Making Democracy Work: Civic Traditions in Modern Italy* (Princeton, N.J.: Princeton University Press, 1993); Charles Sabel, "Studied Trust: Building New Forms of Cooperation in a Volatile Economy," in Frank Pyke and Werner Sengenberger, eds., *Industrial Districts and Local Economic Regeneration* (Geneva: International Institute for Labour Studies, 1992).

20. The British cotton textile industry is typically seen as a classic example; see Bernard Elbaum and William Lazonick, eds., *The Decline of the British Economy* (New York: Oxford University Press, 1986). However, even there

the story is more complex. According to Cobrin, "Two Paths of Industrial Adjustment," the textile firms in Yorkshire adjusted far more successfully to the competitive dislocations of the 1970s and 1980s than the more atomistic Lancashire-based mass producers because of a local industrial system comparable to that of Silicon Valley.

21. This appears to be what happened to the U.S. automobile industry. See Susan Helper, "Comparative Supplier Relations in the U.S. and Japanese Auto Industries: An Exit/Voice Approach," *Business and Economic History* 19 (1990), 153–161.

1. Genesis: Universities, Military Spending, and Entrepreneurs

1. For a view of New England as an agglomeration that periodically generates technologically innovative industries, see John S. Hekman and John S. Strong, "The Evolution of New England Industry," *New England Economic Review* (March/April 1981), 35–46.

2. In 1886, for example, an MIT chemist founded Arthur D. Little, Inc., a research and management consulting firm which now has operations around the world. And the first chair of the electrical engineering department said that he expected young professors to earn twice their salaries from consulting.

3. Susan Rosegrant and David R. Lampe, *Route 128: Lessons from Boston's High-Tech Community* (New York: Basic Books, 1992). Jackson quoted in David F. Noble, *America By Design: Science, Technology, and the Rise of Corporate Capitalism* (New York: Knopf, 1977), 138.

4. Henry Etzkowitz, "The Making of an Entrepreneurial University: The Traffic among MIT, Industry and the Military, 1860–1960" in *Science, Technology, and the Military,* ed. Everett Mendelsohn et al., vol. 2 (Boston: Kluwer Academic Publishers, 1988), 515–540.

5. Otto J. Scott, *The Creative Ordeal: The Story of Raytheon* (New York: Atheneum, 1974); Russell B. Adams, Jr., *The Boston Money Tree* (New York: Thomas Y. Crowell, 1977).

6. This money went to 25 universities and nonprofit institutes. MIT's share was nearly $117 million; Harvard received $31 million. Rosegrant and Lampe, *Route 128,* 80.

7. Etzkowitz, "Entrepreneurial University," 531.

8. Scott, *The Creative Ordeal.*

9. Quoted in Gene Bylinsky, *The Innovation Millionaires: How They Succeed* (New York: Scribner, 1976), 77.

10. Edward B. Roberts, *Entrepreneurs in High Technology: MIT and Beyond* (New York: Oxford University Press, 1991); Etzkowitz, "Entrepreneurial University"; Roberts, *Entrepreneurs in High Technology;* Adams, *Boston Money Tree.*

11. Rosegrant and Lampe, *Route 128,* 134.

12. Matthew Bullock, *Academic Enterprise, Industrial Innovation, and the Develop-*

ment of High Technology Financing in the United States (London: Brand Brothers, 1983); Richard Florida and Martin Kenney, "Venture Capital and High Technology Entrepreneurship," Working Paper 87–27, School of Urban and Public Affairs, Carnegie Mellon University (October 1987).

13. See Christopher Rand, *Cambridge, USA: Hub of a New World* (New York: Oxford University Press, 1964); and Paula G. Leventman, *Professionals Out of Work* (New York: Free Press, 1981).

14. Everett C. Burtt, Jr., "Changing Labor Supply Characteristics along Route 128," Research Report to the Federal Reserve Bank of Boston, no. 17 (July 1961); Rosegrant and Lampe, *Route 128*, 122, 130.

15. Edward B. Roberts and H. A. Wainer, "New Enterprises along Route 128," *Science Journal* 2 (Dec. 1968), 79–83; Edward B. Roberts, "A Basic Study of Innovators; How to Keep and Capitalize on Their Talents," *Research Management* 11, no. 4 (July 1968), 249–267; Adams, *Boston Money Tree;* Bylinsky, *Innovation Millionaires,* 81.

16. Roberts, "New Enterprises," reports that most spin-offs of MIT and its labs during the 1960s found their first markets in the military.

17. Rosegrant and Lampe, *Route 128,* 93; R. C. Estall, "The Electronic Products Industry of New England," *Economic Geography* 39, no. 3 (July 1963), 189–216.

18. Mass production of consumer electronics concentrated primarily in the New York and Chicago areas, which were closer to consumers and offered ample supplies of low-wage labor. Albert H. Rubenstein and Victor L. Andrews, "The Electronics Industry of New England to 1970," Research Report to the Federal Reserve Bank of Boston (December 1959).

19. In accounting for the region's increasing share of the military electronics business, Raytheon's president remarked in 1959: "The nature of the military business is considerably different from that of commercial business . . . in that its key franchise strength is derived from experienced engineers and engineering leadership in frontier areas of science rather than from a consumer market franchise, a patent franchise, or from low cost heavy plant facilities, as are often found in commercial industry." Quoted in Rubenstein and Andrews, "Electronics Industry," 11.

20. David R. Lampe, ed., *The Massachusetts Miracle: High Technology and Economic Revitalization* (Cambridge: MIT Press, 1988); Bylinsky, *Innovation Millionaires,* 83; Bennett Harrison, "Rationalization, Restructuring, and Industrial Reorganization in Older Regions: The Economic Transformation of New England Since World War II," Working Paper no. 72, Joint Center for Urban Studies of MIT and Harvard University (Feb. 1982).

21. Nancy S. Dorfman, "Route 128: The Development of a Regional High Technology Economy," *Research Policy* 12, no. 6 (Dec. 1983), 299–316.

22. On the origins of the computer industry, see Kenneth Flamm, *Creating the Computer: Government, Industry, and High Technology* (Washington, D.C.: Brookings Institution, 1988). The best account of DEC's early history is

found in Glenn Rifkin and George Harrar, *The Ultimate Entrepreneur: The Story of Ken Olsen and Digital Equipment Corporation* (Rocklin, Calif.: Prima Publishing, 1990).

23. "Digital Equipment Rides Wave of Success From Minicomputers," *Wall Street Journal*, 18 July 1978, 1.

24. John S. Hekman, "The Future of High Technology Industry in New England: A Case Study of Computers," *New England Economic Review*, Jan./Feb. 1980, 5–17; quote from Dorfman, "Route 128," 308.

25. Tony Perkins and Rich Karlgaard, "Inside Upside," *Upside* 3, no. 5 (June 1991), 5. Terman similarly arranged for the Varian brothers to use Stanford's physics labs without charge while their firm was getting off the ground.

26. Over the next thirty years Stanford collected almost $2 million in royalties from the arrangement. Edward Ginzton, "The $100 Idea," *IEEE Spectrum* 10 (Feb. 1975), 30–39.

27. Arthur L. Norberg, "The Origins of the Electronics Industry on the Pacific Coast," *Proceedings of the Institute of Electrical and Electronics Engineers* 64, no. 9 (Sept. 1976), 1314–1322; Tim J. Sturgeon, "The Origins of Silicon Valley: The Development of the Electronics Industry in the San Francisco Bay Area" (Master's thesis, University of California at Berkeley, 1992).

28. Food Machinery Corporation (FMC) in San Jose, for example, converted its factories from assembling tractors to making tanks and armored personnel carriers, which it continues to manufacture to this day.

29. Kenneth W. Clarfield, "Packard Urges Strong Commitment to Industry Research, Development," *Northern California Electronics News*, Oct. 2, 1978.

30. Sandra Blakeslee, "Want to Develop a World Center of Innovative Technology? It's Simple. Get Yourself a Fred Terman," *Stanford Observer*, Nov. 1977, 3; Frederick Terman, "Dean's Report, School of Engineering, 1946–47," in Stuart W. Leslie, "How the West Was Won: The Military and the Making of Silicon Valley" (manuscript, Department of History, Johns Hopkins University).

31. Terman quoted in Alan Bernstein et al., *Silicon Valley: Paradise or Paradox?* (Mountain View, California: Pacific Studies Center, 1977); Stuart W. Leslie, "From Backwater to Powerhouse," *Stanford*, March 1990, 55–60.

32. Blakeslee, "Terman," 8; Bylinsky, *Innovation Millionaires*, 52–54.

33. Cited in Michael I. Luger and Harvey A. Goldstein, *Technology in the Garden: Research Parks in Regional Economic Development* (Chapel Hill: University of North Carolina Press, 1991), 124.

34. Ibid., 125.

35. Bylinsky, *Innovation Millionaires*, 54. Leland Stanford's bequest of his 8,100 acre farm to the university prohibited the sale of the land. By 1974 the university had received $18 million in prepaid leases, which produced $1 million in investment income yearly. It also benefited through the growth of corporate contributions, which reached half a million dollars annually

in 1955 and topped $2 million in 1965. By 1977 the park housed 75 tenants and employment exceeded 19,000. Blakeslee, "Fred Terman," 8.

36. See Erica Schoenberger, "Corporate Transformations and Regional Development: Lockheed and the Pre-History of Silicon Valley" (manuscript, Johns Hopkins University, 1992).

37. Later in the decade, the magnetic data-storage disk (the Winchester drive) was invented at this facility. The hard disk drive offered a spectacular advance in the density of data storage and the speed of data retrieval, and vastly increased the market for computers. Numerous people left IBM to form independent disk-making firms in the area, in a spin-off process that foreshadowed the later and more widely celebrated process in the semiconductor industry.

38. By 1964 Lockheed Missiles and Space employed over 12,000 workers in the county, including some 2,200 research scientists, while Sylvania's Electronics Defense Laboratory employed 1,300, including more than 500 scientists and engineers.

39. Diodes and rectifiers were produced before World War II, but the semiconductor industry's real origins date to 1951, the year the transistor was commercially introduced.

40. The name was coined by the journalist Don C. Hoefler. As used here, it refers to Santa Clara County and to high technology activity in the adjacent counties of San Mateo, Alameda, and Santa Cruz.

41. Shockley moved to Boston to serve as a consultant to Raytheon and proposed a semiconductor start-up. When Raytheon management proved unwilling to guarantee the $1 million over a three-year period that his financial plan called for, Shockley left.

42. See Richard C. Levin, "The Semiconductor Industry," in *Government and Technical Progress: A Cross-Industry Analysis,* ed. Richard R. Nelson (New York: Pergamon Press, 1982).

43. Scott, *Creative Ordeal,* 319.

44. In 1968 the computer market accounted for 35 percent of total semiconductor sales, industrial products 20 percent, consumer products markets 10 percent, and military and aerospace markets 35 percent (when classified by end use, not direct purchases). By 1979 the military aerospace market had fallen to 10 percent. Levin, "Semiconductor Industry," 19.

2. Silicon Valley: Competition and Community

1. Thanks to Mark Granovetter for pointing this out. Even decades later, as the electronics industry began to spread up the east side of the Bay and south into Santa Cruz County, high land costs reinforced an unusually dense pattern of development.

2. Tom Wolfe, "The Tinkerings of Robert Noyce: How the Sun Rose on the Silicon Valley," *Esquire,* Dec. 1983, 346–374.

3. "Silicon Summit," *Electronic News,* 26 Sept. 1969, 1; Michael S. Malone, *The*

Big Score: The Billion-Dollar Story of Silicon Valley (New York: Doubleday, 1985), 113.

4. See, for example, Andrew Pollack, "Fathers of Silicon Valley Reunited," *New York Times,* 16 April 1988, B1.

5. Several journalistic accounts of Silicon Valley's origins capture this complex mix of social solidarity and entrepreneurial competition. See, for example, Malone, *The Big Score;* Paul Frieberger and Michael Swaine, *Fire in the Valley: The Making of the Personal Computer* (Berkeley, Calif.: Osborne-McGraw Hill, 1984); Everett M. Rogers and Judith K. Larsen, *Silicon Valley Fever: Growth of High-Technology Culture* (New York: Basic Books, 1984); and Dirk Hanson, *The New Alchemists: Silicon Valley and the Microelectronics Revolution* (Boston: Little, Brown, 1982).

6. Hoefler coined the term in a three-part series that he described as "a behind-the-scenes report of the men, money and litigation which spawned 23 companies—from the fledgling rebels of Shockley Transistor to the present day." Don C. Hoefler, "Silicon Valley—U.S.A.," *Electronic News,* Jan. 11, 18, and 25, 1971, rpt. in U.S. Congress, Joint Economic Committee, Subcommittee on Economic Growth, *Technology and Economic Growth,* 94th Cong., 1st sess., 1976, 172–173.

7. James J. Mitchell, "H-P Sets the Tone for Business in the Valley," *San Jose Mercury News,* Jan. 9, 1989, 1D–2D.

8. Gene Bylinsky, *The Innovation Millionaires: How they Succeed* (New York: Scribner, 1976), 67.

9. Ernest Braun and Stuart Macdonald, *Revolution in Miniature: The History and Impact of Semiconductor Electronics* (Cambridge: Cambridge University Press, 1978), 127. See also Rogers and Larsen, *Silicon Valley Fever;* Malone, *The Big Score;* and Kathleen Gregory, "Signing Up: The Culture and Careers of Silicon Valley Computer People" (Ph.D. diss., Northwestern University, 1984).

10. Wolfe, "Robert Noyce," 362.

11. Semiconductor executive William Winter quoted in Braun and Macdonald, *Revolution in Miniature,* 130; Bylinsky, *Innovation Millionaires,* 67; Irwin Federman, US Venture Partners, interview by author, Aug. 22, 1990. Federman served as the Chief Financial Officer of semiconductor manufacturer Monolithic Memories, Inc., from 1971 through 1979, and as Chairman of the Board until 1987.

12. Larry Jordan, Integrated Device Technology (IDT), interview by author, Sept. 15, 1990.

13. Robert Lorenzini, Siltec Corporation, in *Regional Cultures, Managerial Behavior and Entrepreneurship: An International Perspective,* ed. Joseph W. Weiss (New York: Quorum Books, 1988), 38.

14. Stephen Levy, *Hackers: Heroes of the Computer Revolution* (Garden City, N.Y.: Anchor Press/Doubleday, 1984), 194. See also Frieberger and Swaine, *Fire in the Valley,* and Rogers and Larsen, *Silicon Valley Fever.*

15. Quoted in Gregory, "Signing Up," 445.

16. "Statement of Pat Hill Hubbard," in *Technical Employment Projections* (Palo Alto: American Electronics Association, 1981); engineer quoted in Gregory, "Signing Up," 216. A more recent survey found that some 80 percent of the semiconductor production engineers who quit their jobs in Silicon Valley moved to other firms within the local labor market—far more than in other regions of the country. David P. Angel, "The Labor Market for Engineers in the U.S. Semiconductor Industry," *Economic Geography* 65, no. 2 (April 1989), 99–112.

17. Quotes from Rosenberg, "Technology Pushed to the Limit by Silicon Valley Start-Ups," *Boston Globe*, 15 Nov. 1982, 1, 37; and Braun and Macdonald, *Revolution in Miniature*, 137.

18. Gregory, "Signing Up," 473.

19. See Gregory, "Signing Up"; and David P. Angel, "High-Technology Agglomeration and the Labor Market: The Case of Silicon Valley," *Environment and Planning A*23, no. 10 (Oct. 1991): 1501–1516. Quotes from Hanson, *New Alchemists*, 113; Rosenberg, "Silicon Valley Start-Ups."

20. Gregory, "Signing Up," 205.

21. See Mark Granovetter, "The Strength of Weak Ties," *American Journal of Sociology* 78, no. 6 (1973), 1360–1380.

22. Rob Walker, LSI Logic Corporation, interview by author, May 2, 1988; Robert Swanson, Linear Technology Corp., interview by author, June 24, 1991; Corrigan quoted in John Markoff, "Silicon Valley Faces a Midlife Crisis," *New York Times*, Sept. 28, 1992, C1, C5. Walker worked at Philco-Ford, Fairchild, and Intel for twenty years before helping to found LSI Logic in 1980.

23. A study of 182 companies started in Silicon Valley between 1977 and 1982 showed that 75 percent of their founders had already been working on the technologies that formed the core of the firm's knowledge base and 54 percent had worked on similar products. "The New Entrepreneurs," *Economist*, Dec. 24, 1984, 61–73. See also Edward Roberts, *Entrepreneurs in High Technology: Lessons from MIT and Beyond* (New York: Oxford University Press, 1991).

24. Larry Jordan, interview by author, March 22, 1988. Jordan's career is typical of Silicon Valley: Before moving to IDT in 1987, Jordan had been a founding member of Laser Path and Seeq Technology, and had worked for Intel, National Semiconductor, Monolithic Memories, Fairchild, Raytheon, International Rectifier, and Curoff Electronics.

25. Each generation of technology produces new heroes in Silicon Valley. David Packard and William Hewlett were the original garage-entrepreneur heroes. They were joined in the 1970s by Robert Noyce of Intel Semiconductor, Jerry Sanders of Advanced Micro Devices, and Charlie Sporck of National Semiconductor. The early 1980s saw the rise of Apple Computer's Stephen Jobs and Steve Wozniak. See Malone, *Big Score*.

26. For example, Zilog, Inc., founded in 1974, is referred to as Zilog University

because it spawned a collection of spin-offs which focused on networking hardware and software, including Ungermann-Bass, 3Com, Novell, Bridge Communications, and Network Computing Devices.

27. Gene Bylinsky, "Jerry Sanders's Act Is Cleaning Up," *Fortune*, Oct. 15, 1984, 210–220. See also Malone, *Big Score*.

28. Jeffrey Kalb, MasPar Computer Corp., interview by author, Jan. 10, 1991; Doug Pelzer, Chips and Technologies, Inc., interview by author, Aug. 7, 1990. Kalb worked for DEC in Massachusetts during the 1980s and moved to Silicon Valley to start MasPar in 1988. Pelzer founded a business called Tactical Fabs to consult on the design and operation of semiconductor fabrication lines in the early 1980s.

29. Failure was not uncommon. One study of 250 Silicon Valley firms started during the 1960s found that by 1988 50 percent had failed, 32 percent had merged or been acquired, and 18 percent had survived as independent businesses. Albert V. Bruno, Edward F. McQuarrie, Carol G. Torgrimson, "The Evolution of New Technology Ventures over 20 Years: Patterns of Failure, Merger, and Survival," *Journal of Business Venturing* 7 (1992), 291–302.

30. Quoted in Bylinsky, *Innovation Millionaires*, 64.

31. Quoted in Malone, *Big Score*, 289.

32. Robert Noyce, "Competition and Cooperation—A Prescription for the Eighties," *Research Management*, March 1982, 15.

33. Lawrence M. Friedman, Robert W. Gordon, Sophie Pirie, and Edwin Whatley, "Law, Lawyers, and Legal Practice in Silicon Valley: A Preliminary Report," *Indiana Law Journal* 64 (Summer 1989), 555–567.

34. Frederick E. Terman, "A Brief History of Electrical Engineering Education," *Proceedings of the IEEE* 64, no. 9 (Sept. 1976), 1403–1405.

35. See Elizabeth L. Useem, *Low Tech Education in a High Tech World: Corporations and Classrooms in the New Information Society* (New York: Free Press, 1986).

36. Quoted in Tom Forester, *The Microelectronics Revolution* (Cambridge: MIT Press, 1981).

37. See Noyce, "Competition and Cooperation."

38. Ibid., 15.

39. Rogers and Larson, *Silicon Valley Fever*, 58–59.

40. Irwin Federman, interview by author, Aug. 22, 1988; Larry Jordan, interview by author, March 24, 1988; Michael Krey, "Sandra Kurtzig: A Role Model Who Is at Odds with Symbols," *Business Journal: San Jose and Silicon Valley*, March 18, 1991.

41. Noyce, "Competition and Cooperation," 14. This open dissemination of technology is attributable in part to the 1965 consent decree in the Justice Department's antitrust suit against AT&T, in which the firm agreed to license its existing patents royalty free to any interested domestic company and all future patents at reasonable royalties. AT&T's Bell Labs, where the transistor was invented, thus liberally licensed its technology and dissemi-

nated its semiconductor know-how widely through industry symposia, technical publications, and plant tours, and maintained a lenient attitude toward personnel defections. See John E. Tilton, *International Diffusion of Technology: The Case of Semiconductors* (Washington, D.C.: Brookings Institution, 1971).

42. P. Carey and A. Gathright, "The Silicon Valley Ethic: By Work Obsessed," *San Jose Mercury News*, Feb. 17–18 and 20–23, 1985.

43. See AnnaLee Saxenian, "In Search of Power: The Organization of Business Interests in Silicon Valley and Route 128," *Economy and Society* 18 (1989), 25–70.

44. Unlike the typical engineer-turned-entrepreneur, Packard was no newcomer to politics. He was among the founders of the West Coast Electronics Manufacturers Association, which later became the AEA, in 1943, and his international reputation earned as Deputy Secretary of Defense under Richard Nixon and his connections, political stature and savvy, and personal wealth set him apart from the rest of the local business community.

45. When the West Coast Electronics Manufacturers Association (WCEMA) moved to Palo Alto in 1964 from Los Angeles it changed its name to Western Electronics Manufacturers Association. In 1969 the name was changed once more, this time to WEMA to eliminate the words "electronics manufacturers" and enable software firms to join. This also allowed them to expand membership outside of the thirteen Western states. Finally in 1978 the name was changed to American Electronics Association (AEA). See AnnaLee Saxenian, "Contrasting Patterns of Business Organization in Silicon Valley," *Environment and Planning D: Society and Space* 10 (1992), 377–391.

46. James J. Mitchell, "A Valley Hero Readies to Retire," *San Jose Mercury News*, Jan. 20, 1985. The column was on the retirement of E. E. Ferrey, who was president of the AEA from 1960 to 1985.

47. After the recession of the mid-1980s, however, the AEA changed its course significantly, opening up a Washington office and becoming heavily involved in traditional lobbying activities.

48. In 1986, 66 percent of SEMI's 900 U.S. members had fewer than 100 employees and annual sales of less than $10 million. *SEMI Membership Profile* (Mountain View, Calif.: SEMI, 1986).

49. Richard O. von Werssowetz and Michael Beer, "Human Resources at Hewlett-Packard," Harvard Business School Case 9–482–125, 1982, 712.

50. William Krause, 3Com Corp., interview by author, Oct. 13, 1990.

51. Thomas J. Peters and Robert H. Waterman, Jr., *In Search of Excellence: Lessons from America's Best Run Companies* (New York: Harper and Row, 1982), 123.

52. Gregory, "Signing Up," 105.

53. "Creativity by the Numbers: An Interview with Robert Noyce," *Harvard Business Review* 58, no. 3 (May–June 1980), 130.

54. William Unger, Mayfield Fund, quoted in Ron Wolf, "Valley Execs Take Stock—and Moderate Salaries," *San Jose Mercury News*, June 29, 1992, 2D.
55. Andre Delbecq and Joseph Weiss, "The Business Culture of Silicon Valley: Is It a Model for the Future?" in Weiss, *Regional Cultures*, 23–41; and Joseph Weiss and Andre Delbecq, "High Technology Cultures and Management: Silicon Valley and Route 128," *Group and Organization Studies* 12, no. 1 (March 1987), 39–54.
56. Irwin Federman, Monolithic Memories, Inc., and Robert Lorenzini, Siltec Corporation, quoted in Weiss and Delbecq, "High Technology Cultures," 33.
57. Paul Wythes, Sutter Hills Ventures, and Kenneth Oshman, Rolm Corporation, ibid., 32.
58. John Sculley, Apple Computer, Inc., ibid., 37.
59. Robert Swanson interview, June 24, 1991. Swanson worked for Route 128–based Transitron in the late 1950s and early 1960s, then moved to Silicon Valley where he worked for Fairchild and National Semiconductor before starting Linear Technology in 1981.
60. Delbecq and Weiss, "Business Culture," 34.
61. Membership estimates from AFL-CIO Central Labor Councils. Established defense contractors in Silicon Valley (such as Lockheed, Westinghouse, FMC, and GE) and elsewhere commonly recognized unions in the postwar period because labor often had the political clout to influence defense contract awards and because companies paid little if any competitive penalty for high labor costs.
  The general failure to organize Silicon Valley's technology firms was due in part to effective prevention by management and in part to weak enforcement of federal labor laws. Equally important, however, was the failure of industrial unions to develop innovative approaches to organizing and representing highly skilled employees in a fast-changing industry. Steeped in the experience of stable, mass production industries, unions have overlooked the needs of professional and technical employees who work in a highly decentralized industrial setting.
62. Wolfe, "Robert Noyce," 368.

3. Route 128: Independence and Hierarchy

1. See E. Digby Baltzell, *Puritan Boston and Quaker Philadelphia: Two Protestant Ethics and the Spirit of Class Authority and Leadership* (New York: Free Press, 1979).
2. Jeffrey Kalb, MasPar Computer Corp., interview by author, Jan. 10, 1991; Tom Furlong, Digital Equipment Corporation, interview by author, Feb. 11, 1991.
3. Sterling Hager, "Wild West Public Relations Invades Entrenched East Coast," *Upside,* Dec. 1990, D-27.

4. See Stephen Levy, *Hackers: Heroes of the Computer Revolution* (Garden City, N.Y.: Anchor Press/Doubleday, 1984).

5. Kenneth H. Olsen, *Digital Equipment Corporation: The First Twenty-Five Years* (New York: Newcomer Society in North America, 1983); Glenn Rifkin and George Harrar, *The Ultimate Entrepreneur: The Story of Ken Olsen and Digital Equipment Corporation* (Rocklin, Calif.: Prima Publishing, 1990).

6. Ray Stata, chairman of Analog Devices (founded in 1965), for example, drives himself to work in a twenty-year-old Oldsmobile, flies tourist or business class, and eats breakfast in the company cafeteria or at his desk. Jeremy Main, "A Chipmaker Who Beats the Business Cycle," *Fortune*, Dec. 23, 1985, 114.

7. Paul DeLacey, Boston Technology, Inc., interview by author, Feb. 4, 1991.

8. Robert Swanson, Linear Technology Corp., interview by author, June 24, 1991.

9. P. Andrews McLane, TA Associates, quoted in Ronald Rosenberg, "Technology Pushed to the Limit by Silicon Valley 'Start-Ups,'" *Boston Globe*, Nov. 15, 1982, 37.

10. Olsen was CEO of DEC for 35 years, until he was forced to resign in 1992; DeCastro remained chairman of Data General almost 25 years after its founding, until he was forced to resign in 1990; and Wang remained president and CEO of Wang for 40 years, until his death in 1991.

11. Edward B. Roberts, *Entrepreneurship in High Technology: MIT and Beyond* (New York: Oxford University Press, 1991); A. Cooper, "Technical Entrepreneurship: What Do We Know?" *R&D Management* 3, no. 2 (1973), 59–64. See also E. B. Roberts and H. A. Wainer, "New Enterprises along Route 128," *Science Journal* 2 (Dec. 1968), 79–83.

12. Of the $1.4 billion in total venture capital investments made during 1981, 12 percent went to Massachusetts-based companies and 38 percent went to California. *Venture Capital Journal* (Needham, Mass.: Venture Economics Inc., 1982).

13. Henry Etzkowitz, "The Making of an Entrepreneurial University: The Traffic among MIT, Industry, and the Military, 1860–1960," in *Science, Technology, and the Military*, ed. Everett Mendelsohn et al., vol. 12 (New York: Kluwer Academic Publishers, 1988), 515–540; Russell B. Adams, Jr., *The Boston Money Tree* (New York: Thomas Y. Crowell, 1977), 300.

14. Alan Michels, quoted in Rosenberg, "Silicon Valley Start-Ups." 37.

15. C. Gordon Bell, Bell-Mason Group, interview by author, March 24, 1993. Bell joined DEC as a computer engineer in 1960 and left as vice president of engineering in 1983. He is credited with masterminding most of DEC's minicomputers.

16. Cheryl Vedoe, Sun Microsystems, interview by author, June 5, 1991; Jeffrey Kalb interview, Jan. 10, 1991.

17. By 1990 the Stanford Instructional Television Network served some 200 Silicon Valley companies and 4,500 students annually. Taking advantage

of technological advances, students now ask questions and participate in class discussions through interactive video. Ronald Rosenberg, "The Learning Center at the Top End of Silicon Valley," *Boston Globe*, Nov. 16, 1982.

18. See Elizabeth Useem, *Low Tech Education in a High Tech World* (New York: Free Press, 1986).

19. C. Gordon Bell interview, March 24, 1993.

20. Carey Kimmel, Xerox Corp., interview by author, June 19, 1991.

21. Useem, *Low Tech Education*. The Bay State Skills Corp. was established in 1981 to bring together several community colleges and high technology companies in joint training efforts.

22. Sterling Hager, "New England vs. Silicon Valley: Toe-to-Toe in Technology," *Business Journal* (San Jose), March 27, 1989, 26.

23. Quoted in Rosegrant and Lampe, *Route 128*, 141.

24. See AnnaLee Saxenian, "In Search of Power: The Organization of Business Interests in Silicon Valley," *Economy and Society* 18, no. 1 (Feb. 1989), 25–70.

25. The Route 128 Venture Group's monthly meetings, for example, typically drew only 20 percent repeat attendees. See Amy Bemar, "How MIT Helps the Enterprising," *Upside*, May 1990, 57–84; and Nitin Nohria, "Creating New Business Ventures: Network Organization in Market and Corporate Contexts" (Ph.D. diss., MIT, 1988).

26. The classic description of this corporate model appears in Alfred D. Chandler, Jr., *The Visible Hand: The Managerial Revolution in American Business* (Cambridge, Mass.: Harvard University Press, 1977).

27. Route 128's largest military contractor, Raytheon, reduced its sales to the government from 87 percent of its total business in 1964 to 55 percent in 1967 and to 37 percent in 1975. Otto J. Scott, *The Creative Ordeal: The Story of Raytheon* (New York: Atheneum, 1974); Michael Porter, "Raytheon Co.: Diversification," Harvard Business School Case 0–377–055, rev. 5/85.

28. Jim Campbell, quoted in Harold Seneker, "Data General—Life in the Fast Lane," *Forbes*, March 3, 1980, 72–74; Dave Weischaar, Sun Microsystems, interview by author, Jan. 31, 1991. Weischaar worked for DEC and two Route 128 start-ups during the 1980s.

29. Rifkin and Harrar, *Ultimate Entrepreneur*, 101; "Data General's Management Trouble," *Business Week*, Feb. 9, 1981, 58–61.

30. Intel employed 15,000 workers in 1980. Noyce said the company was "run out of the collective experience of everyone. . . and consequently we feel that we're plowing new ground in terms of how we organize, how we do things, how we keep focus." Noyce quoted in "Creativity by the Numbers," *Harvard Business Review* 58, no. 3 (May/June 1980), 123.

31. Rifkin and Harrar, *Ultimate Entrepreneur*, 95.

32. Ibid., 257, 106.

33. C. Gordon Bell interview, March 24, 1993; Sam Fuller, Digital Equipment Corporation, interview by author, Jan. 16, 1991.

34. Bro Uttal, "The Gentlemen and the Upstarts Meet in a Great Mini Battle,"

Fortune, April 23, 1979, 106; William Foster, Stratus Computer, interview by author, Jan. 9, 1991. See also "Espionage in the Computer Business," *Business Week*, July 28, 1975, 60–62.

35. Tracy Kidder, *Soul of a New Machine* (Boston: Little, Brown, 1981). Thanks to Peter Evans for this observation.

36. Joe DeNucci, MIPS Computer Systems, interview by author, March 25, 1991.

37. Edson DeCastro, Data General, interview by author, Jan. 17, 1991.

38. John S. Hekman, "The Future of High Technology Industry in New England: The Case of Computers," *New England Economic Review*, Jan./Feb. 1980, 5–17.

39. Michael Weinstein, quoted in Rifkin and Harrar, *Ultimate Entrepreneur*, 133.

40. Gideon Kunda, *Engineering Culture: Control and Commitment in a High-Tech Corporation* (Philadelphia: Temple University Press, 1992).

41. Edgar H. Schein, *Organizational Culture and Leadership* (San Francisco: Jossey-Bass, 1985), 220; Rifkin and Harrar, *Ultimate Entrepreneur*, 119, 106. Wang Laboratories also developed a highly paternalistic, familial culture during this era, with An Wang often described as a benevolent dictator.

42. Rifkin and Harrar, *Ultimate Entrepreneur*, 121.

43. Schein, *Organizational Culture and Leadership*.

44. Edgar Schein, Professor of Management, MIT, interview by author, June 3, 1991; Paul DeLacey interview, Feb. 4, 1991. DeLacey was with Honeywell for more than twenty years before leaving to join start-up Boston Technology.

One study found that most Silicon Valley CEOs sold their shares and ceded control over operations within the company's first five years. Claudia Schoonhoven and Kathleen Eisenhardt, "Regions as Industrial Incubators of Technology-based Ventures," in Edwin Mills and John MacDonald, eds., *Sources of Metropolitan Growth* (New Brunswick, N.J.: Center for Urban Policy Research, 1992).

45. William Foster interview, Jan. 9, 1991.

46. "Computer Slump Stalls Boston's Pace," *San Jose Mercury News*, Aug. 3, 1989, 1E–2E.

47. Paul DeLacey interview, Feb. 4, 1991; Rifkin and Harrar, *Ultimate Entrepreneur*, 89. After the exodus of engineers to Data General in 1968, DEC liberalized its policy on the provision of stock options.

48. Tod Basche, Sun Microsystems, interview by author, Feb. 12, 1991.

49. Receiving tubes were the first electronic components that were capable of detecting, modifying, and amplifying electrical signals. Solid state technology, which conducts and controls the movement of electrical current within solid materials, began to compete with receiving tubes for use in electronic products in the 1960s. All silicon semiconductors are solid state devices.

In 1959, Sylvania, Raytheon and CBS-Hytron together employed 6,000 workers and accounted for 85 percent of all electronic component manufacture in New England; start-up Transitron employed more than 1,500. R. C. Estall, "The Electronic Products Industry of New England," *Economic Geography* 39, no. 3 (July 1963), 189–216.

50. John E. Tilton, *International Diffusion of Technology: The Case of Semiconductors* (Washington, D.C.: Brookings Institution, 1971), 65–66.

51. "Route 128 firms started in the 1950s and 1960s depended on defense and space business to an extent unknown in Silicon Valley." Gene Bylinsky, *The Innovation Millionaires: How They Succeed* (New York: Scribner, 1976), 82. The federal government accounted for between a quarter and half of the total semiconductor market during the 1950s and 1960s and was an important sponsor of new as well as established semiconductor ventures. See Tilton, *International Diffusion,* 90. Semiconductor start-ups that were started or grew in the 1950s and 1960s on the basis of military contracts included Bomac Laboratories, Micro-wave Associates, Analog Devices, and Teradyne on Route 128 and Siliconix, Molectro, General Micro-electronics, and Signetics in Silicon Valley.

52. Tilton, *International Diffusion,* 66.

53. Quote from Albert H. Rubenstein, "Problems of Financing and Managing New Research-Based Enterprises in New England," Research Report to the Federal Reserve Bank of Boston, no. 3, April 7, 1958.

54. Kathryn Harrigan and Michael Porter, "The Receiving Tube Industry in 1966," Harvard Business School Case 9–379–181, rev. 6/88.

55. Ibid.

56. Ernest Braun and Stuart Macdonald, *Revolution in Miniature: The History and Impact of Semiconductor Electronics* (Cambridge: Cambridge University Press, 1978), 145.

57. Tom Hinkleman, quoted in Dirk Hanson, *The New Alchemists: Silicon Valley and the Microelectronics Revolution* (Boston: Little, Brown, 1982), 110.

58. See Robert W. Wilson, Peter K. Ashton, and Thomas P. Egan, *Innovation, Competition, and Government Policy in the Semiconductor Industry* (Lexington, Mass.: Lexington Books, 1980).

59. Ibid., 55.

60. Rob Walker, *Silicon Destiny: The Story of Application Specific Integrated Circuits and LSI Logic Corporation* (Milpitas, Calif.: C.M.C. Publications, 1992); "Transitron Sets Investors Agog," *Business Week,* Dec. 5, 1959, 123–124; Braun and Macdonald, *Revolution in Miniature.*

4. BETTING ON A PRODUCT

1. Robert Noyce, "Microelectronics," *Scientific American* 237, no. 3 (Sept. 1977), 68. Worldwide semiconductor production increased tenfold, from $1.7 billion in 1970 to over $17 billion in 1980. Mel Eklund and William Strauss, eds., "Status '80: A Report on the Integrated Circuit Industry" (Scottsdale, Ariz.: Integrated Circuit Corporation, 1980), 51. Military sales accounted for 55 percent of the integrated circuits market in 1965 but fell

to less than 25 percent by 1972. Michael G. Borrus, *Competing for Control: America's Stake in Microelectronics* (Cambridge, Mass.: Ballinger, 1988).

2. "Cashing in on a New Generation of Chips," *Business Week*, March 27, 1971, 50. Development of bipolar chips in the early 1960s focused on standardized, off-the-shelf products, but most producers learned from the experience of Philco (described in Chapter 3) to avoid investments in automation.

3. Quote from Robert W. Wilson, Peter K. Ashton, and Thomas P. Egan, *Innovation, Competition, and Government Policy in the Semiconductor Industry* (Lexington, Mass.: Lexington Books, 1980). For example, in 1972 the Micromosaic group at Fairchild completed 70 customer-specific circuit designs and expected to turn out some 500 devices per week. In an early version of gate-array techniques, they built wafers containing different logic gate designs that could later be processed to connect the gates to meet the customer's unique requirements. Rob Walker, *Silicon Destiny: The Story of Application Specific Integrated Circuits and LSI Logic Corporation* (Milpitas, Calif.: C.M.C. Publications, 1992).

4. M. S. Peterson, "The Semiconductor Industry: Why the Past Isn't Necessarily Prologue," Industry Series SI1944.84, First Boston Research (New York: First Boston Corporation, Nov. 1984). Noyce, in "Microelectronics," 66, estimates the learning curve at 28 percent cost reduction with every doubling of cumulative output. The learning curve was widely promoted by management science of the time. See, for example, Frank Andress, "The Learning Curve as a Production Tool," *Harvard Business Review*, Jan.–Feb. 1954, and Winifred Hirschmann, "Profit from the Learning Curve," *Harvard Business Review*, Jan.–Feb. 1964.

5. See Walker, *Silicon Destiny.*

6. Grove quoted in Gene Bylinsky, *The Innovation Millionaires: How They Succeed* (New York: Scribner, 1976), 156–157, and in *San Jose Mercury News*, May 4, 1980; Robert N. Noyce, "Large-Scale Integration: What Is Yet to Come?" *Science* 195 (March 1977), 1105. Grove called Intel "a manufacturer of high technology jelly beans" and drew a parallel with McDonald's, "a very successful manufacturer of medium-technology jelly beans."

7. This created tensions between the semiconductor makers and their customers, who still demanded special-purpose chips. At a 1980 industry symposium, Silicon Valley industry leaders told computer and equipment makers that in-house production was their only alternative. See Arthur L. Robinson, "Are VLSI Microcircuits Too Hard to Design?" *Science* 208 (July 11, 1980).

8. "Rolling with the Recession in Semiconductors," *Business Week*, July 21, 1980, 189–192.

9. "Clouds over Silicon Valley," *Far Eastern Economic Review*, Dec. 14, 1979, 107–108.

10. Thomas Skornia, Advanced Micro Devices, interview by author, Feb. 27,

1980; Lester Hogan, quoted in *Business Journal* (San Jose), Sept. 8, 1986; Arthur L. Robinson, "Giant Corporations from Tiny Chips Grow," *Science* 208 (May 2, 1980), 480–484.

11. U.S. Bureau of the Census, *County Business Patterns* (Washington, D.C.: Government Printing Office, 1970, 1980). National Semiconductor was known as the classic low-cost producer of commodity "jelly bean" memories, Intel was the market leader in design-intensive microprocessors, while AMD depended on second-sourcing microprocessors. Both AMD and Intel also mass-produced memory products and related peripherals. By 1980 Intel and National reported some $600 million in sales, while Fairchild and AMD exceeded $250 million. All ranked among the nation's ten largest integrated circuit suppliers. U.S. Department of Commerce, *A Report on the U.S. Semiconductor Industry* (Washington, D.C.: U.S. Government Printing Office, 1979), 89.

12. This process culminated in 1979 when the French conglomerate Schlumberger acquired the grandfather of Silicon Valley, Fairchild Semiconductor. See "Can Semiconductors Survive Big Business?" *Business Week*, Dec. 3, 1979, 66–86.

13. The limits of the traditional American approach to mass production were already becoming apparent in the auto industry, where U.S. producers had lost market share during the 1970s to the more flexible and efficient Japanese producers. See William Abernathy, Kim Clark, and Alan Kantrow, *Industrial Renaissance: Producing a Competitive Future for America* (New York: Basic Books, 1983); James Womack, Daniel Jones, and Daniel Roos, *The Machine That Changed the World: Based on the Massachusetts Institute of Technology 5-Million Dollar 5-Year Study on the Future of the Automobile* (New York: Rawson Associates, 1990).

14. See Annette Lamond, "The Loss of U.S. Dominance in DRAMS: A Case History (1976–1984)," Harvard Business School Case 9–689–067, 1989; and Borrus, *Competing for Control*. U.S. producers, especially Intel, continued to dominate microprocessor and microcontroller markets, partly because of design superiority and partly because of their proprietary products used in personal computers.

15. See "America's High Tech Crisis: Why Silicon Valley Is Losing Its Edge," *Business Week*, March 1985, 56–67.

16. The preference of the SIA for lobbying Washington marked an important departure from the regional activities of Silicon Valley's older business associations. Following the SIA model, the AEA began to shift its attention away from the region during the 1980s, devoting more and more attention to lobbying for "competitiveness" policies and less and less to management education and training programs. See AnnaLee Saxenian, "Contrasting Patterns of Business Organization in Silicon Valley," *Environment and Planning D: Society and Space* 10 (1992), 377–391.

17. The SIA was increasingly isolated from the wider electronics community

in Silicon Valley during the 1980s, just when it was gaining national political support. Moreover, the SIA victory appears to have been pyrrhic. Most observers have concluded that the trade agreement simply provided Japanese semiconductor producers with windfall profits that they used to finance investment in the next generation of semiconductor products and processes. See, for example, David Mowery and Nathan Rosenberg, "New Developments in U.S. Technology Policy: Implications for Competitiveness and International Trade Policy," *California Management Review* 32 (1984), 107–124; A. Erdilek, "The U.S.–Japan Semiconductor Trade Agreement and the Globalization of Dynamic and Imperfect Competition," in *Industrial Dynamics*, ed. Bo Carlsson (Boston: Kluwer-Nishoff, 1989), 211–238.

18. See Borrus, *Competing for Control.*

19. Quote from Arthur L. Robinson, "Perilous Times for U.S. Microcircuit Makers," *Science*, May 1980, 585. Cost reduction in the complex process of manufacturing integrated circuits derives primarily from the ability to increase the yield from a given batch of wafers. Yields for new products can be as low as 10 percent, but they increase rapidly with production experience, typically reaching 90 percent for mature products. Since the cost of processing a batch of wafers is essentially fixed, an increase in yields from 10 to 20 percent cuts marginal fabrication cost per circuit in half. Such savings are essential to commodity producers, who must compete on the basis of cost.

20. Jay Stowsky, "The Weakest Link: Semiconductor Equipment, Linkages, and the Limits to International Trade," Working Paper no. 27, Berkeley Roundtable on the International Economy, University of California at Berkeley, 1987.

21. Elizabeth A. Hass, "Applying the Lessons: Networking Semiconductor Companies," *Entrepreneurial Economy* 6, no. 1 (July/Aug. 1987), 40–41.

22. See Borrus, *Competing for Control.*

23. Doug Peltzer, Chips and Technologies, interview by author, Aug. 7, 1990. Peltzer began his career building epitaxial reactors for Fairchild and later worked as a semiconductor process consultant before joining C&T.

24. Ronald Whittier, Intel Corporation, quoted in Michael Schrage, "Hard Times Descend on Silicon Valley," *Washington Post*, April 28, 1985.

25. The low-trust, arms-length supplier relations adopted by the chipmakers, for example, reflected the pattern established in the U.S. auto industry, which was widely viewed as the model of mature mass production. See Susan Helper, "Supplier Relations and Technical Change: Theory and Application to the U.S. Auto Industry" (Ph.D. diss., Harvard University, 1987).

26. Stowsky, "The Weakest Link."

27. Henri Jarrat, "A Look at the Semiconductor Industry in the 1990s," speech presented to the 1990 Semiconductor Conference, Robertson, Colman and Stephens, Sept. 23, 1987; A. Hayashi, "The New Intel: Moore Mature, Moore Competitive," *Electronic Business*, Nov. 15, 1987. Intel, National Semiconductor, and Fairchild all began producing electronic digital

watches during the 1970s. National also entered the calculator business. These efforts at forward integration proved to be costly failures: the chip producers lacked the understanding of the market or the distribution network needed to compete in the consumer electronics business.

28. Intel, for example, adopted (and later abandoned) a matrix organization. It was, according to former managers, a dismal failure because it created so many lateral committees that nothing ever got done. Gordon Campbell, Chips and Technologies, interview by author, Jan. 8, 1987.

29. "Why They're Jumping Ship at Intel," *Business Week,* Feb. 14, 1983, 107–108; "Behind the Exodus at National Semiconductor," *Business Week,* Sept. 21, 1981, 95–100; Robert Swanson, Linear Technology Corp., interview by author, June 24, 1991; Gordon Campbell, Chips and Technologies, interview by author, June 24, 1991.

30. C. Makridis and N. Berg, "Manufacturing Offshore Is Bad Business," *Harvard Business Review,* Sept.–Oct. 1988, 113–120.

31. Dieter Ernst, "Programmable Automation in the Semiconductor Industry: Reflections on Current Diffusion Patterns," paper presented at an OECD Conference on Programmable Automation, Paris, April 2–4, 1987.

32. The Korean government invested more than $4 billion in computer memory technology between 1987 and 1992, and Korean firms controlled 15 percent of the world memory market by 1992. Samsung became one of the largest producers of DRAMs in the world, and the leading DRAM supplier in the U.S. Andrew Pollack, "US Chip Makers Stem the Tide in Trade Battles with Japanese," *New York Times,* April 9, 1992, A1; and John Markoff, "Rethinking the National Chip Policy," *New York Times,* July 14, 1992.

33. *Architecture* is the complex of standards and rules that define how programs and commands will work and how data will move around a system (including, for example, the communications protocols that hardware components must follow, the rules for exchanging data between applications software and the operating system, and the allowable font descriptions that can be communicated to printers).

34. DEC, for example, grew from 5,800 to 56,000 employees between 1970 and 1980, while DG grew from 240 to 14,370. Harold Seneker, "Data General—Life in the Fast Lane," *Forbes,* March 3, 1980, 72–74.

35. DeCastro quoted in "The Long Hairs vs. the Stuffed Shirts," *Forbes,* Jan. 15, 1976, 30.

36. By 1981 DG designed and manufactured more than 80 percent of the components for its minicomputers. Ralph Emmett, "DG's High Stakes Gambling," *Datamation,* July 1981, 34.

37. In 1977 the top four firms in the industry accounted for 65 percent and the top eight firms for 85 percent of unit sales. Elaine Romanelli, "New Venture Strategies in the Minicomputer Industry," *California Management Review,* Fall 1987, 160–175.

38. "Ken Olsen Talks about Digital," *Mass High Tech,* Oct. 28, 1985, 14.

39. DEC and military-oriented Raytheon each employed approximately 30,000 workers locally in the late 1980s, making them the largest employers in Massachusetts. Sarah Kuhn, "Computer Manufacturing in New England: Structure, Location, and Labor in a Growing Industry," Joint Center for Urban Studies of MIT and Harvard University, April 1982, 99.

40. Defense electronics, the other leading manufacturing sector in the region, remained healthy throughout most of the 1980s as a result of high levels of military spending.

41. See David Manasian, "Within the Whirlwind: A Survey of the Computer Industry," *Economist*, Feb. 27, 1993. In developing the PC, IBM bought its microprocessor from Intel, its operating system from Microsoft, and its disk drives, monitors, and add-in boards off the shelf from a variety of third-party suppliers.

42. Quotes from Glenn Rifkin and George Harrar, *The Ultimate Entrepreneur: The Story of Ken Olsen and Digital Equipment Corporation* (Chicago: Contemporary Books, 1988), 194–195; and John Markoff, "The Big Squeeze Facing Digital," *New York Times*, April 5, 1988, D1. Edgar Schein describes DEC's arrogance toward customers and its assumption that engineers know what customers want better than the customers do. Edgar H. Schein, *Organizational Culture and Leadership* (San Francisco: Jossey-Bass, 1985), 229.

43. In 1990 profit margins on computers running on proprietary systems were consistently 60 percent or more, compared to less than 40 percent (and shrinking rapidly) for standard Unix workstations. Stratford P. Sherman, "Digital's Daring Comeback Plan," *Fortune*, Jan. 14, 1991, 100–103.

44. See Schein, *Organizational Culture*, 217–219; and Rifkin and Harrar, *Ultimate Entrepreneur*.

45. John Teresko, "Can DEC Rise Again?" *Industry Week* 14 (Nov. 1983), 87; Jeffrey Kalb, MasPar Computer Corp., interview by author, Jan. 31, 1991; Miller quoted in Rifkin and Harrar, *Ultimate Entrepreneur*, 210–211.

46. Susan Traker, "How DEC Got Decked," *Fortune*, Dec. 12, 1983, 83–92.

47. Rifkin and Harrar, *Ultimate Entrepreneur*.

48. Michael H. Best, *The New Competition: Institutions of Industrial Restructuring* (Cambridge, Mass.: Harvard University Press, 1990), 264; Joe DeNucci, MIPS Computer Systems, interview by author, Sept. 18, 1990.

49. "Can Minicomputers Sustain Their Recovery?" *Business Week*, Jan. 13, 1984, 50–57; William M. Bulkeley, "Wang, Bogged Down By Debt, Could Face Loss of Independence," *Wall Street Journal*, July 14, 1987.

50. "Minicomputers," 57; Traker, "DEC Got Decked," 92.

5. Running with Technology

1. There were 35 public technology companies headquartered in each region in 1980; by 1990 there were 132 in Silicon Valley and only 82 in Route 128. Compustat PC+ Database, Standard and Poors Corporation, 1992.

These numbers understate Silicon Valley's performance for two reasons. First, they include only public companies, a small subset of the total population of firms in both regions. Second, the definition of high technology used here excludes companies in several SIC codes that are disproportionately represented in Silicon Valley, such as semiconductor equipment manufacturers. See Definitions and Data Sources.

2. *Venture Capital Journal* (Needham, Mass.: Venture Economics, Inc.).

3. See Carolyn Sherwood-Call, "Changing Geographical Patterns of Electronic Components Activity," *Federal Reserve Bank of San Francisco Economic Review*, no. 2 (1992), 25–35; Robert Tannenwald, "Rating Massachusetts' Tax Competitiveness," *New England Economic Review*, Nov./Dec. 1987, 33–45.

4. Regis McKenna, *Who's Afraid of Big Blue? How Companies Are Challenging IBM—and Winning* (Reading, Mass.: Addison-Wesley, 1989), 85.

5. Richard Florida and Martin Kenney, in *The Breakthrough Illusion: America's Failure to Move from Innovation to Mass Production* (New York: Basic Books, 1990), cite the hard disk drive industry as an example of the excessive costs of "start-up mania." Yet intense competition in the industry helped U.S. producers—mainly located in Silicon Valley—to capture 76 percent of the world market for hard drives in 1990. See AnnaLee Saxenian, "A Response to Richard Florida and Martin Kenney," *California Management Review*, Spring 1991, 136–142.

6. Jack Yelverton, quoted in Cheryll Aimee Barron, "Silicon Valley Phoenixes," *Fortune*, Nov. 23, 1987, 130–134; Gilder quoted in Richard Karlgaard, "George Gilder Interview," *Upside*, Oct. 1990, 52.

7. Larry Jordan, Integrated Device Technology, interview by author, Aug. 7, 1990.

8. Quoted in David Sheff, "Don Valentine Interview, Part Two," *Upside*, June 1990, 52. George Gilder similarly notes that "most studies show that money ranks third or fourth as a driving factor for entrepreneurs." Karlgaard, "Gilder Interview," 52.

9. The relationship between Silicon Graphics and MIPS was so close that when MIPS fell into trouble in the early 1990s, the two firms merged. This merger has been a great success, in part because of their history of collaboration and in part because MIPS has remained a highly autonomous division that continues to sell its microprocessors to a wide range of Japanese, European, and American computer companies. Jim Nash, "A Merger Success: SGI-MIPS," *Business Journal* (San Jose and Silicon Valley), April 5, 1993, 1, 28.

10. The study also concluded that the Bay Area had by far the largest concentration of hardware engineering vendors of any locale in the country. "Assessing Northern California's Engineering Strength in Selected Technical Fields," Center for Economic Competitiveness, SRI International, Menlo Park, Calif., Sept. 1988.

11. Les Denend, 3Com Corp., interview by author, Oct. 13, 1990.

12. The average waiting time from firm founding to the first working prototype was 12.4 months in Silicon Valley, compared to over 20 months for firms elsewhere in the United States. Similarly, Silicon Valley firms took only 17.5 months after founding, on average, to ship their first products, while firms in other regions took closer to 25 months. Claudia Bird Schoonhoven and Kathleen M. Eisenhardt, "Regions as Industrial Incubators of Technology-based Ventures," in *Sources of Metropolitan Growth*, ed. Edwin Mills and John McDonald (New Brunswick, N.J.: Center for Urban Policy Research, 1992), 210–252.

13. Howard Anderson, Yankee Group and Battery Ventures, interview by author, Dec. 18, 1990.

14. Hans Schwarz, Chips and Technologies, interview by author, July 25, 1990.

15. Larry Jordan, Integrated Device Technology, interview by author, Sept. 5, 1990.

16. Jim Jubak, "Venture Capital and the Older Company," *Venture*, Sept. 1988, 14–15; Jeffrey Kalb, Maspar Computer Corp., interview by author, Jan. 31, 1991.

17. Jeffrey Kalb, MasPar Computer Corp., interview by author, Jan. 10, 1991.

18. Tod Basche, Sun Microsystems, interview by author, Feb. 12, 1991.

19. As one HP veteran claimed: "Anyone on the computer side of HP has been involved in at least one divisional start-up. When I came to Datalex, I already knew how to start a new venture and which people I needed." Carolyn J. Morris, Datalex Corp., quoted in "HP Alumni: A Who's Who of Silicon Valley Start-ups," *Business Week*, Dec. 6, 1982, 75. See also James J. Mitchell, "HP Sets the Tone for Business in the Valley," *San Jose Mercury News*, Jan. 9, 1989.

20. Ted Dintersmith, Aegis Fund, interview by author, Dec. 11, 1990.

21. Howard Anderson, quoted in "Stalwart Venture Capitalists Keep Eyes on Future," *Mass High Tech*, March 11, 1991, 3.

22. Data from a study of the 25 largest metropolitan areas in the country. The location quotient for highly skilled manufacturing workers in the San Jose SMSA was 6.12, while for Boston it was 2.02. Richard Barff and Mark Ellis, "The Operation of Regional Labor Markets for Highly Trained Manufacturing Workers in the United States," *Urban Geography* 12 (1991), 339–362.

23. This wave of start-ups was spurred at least in part by the 1978 reduction of the capital gains tax from 49 percent to 28 percent, although estimates by local venture capitalists that the tax change generated a tenfold increase in venture capital funds seem excessive.

24. A total of 157 semiconductor firms were started in the United States from 1977 to 1987, compared to 60 between 1966 and 1976 and 10 between 1956 and 1965. Dataquest Inc., San Jose, Calif., 1989.

25. Intel also contributed directly to the region's revitalization because it recovered quickly from the loss of the memory business by concentrating

on the lucrative and proprietary microprocessor business. By the early 1990s Intel was the largest semiconductor manufacturer in the world.

26. In interviews and public statements, the founders of the 1980s semiconductor start-ups described the companies that they had left as "stifling," even "moribund," and complained about their bureaucratic sluggishness and inability to identify new markets or assimilate new ideas. See, for example, T. J. Rodgers, "Return to the Microcosm," *Harvard Business Review,* July/Aug. 1988, 139–140.

27. See Brenton R. Schendler, "Chipper Days for U.S. Chipmakers," *Fortune,* May 6, 1991, 90–96; Bernard C. Cole, "ASIC Houses Revise Their Strategies," *Electronics,* Aug. 6, 1987, 73–74.

28. By 1990 Cypress was producing 142 products, which, with various packaging options, yielded close to 1,000 distinct variants. See T. J. Rodgers, "Landmark Messages from the Microcosm," *Harvard Business Review,* Jan./Feb. 1990, 24–30; John McCreadie and Valerie Rice, "Nine New Mavericks," *Electronic Business,* Sept. 4, 1989, 30–35; Bill Arnold, "Cirrus Takes PC Market by Storm," *Upside,* Aug. 1993, 40–50.

29. Lowell Turriff, Cypress Semiconductor, interview by author, Jan. 21, 1988; Thomas Longo, Performance Semiconductor, interview by author, July 31, 1990.

30. Chips and Technologies, for example, was one of the first firms to use advanced computer-aided-design tools for rapid design of complex integrated circuits. Its first product was a five-piece chip set that did the work of five dozen chips in an IBM personal computer; it also introduced a four-chip set that handled the primary graphics functions of an IBM graphics board. By 1989 it offered some four dozen different chips and chip sets. Kathleen Sullivan, "Maintaining a Competitive Edge," *San Francisco Examiner,* Oct. 8, 1989, D-1, D-12.

31. Ironically, many of these start-ups subcontracted to Japanese fabs, largely because the large U.S. semiconductor producers were unwilling to open up their manufacturing facilities to outsiders.

32. David Laws, Altera Corporation, interview by author, May 10, 1988. Altera paid $7.4 million for an equity interest in the facility of a Cypress subsidiary. This guaranteed Altera manufacturing capacity and access to Cypress's next generation of process technology. Cypress gained the rights to produce and sell Altera products, a sizable cash investment, and the chance to run its fab closer to capacity. John Case, "Intimate Relations," *Inc.,* Aug. 1990, 64–72.

33. M. Mehler, "Minifabs Reshape IC Production," *Electronics Business,* June 1, 1987; Bernard C. Cole, "Getting to the Market on Time," *Electronics,* April 1989, 62–67. By the late 1980s Japanese producers had pushed the logic of the mass production strategy to its extreme with very large scale and highly dedicated automated "monster" fabs that allowed for vastly superior productivity and significantly lower unit production costs—but at the cost

of total inflexibility. These firms produced only 1 to 2 products per line, and were extremely costly to scale down to shorter runs. See Michael G. Borrus, *Competing for Control: America's Stake in Microelectronics* (Cambridge, Mass.: Ballinger, 1988); Dieter Ernst, "Programmable Automation in the Semiconductor Industry," paper presented at an OECD Conference on Programmable Automation, Paris, April 2–4, 1987.

34. CEO T. J. Rodgers claimed that his aim was to become a $1 billion company made up of ten loosely linked $100 million subsidiaries. The four subsidiaries, Aspen Semiconductor, Cypress Semiconductor (Texas), Multichip Technology, and Ross Technology, all receive cash, management advice, and contacts (as in a traditional venture capital arrangement), as well as access to one another's sales and distribution channels and fabrication facilities. See Julie Cortino, "Spin-offs Keep Big Guys Thinking Small," *Upside,* June 1990, 56–60.

35. McCreadie and Rice, "Nine New Mavericks," 32.

36. See Andrew Rappaport, "The Dawning of the Age of Free Silicon," *Technology Research Group Newsletter* 4, no. 4 (Feb. 1990), 2–8.

37. Art Collmeyer, Weitek Corporation, interview by author, Aug. 19, 1986; Valerie Rice, "Where They Are Now: 1987's Superstars Revisited," *Electronic Business,* Sept. 4, 1989, 36–38. Some analysts have suggested that the specialty segment of the industry was dependent upon or parasitic of the commodity segment. The "technology driver" argument asserts that high-volume production of memory chips drives process development and accelerates movement down the learning curve. In this view, specialty chipmakers would be uncompetitive without the production of high-volume memories. But the manufacturing processes and organizational forms in specialty production have diverged so greatly from those used in commodity production that these claims are no longer supportable. See Rappaport, "Free Silicon," 5.

38. Schendler, "Chipper Days"; Michael Leibowitz, "ASIC Strategies for the Big Five," *Electronic Business,* Oct. 15, 1988, 107–112; investment report by Alex Brown and Sons, Baltimore, cited in J. Goldman, "Nine Valley Chip Companies Recommended by R&D Firm," *San Jose Business Journal,* Oct. 30, 1989.

39. Rizzo quoted in Valerie Rice, "The Upstart Start-ups," *Electronic Business,* Aug. 15, 1987, 46–64; Bernard C. Cole, "By the Mid-90's the Memory Market Will Look Like the Logic Business," *Electronics,* Aug. 1988, 55.

40. In 1975 Route 128 companies employed just over 41,000 workers. Data for SIC 357, Computing and Office Equipment, *County Business Patterns* (Washington, D.C.: U.S. Government Printing Office, 1975 and 1990). The changes may be slightly exaggerated by the 1987 changes in SIC code definitions, but the data remain comparable across regions.

41. Industry leader IBM's share of world computer revenues fell from 37 percent in 1975 to 20 percent in 1989. The top ten companies in the

industry accounted for 65 percent of total sales in 1975 and only 48 percent in 1989, in spite of major consolidations, such as Burroughs and Sperry. Ron Bohlin and Joanne Guiniven, "Challenges for the Computer Industry in the 1990s," *McKinsey Quarterly,* no. 1 (1991), 109.

42. The growth rates of these segments during the 1980s suggested the continued decline of the traditional large systems. From 1986 to 1991 sales of personal computers and workstations grew 21 percent annually, versus 3.3 percent for mainframes and minicomputers. Charles H. Ferguson and Charles R. Morris, *Computer Wars: How the West Can Win in a Post-IBM World* (New York: New York Times Books, 1993).

43. Rob Walker, LSI Logic Corporation, interview by author, May 19, 1988. ASICs offer both cost and performance advantages: by condensing complex multichip circuits into a single chip they conserve space, reduce weight, increase machine speed and reliability, and reduce power consumption, while optimizing circuit performance to a particular system. A company can make its computer run twice as fast with the careful use of ASICs, or reduce system design costs by up to 90 percent if quantities are great enough to amortize initial development costs. In addition, the development time for ASICs is significantly shorter than that for standard products, a factor that is more important to most systems firms than lower unit costs. See "Special ASIC Issue" *Electronics,* Aug. 6, 1987.

44. Edward McCracken, Silicon Graphics, interview by author, Aug. 23, 1990.

45. See Dwight B. Davis, "Reliability Spells Edge in Competitive Drive Market," *Electronic Business,* April 17, 1989, 47–50; and Alden M. Hayashi, "Hard Times for Hard Drives," *Electronic Business,* Nov. 15, 1988, 33–37.

46. Robert Graham, "Seven Paths to Profit in IC Production Gear," *Electronic Business,* May 15, 1989, 121.

47. David Manasian, "Within the Whirlwind: A Survey of the Computer Industry," *Economist,* Feb. 27, 1993.

48. Bruce A. Kirchoff and Robert E. McAuliffe, "Economic Redevelopment of Mature Industrial Areas," report prepared for U.S. Department of Commerce, Economic Development Administration, Technical Assistance and Research Division, Oct. 1989.

49. Ted Dintersmith, Aegis Fund, quoted in "Stalwart Venture Capitalists Keep Eyes on the Future," *Mass High Tech,* March 11, 1991, 3.

50. Allison Bell and Ellen Corliss, "Apollo Falls to the West," *Mass High Tech,* April 24, 1989.

51. One survey of semiconductor start-ups concluded that the heterogeneity of industry experience in the founding management team was correlated with higher growth. Kathleen M. Eisenhardt and Claudia Bird Schoonhoven, "Organizational Growth: Linking Founding Team Strategy, Environment, and Growth among U.S. Semiconductor Ventures, 1978–1988," *Administrative Science Quarterly* 35, no. 3 (Sept. 1990), 504–529.

52. The central processor (CPU) is the section of a computer that controls

interpretation and execution of instructions. The CPU in workstations and personal computers is a microprocessor.

53. A RISC microprocessor executes fewer, less complex instructions than the traditional microprocessor, thus streamlining and accelerating the entire chip.

54. David Sheff, "A New Ballgame for Sun's Scott McNealy," *Upside*, Nov./Dec. 1989, 46–54. In 1986 Sun's cheapest machine sold for $4995, or half the price of Apollo's cheapest. William M. Bulkeley, "Culture Shock: Two Computer Firms with Clashing Styles Fight for Market Niche," *Wall Street Journal*, July 6, 1987.

55. Tod Basche, Sun Microsystems, interview by author, Feb. 12, 1991. Basche worked for almost a decade on Route 128 and was one of the earliest employees of Apollo, where he stayed for four years before moving to Silicon Valley.

56. Alex Beam and Marc Frons, "How Tom Vanderslice Is Forcing Apollo Computer to Grow Up," *Business Week*, March 25, 1985, 96–98.

57. Bulkeley, "Culture Shock."

58. Tod Basche interview, Feb. 12, 1991; Eric Nee, "Stardent, 'For Better or For Worse,'" *Upside*, Nov. 1990, 30–65.

59. According to Foster: "Data General was a horrible place to work . . . It was easy to leave because you always felt as if you were being used. I knew it was time to leave when I realized that I'd never let my son work there." William Foster, Stratus Computer, interview by author, Jan. 9, 1991. On details of the founding and financing of Stratus Computer, see "Stratus Computer," Harvard Business School Case 682–030, 1981.

60. This was in part a reaction to the exploitative vendor relations he observed at Data General. Foster claimed that the firm "beat vendors up on price, didn't pay them on time, and abandoned them when times got tough," comparing it to the way HP nurtured long-term relations with suppliers. William Foster, Stratus Computer, interview by author, Jan. 22, 1991. Also see Andrea L. Larsen, "Cooperative Alliances: A Study of Entrepreneurship" (Ph.D. diss., Harvard University, 1988).

61. The firm also adopted what became known as the "Stratapizza" tradition in 1981 when a group of programmers ordered pizza once a month and held lunch meetings on a loading dock. By 1989 it took three pizzerias to deliver more than 400 pies to feed the 1,200 employees at the company headquarters. Keith H. Hammonds and Jonathan B. Levine, "Can Stratus Fly in a Higher Sphere? The Mini Maker Takes on Bigger Market—with Bigger Rivals," *Business Week*, April 3, 1989, 76.

62. The original statement of the product life cycle model is Raymond Vernon, "International Investment and International Trade in the Product Cycle," *Quarterly Journal of Economics* 80 (1966), 190–207; see also Ann R. Markusen, *Profit Cycles, Oligopoly, and Regional Development* (Cambridge, Mass.: MIT Press, 1985); and for critiques, Michael Storper, "Oligopoly and

the Product Cycle: Essentialism in Economic Geography," *Economic Geography* 61, no. 3 (1985), 260–282; and Raymond Vernon, "The Product Cycle Hypothesis in a New International Environment," *Oxford Bulletin of Economics and Statistics*, 1979, 255–267.

6. Inside Out: Blurring Firms' Boundaries

1. Lockheed Missile and Space and Raytheon Corporation were the largest employers in Silicon Valley and Route 128, respectively. However, they were military contractors that remained largely detached from the commercial technology businesses of the regions.
2. Harold Edmondson, Hewlett-Packard Corporation, interview by author, Feb. 5, 1988. See also Dwight B. Davis, "Beating the Clock," *Electronic Business*, May 29, 1989, 21–28.
3. See, for example, Ron Bohlin and Peter Mendelman, "Daring to Be Different in a New World of Standards," *Electronic Business*, May 29, 1989, 51–54. Silicon Graphics CEO Edward McCracken claims that open standards allowed his company to minimize its investments in computer hardware while investing heavily in the graphics that differentiate its systems from others. Silicon Graphics put half of its resources into developing graphics software and half into systems to integrate the graphics. This would have been impossible without standards that eliminated the risk of incompatibility between the firm's products and the software and hardware products supplied by other specialists. Edward McCracken, Silicon Graphics, interview by author, May 19, 1988.
4. "The Electronic Business 200," *Electronic Business*, July 22, 1991, 42–43.
5. Cheryl Vedoe, Sun Microsystems, interview by author, Dec. 19, 1990. With over 30,000 employees in Massachusetts by 1990, DEC accounted for almost 20 percent of regional high technology employment, while HP's 20,000 Silicon Valley employees were only 8 percent of the regional total.
6. The other leading producer, Sun, led only in workstations, with a 32 percent share. In the RISC and Unix computer systems markets, Sun lagged behind DEC with market shares of 30 percent and 11 percent. Eric Nee, "Back to Basics at Hewlett-Packard," *Upside*, June 1991, 38–78.
7. Stuart Gannes, "Back-to-Basics Computers with Sports Car Speed," *Fortune*, Sept. 30, 1985, 98–101; Mary Jo Foley, "HP Turns to RISC and Unix to Turn Around the Company," *Electronic Business*, Aug. 1, 1988, 46–48; quote from Tony Greene, "Can HP Find the Right Direction for the '90s?" *Electronic Business*, Jan. 22, 1990, 26–29.
8. Cheryl Vedoe, Sun Microsystems, interview by author, Feb. 4, 1991.
9. Stephen K. Yoder, "A 1990 Reorganization at Hewlett-Packard Already Is Paying Off: HP Cuts Bureaucracy, Costs, Undoing Past Blunders," *Wall Street Journal*, July 22, 1991, A1.
10. Only in 1988, after some of the firm's largest customers began demanding

independence from individual vendors and defecting to Unix, did DEC abandon the vision of a single, proprietary VMS operating system and VAX architecture for all of its systems. Joe DeNucci, MIPS Computer Systems, interview by author, Sept. 18, 1990.

11. Tod Basche, Sun Microsystems, interview by author, Feb. 12, 1991. Tom Furlong, DEC Palo Alto, interview by author, Feb. 11, 1991. The RISC processor, Titan, which was developed by a group of defectors from Xerox PARC, tripled the performance speed of the VAX, but ran under Unix rather than VMS. See Richard Comerford, "How DEC Developed Alpha," *IEEE Spectrum*, July 1992, 26–31.

12. By June 1988 the Prism team did not yet have a launchable 32-bit RISC machine. Comerford, "How DEC Developed Alpha," 26.

13. Gary McWilliams, "Crunch Time at DEC," *Business Week*, May 4, 1992, 30–33.

14. Joe DeNucci, MIPS Computer Systems, interview by author, March 25, 1991.

15. Tom Furlong, Digital Equipment Corporation, interview by author, Feb. 11, 1991.

16. HP's longstanding partnership with the database software developer Informix Software culminated in a decision to build and staff a joint research and development lab at Informix's Silicon Valley headquarters. "Technology Roundup: HP and Informix," *Business Journal* (San Jose and Silicon Valley), July 5, 1993, 9. John Eton, HP, quoted in David Tuller, "HP Plans to Buy 10% Stake in Octel," *San Francisco Chronicle*, Aug. 12, 1988.

17. Jim Nash and Mary Hayes, "Key DEC Project Moving to Palo Alto," *Business Journal* (San Jose and Silicon Valley), July 19, 1993, 1, 17.

18. Sun began assembling some of its most advanced printed circuit boards internally in the late 1980s.

19. Bean quoted in "For Flexible, Quality Manufacturing, Don't Do It Yourself," *Electronic Business*, March 15, 1987.

20. Quoted in Regis McKenna, *Who's Afraid of Big Blue? How Companies Are Challenging IBM—and Winning* (Reading, Mass.: Addison-Wesley, 1989), 157.

21. Andy Grove, "How Intel Makes Spending Pay Off," *Fortune*, Feb. 22, 1993, 58.

22. Sources: The Electronic Business 200; Annual 10K Reports.

23. Edward McCracken, Silicon Graphics, interview by author, Aug. 23, 1990.

24. Sun Microsystems Computer Corporation (SMCC) designs and builds the hardware for Sun workstations; SunSoft develops and markets Solaris, Sun's Unix-based operating system; SunTech Enterprises is a holding company of enterprises concerned with developing all workstation software products aside from Solaris; SunExpress runs a mail-order distribution service for Sun products; and Sun Laboratories does research and advanced development on high-risk product concepts that could be important to the company's future.

While all of the established computer companies began to decentralize and create autonomous business units in the 1990s, Sun went a step further. Even IBM's reorganization left its unified sales force largely untouched. Without the freedom to create their own independent—and if necessary competing—sales forces, IBM's new units would not achieve the degree of independence needed in today's markets. Mark Stahlman, "The Failure of IBM: Lessons for the Future," *Upside*, March 1993, 28–50.

25. McCracken interview, Aug. 23, 1990.
26. McCracken interview, May 19, 1988.
27. See, for example, William Bluestein, "How Sun Microsystems Buys for Quality," *Electronics Purchasing*, March 1988, 47–51; Robert Faletra and Marc Elliot, "Buying in the Microcomputer Market," *Electronics Purchasing*, Oct. 1988, 40–45.
28. The one-year collaboration between a team of Sun and Cypress engineers to develop SPARC was a model of complementary innovation, combining Sun's knowledge of systems architecture and software design with Cypress's integrated circuit design and advanced fabrication capabilities. Sun licensed SPARC production to Fujitsu, Texas Instruments, LSI Logic, Bipolar Integrated Technologies, and Cypress.
29. John Case, "Intimate Relations," *Inc.*, Aug. 1990, 66.
30. See McKenna, *Big Blue*, 155–156; and Evelyn Richards, "IBM Pulls the Strings," *San Jose Mercury News*, Dec. 31, 1984.
31. See Dwight B. Davis, "Making the Most of Your Vendor Relationships," *Electronic Business*, July 10, 1989, 42–47. Quote from Adrienne Pauly, "What JIT Buyers Want from Suppliers," *Electronics Purchasing*, Jan. 1987, 52.
32. For a typical computer maker, this privileged group included between fifteen and thirty producers of integrated circuits, printed circuit boards, disk drives, power supplies, and other components and software that were critical to product quality and performance. See, for example, Davis, "Vendor Relationships"; Sylvia Tierston, "The Changing Face of Purchasing," *Electronic Purchasing*, March 20, 1989, 22–27.
33. When HP introduced JIT in the early 1980s, for example, the firm's cost reductions and improvements in manufacturing efficiency were widely publicized in Silicon Valley. JIT has since been widely adopted in the region. See "Hewlett-Packard Swears by 'Just-in-Time' System," *Business Journal* (San Jose), June 10, 1985, 22. Also see Marilyn J. Cohodas, "What Makes JIT Work," *Electronics Purchasing*, Jan. 1987, 47–51.
34. Quoted in Davis, "Vendor Relationships," 44.
35. Edmondson quoted in Tierston, "Changing Face," 22–27; Jack Faber, Hewlett-Packard, interview by author, May 9, 1988.
36. John Sims, Tandem Computers, interview by author, Nov. 9, 1990; Kitrosser quoted in Davis, "Vendor Relationships," 43.
37. Jeffrey Miller, Adaptec Corporation, interview by author, May 10, 1988.
38. Tod Frohnen, Tandem Computers, interview by author, July 24, 1990.

Frohnen said in another interview on Aug. 2, 1990: "If one of their suppliers drops off the face of the earth, we're in big trouble."

39. Quotes from Marilyn Cohodas, "How Apple Buys Electronics," *Electronics Purchasing,* Nov. 1986, 46–53; Davis, "Vendor Relationships," 47.

40. Quote from Henri Jarrat, VLSI Technology, interview by author, May 10, 1988.

41. Steve Kitrosser, in Davis, "Vendor Relationships," 46.

42. McCracken interview, Aug. 23, 1990.

43. Robert Todd, Flextronics, Inc., interview by author, Feb. 2, 1988. See also Adrienne Pauly, "An Insiders View of Contract Manufacturing," *Electronics Purchasing,* Nov. 1986, 64–67.

44. Quoted in *San Jose Mercury News,* July 25, 1988.

45. Dennis Stradford, Flextronics, Inc., interview by author, March 3, 1988.

46. Todd interview, Feb. 2, 1988. The expansion of Flextronics was too rapid. In 1989 the firm was forced to restructure its worldwide business because of excess manufacturing capacity and significant operating losses which began with a downturn in the disk drive business. The production facilities in Massachusetts, South Carolina, Southern California, and Taiwan were sold or closed. The facilities in Hong Kong and Singapore were geared for labor-intensive products for which low labor costs provided a clear advantage. By 1993 Flextronics International was a highly profitable and fast-growing Singapore-based company with manufacturing facilities in China, Malaysia, and Singapore.

47. Solectron invested more than $18 million in SMT equipment between 1984 and 1988. Guy Lasnier, "Solectron to Acquire 10 Advanced Surface Mount Systems," *San Jose Business Journal,* Feb. 8, 1988, 11.

48. Quote from Stephen Jones, "Hewlett-Packard Inks Major Chip Deal," *San Jose Business Journal,* May 18, 1987, 17.

49. See Nitin Nohria and Robert Eccles, "Face-to-Face: Making Network Organizations Work," in Nohria and Eccles, ed., *Networks and Organizations: Structure, Form, and Action* (Boston: Harvard Business School Press, 1992).

50. Furlong interview, Feb. 11, 1991.

51. The customer in turn increased its purchases of the firm's power supplies more than tenfold. Interview by author, Sept. 1, 1988, name and company withheld.

52. The two firms had worked together for several years. Oracle executives had even lent Ncube $3 million in 1989—but had chosen not to buy a majority of the firm so as not to compromise its ability to work with other hardware producers.

53. Jim Bilodeau, Apple Computer, quoted in Cohodas, "How Apple Buys"; Scott Metcalf, Sun Microsystems, interview by author, March 30, 1988.

54. See Thomas J. Temin, "Why Foreign Sourcing is Obsolete," *Electronics Purchasing,* October 1989, 1; Mike Nevens and Lorraine Harrington, "Management Levers for Global Success," *Business Journal* (San Jose and Silicon Valley), June 24, 1991, 7.

55. Stephanie Yanchinsk, "Why Hewlett-Packard Looked East for Its Computer Innovation," *Financial Times,* July 1, 1987; William Almon, Conner Peripherals, interview by author, Sept. 7, 1990; Winston Chen, Solectron Corp., interview by author, July 31, 1990.

56. Cohodas, "How Apple Buys," 48.

CONCLUSION: PROTEAN PLACES

1. See "Signs of Life: Software, Networking, and Supercomputer Companies Give a Brighter Look to Massachusetts High Tech," *The Gray Sheet: Computer Industry Report* 27, no. 16 (June 12, 1992); and Gary McWilliams, "A Bloom amid New England's Gloom," *Business Week,* Dec. 7, 1992, 93–94.

2. Ron Wolf, "A Growth Surge Recharging the Valley," *San Jose Mercury News,* April 12, 1993, 1E, 7E.

3. This problem is not unique to Silicon Valley. See Carlo Trigilia, "The Paradox of the Region: Economic Regulation and the Representation of Interests," *Economy and Society* 20, no. 3 (Aug. 1991), 306–327.

4. Shmuel Halevi, Technology Research Group, quoted in Don Clark, "Who Polished Apple," *San Francisco Chronicle,* June 19, 1993, B1, B3; John Markoff, "Apple Computer, Faltering, Strives to Refocus," *New York Times,* June 21, 1993, C1, C3.

5. Hayes quoted in Steve Kaufman, "Report: Valley Sliding," *San Jose Mercury News,* Jan. 24, 1992.

6. See Laurence M. Fisher, "Chip Makers Combine to Fight Suits," *New York Times,* Oct. 15, 1990; Jonathan Weisman, "Disk Drive Deal Would Curb Litigation," *Business Journal* (San Jose and Silicon Valley), July 20, 1992.

7. Joint Venture: Silicon Valley's proposals cover everything from local regulatory reform to coordinating the development of fiber-optic links within the Valley. Its initiatives include organizing small companies to join together to fund "customized" community college courses, creating a center for entrepreneurship to support collaborative projects within and between local enterprises as well as public-private partnerships, a coordinated effort to attract hundreds of millions of dollars in funding for collaborative research on flat-panel computer screen technology, streamlining procedure for obtaining business permits, increasing the availability of low-cost housing, providing "fast track" retraining of laid-off defense workers, involving companies in improving the mathematics and science curricula of local public schools, establishing a communications forum to encourage the movement of emerging micromachining technologies from labs into manufacturing, creating a region-wide information and training network for the workforce, and bringing together semiconductor companies, equipment and materials suppliers, and systems companies to exchange information and address common technological challenges. See "Joint Venture: Silicon Valley Progress Report," prepared by PRx Inc. Strategic Marketing Communications, Winter 1993.

8. George F. Gilder, *Microcosm: The Quantum Revolution in Economics and Technology* (New York: Simon and Schuster, 1989), and *Wealth and Poverty* (New York: Basic Books, 1981); Michael L. Rothschild, *Bionomics: The Inevitability of Capitalism* (New York: H. Holt, 1990).

9. Charles H. Ferguson, "Computers and the Coming of the U.S. Keiretsu," *Harvard Business Review* 90, no. 4 (July-Aug. 1990), 55–70; Michael G. Borrus, *Competing for Control: America's Stake in Microelectronics* (Cambridge, Mass.: Ballinger, 1988).

10. The experience of Cambridge, England—where all the ingredients for successful high tech development appear to be present, including ample venture capital and skilled labor, a world-class research university, and entrepreneurial activity—demonstrates the inability of market forces alone to generate dynamic technological growth. See AnnaLee Saxenian, "The Cheshire Cat's Grin: Innovation, Regional Development and the Cambridge Case," *Economy and Society* 18, no. 4 (Nov. 1989), 448–477. Studies of research parks consistently document low success rates; see Michael I. Luger and Harvey A. Goldstein, *Technology in the Garden: Research Parks and Regional Economic Development* (Chapel Hill: University of North Carolina Press, 1991).

11. By 1992 U.S. producers had eliminated Japan's lead in worldwide semiconductor sales, with each nation controlling 43 percent of the total, and U.S. firms controlled 53 percent to Japan's 45 percent of the $10 billion market for semiconductor manufacturing equipment. See Rebecca Smith, "U.S. Chipmakers Surge to Front," *San Jose Mercury News*, Nov. 8, 1992; Don Clark, "The Tactics That Beat Japan," *San Francisco Chronicle*, Feb. 3, 1993. On software and computers, see Andrew S. Rappaport and Shmuel Halevi, "The Computerless Computer Company," *Harvard Business Review*, July–Aug. 1991, 69–80.

12. While proponents of industrial policy point to the contribution of the Japanese Ministry of Industry and Trade (MITI) in promoting Japan's steel, auto, and semiconductor industries, its record in high-value-added, innovative industries has been less auspicious. The Fifth Generation Computer project, for example, failed to keep up with the pace of commercial innovation set by Silicon Valley–based computer firms during the 1980s. See Andrew Pollack, "'Fifth Generation' Became Japan's Lost Generation," *New York Times*, June 5, 1992, C1–C2; Russell J. Hancock, "A Farewell to Japanese Industrial Policy," *Stanford Journal of International Affairs* 2, no. 1 (Fall–Winter 1993), 111–128.

13. The semiconductor trade agreement, for example, is often cited as a model of support for a "strategic" sector, yet it is far from clear that the commodity memory business is critical to the future of the U.S. technology industry. If anything, the trade agreement unnecessarily increased costs for linked sectors such as computer systems. The semiconductor manufacturing consortium, Sematech, may offer a model of the sorts of collaboration needed

by American industry, but there is little evidence that Sematech's efforts have contributed as much to the resurgence of the American semiconductor industry as the independent efforts of Silicon Valley's producers of microprocessors, specialty logic, and semi-custom chips.

14. This model of policy as a catalyst is a far cry from traditional postwar economic development strategies in the United States that focused on smokestack chasing or the ill-fated efforts to "grow" high technology industry. Recent efforts by the state governments of Michigan and Pennsylvania to create regional industrial strategies offer helpful experiences. See Charles F. Sabel, "Studied Trust: Building New Forms of Cooperation in a Volatile Economy," in Frank Pyke and Werner Sengenberger, eds., *Industrial Districts and Local Economic Regeneration* (Geneva: International Institute for Labour Studies, 1992); David Osborne, "Refining State Technology Programs," *Issues in Science and Technology*, Summer 1990, 55–61. John Herbers, "A Third Wave of Economic Development," *Governing*, June 1990, 43–50.

15. On policy for regional network–based industrial systems, see Trigilia, "The Paradox of the Region"; Paul Hirst and Jonathan Zeitlin, "Flexible Specialization vs. Post-Fordism: Theory, Evidence, and Policy Implications," *Economy and Society*, Feb. 1991, 1–56; Michael Storper and Allen J. Scott, "The Wealth of Regions: Market Forces and Policy Imperatives in Local and Global Context," Working Paper no. 398, Lewis Center for Regional Policy Studies, UCLA, June 1993.

16. See AnnaLee Saxenian, "In Search of Power: The Organization of Business Interests in Silicon Valley and Route 128," *Economy and Society* 18, no. 1 (Feb. 1989), 25–70.

HISTORICAL DATA

High technology employment by sector, Silicon Valley and Route 128:
1959, 1975, 1990, 1992 (County Business Patterns)

Type of establishment	1959			1975		
	SV	128	SV/128	SV	128	SV/128
Computing and office equipment	3,611	2,899	1.2	25,837	19,587	1.3
Communications equipment	2,532	16,905	0.1	17,270	27,771	0.6
Electronic components	10,241	27,365	0.4	33,109	14,459	2.3
Guided missiles, space vehicles	n/a	n/a	n/a	17,850	1,750	10.2
Instruments	992	14,240	0.1	17,218	31,019	0.6
Software and data processing	n/a	n/a	n/a	5,387	4,366	1.2
Total	17,376	61,409	0.3	116,671	98,952	1.2

Type of establishment	1990			1992		
	SV	128	SV/128	SV	128	SV/128
Computing and office equipment	57,143	14,630	3.9	45,668	12,951	3.5
Communications equipment	18,239	17,591	1.0	17,138	14,720	1.2
Electronic components	73,446	22,564	3.3	66,472	21,828	3.0
Guided missiles, space vehicles	37,675	7,675	4.9	37,675	3,810	9.9
Instruments	39,459	50,758	0.8	37,113	48,928	0.8
Software and data processing	41,569	37,358	1.1	45,193	38,406	1.2
Total	267,531	150,576	1.8	249,259	140,643	1.8

Number of high technology establishments by sector, Silicon Valley and
Route 128: 1959, 1975, 1990, 1992 (County Business Patterns)

Type of establishment	1959			1975		
	SV	128	SV/128	SV	128	SV/128
Computing and office equipment	7	17	0.4	87	71	1.2
Communications equipment	22	37	0.6	110	91	1.2
Electronic components	38	96	0.4	216	166	1.3
Guided missiles, space vehicles	n/a	n/a	n/a	4	1	4.0
Instruments	42	118	0.4	228	283	0.8
Software and data processing	n/a	n/a	n/a	186	228	0.8
Total	109	268	0.4	831	840	1.0

Type of establishment	1990			1992		
	SV	128	SV/128	SV	128	SV/128
Computing and office equipment	294	120	2.5	317	121	2.6
Communications equipment	150	53	2.8	162	55	2.9
Electronic components	661	t294	2.2	679	281	2.4
Guided missiles, space vehicles	5	4	1.3	9	4	2.3
Instruments	468	426	1.1	518	437	1.2
Software and data processing	1,653	1,271	1.3	2,378	1,615	1.5
Total	3,231	2,168	1.5	4,063	2,513	1.6

DEFINITIONS AND DATA SOURCES

▶ The research for this book was ethnographic in nature, with the empirical material accumulated over the course of nearly a decade living in and observing the two regional economies. The core of the argument is built from more than 160 in-depth interviews with entrepreneurs, industry leaders, corporate executives, and representatives of local business associations, governmental organizations, and universities in Silicon Valley and Route 128. The majority of the interviews were conducted between 1988 and 1991, but some were as early as 1980. The book also draws heavily from the industry and trade press, both local and national, and from corporate documents and a variety of public and private databases.

The high technology sector has been defined for all data presented in this book to include the following industries, identified by their Standard Industrial Codes: Computer and Office Equipment (SIC 357), Communications Equipment (SIC 366), Electronic Components and Accessories (SIC 367), Guided Missiles and Space Vehicles and Parts (SIC 376), Instruments (SIC 38), and Computer Programming and Data Processing (SIC 737).

Scholars who work with SIC codes know of their many weaknesses, particularly in industries whose boundaries are continually redefined. The Census Bureau periodically updates SIC categories to address these changes, making somewhat risky any attempt to compare individual sectors over time. SIC definitions changed in 1972 and 1987. The aggregate data on the high technology industry presented here remain largely unaffected, as do comparisons across regions, because of the use of three-digit categories (the main definitional shifts occurred at the four-digit level) and the aggregation across sectors that were redefined.

While employment data are relatively easy to obtain at the regional level, other information on regional economic performance is scarce. All employment data used in this book are from County Business Patterns, published by the U.S. Bureau of the Census. County Business Patterns offers county-by-county data on the number of employees, payroll, number of establishments, and establishments by employment class size disaggregated to the four-digit SIC code level. It is published and distributed annually. The main drawback of the data is that because firms often have multiple establishments, it is impossible to say anything definitive about the number of firms in a region or about regional differences in distribution of firm size.

It is more difficult to collect data on other aspects of regional economic performance, such as output or profitability. Some information is available at the state, but not the county, level. The Census of Manufacturers and the Census of Services, for example, provide data on the value of shipments for three-digit SIC codes every five years, but only at the state or SMSA level. The Department of Commerce also publishes gross state product data annually.

Corporate data sources contain information on firm-level sales and profitability that can be aggregated by location to analyze regional performance, but they must be used with great caution. Two such sources have been used in this book: the Standard & Poor's PC+ Database and the Corporate Technology Information Service (CorpTech) regional database.

The Standard & Poor's PC+ Database, which contains financial information on all publicly traded firms in the United States, includes annual sales, income, and equity data for a fifteen-year period, as well as a variety of current fiscal indicators. Because the database is limited to public firms, however, it has only limited value for regional analysis. This is particularly a problem for Route 128 and Silicon Valley, where much of the economic activity is in thousands of private firms. Moreover, because the data are reported at the level of the firm rather than the individual unit, it is impossible to assess accurately activity that is generated within the region, as compared to the firms' global operations.

The CorpTech regional databases include financial data for both public and private firms. They also provide data disaggregated to the level of the business unit, allowing for a better, if still not completely accurate, assessment of activity within a particular region. The reporting of disaggregated information, however, varies with the structure of the firm. Hewlett-Packard, for example, is divided into more than a dozen autonomous business units, making it easy to distinguish those that are actually based in Silicon Valley. Digital Equipment Corporation, in contrast, reports data only on global operations; hence it is difficult to separate DEC sales and employment in the Route 128 region from those of units elsewhere.

Although the CorpTech database is more comprehensive than the Standard & Poors, it also has limitations for regional economic analysis. No historical information is reported in the current edition, nor are previous editions available from CorpTech.

There are also regional directories of technology firms, such as the Mass High Tech Guide to Massachusetts Technology Companies and Rich's High-Tech Business Guide to Silicon Valley and Northern California, that provide limited financial data. These directories may well be the most comprehensive listings of regional firms because they are generated locally and updated annually. They can be quite useful for analysis of a single region, although they share the reporting problems described for the CorpTech data and for this reason cannot be used for cross-regional comparisons.

All figures in this book that use employment data from County Business Patterns define the geographic boundaries of Silicon Valley to include four California counties: Santa Clara, San Mateo, Alameda, and Santa Cruz. Route 128 includes four Massachusetts counties: Middlesex, Suffolk, Norfolk, and Essex. For corporate data from the Standard & Poors database and the CorpTech database, Silicon Valley refers to companies headquartered in the 408, 415, or 510 telephone area codes and includes most of the San Francisco Bay Area. Route 128 refers to companies headquartered in either the 617 or 508 telephone area codes and includes all of Eastern Massachusetts.

List of Interviews

I interviewed each person on this list at least once, many two or three times. Individuals are identified here with the company or organization they worked for at the time of the initial interview, but with the high levels of mobility in the industry, some moved to new organizations during the course of my research and many others have moved since that time.

Adaptec, Inc.: Dolores Marciel, Director, Corporate Purchasing

Adaptec, Inc.: Jeffrey A. Miller, Vice President, Marketing

Addington Laboratories, Inc.: Dennis Contois, Division Manager

Advanced Micro Devices, Inc.: George Scalise, Senior Vice President and Chief Administrative Officer

Advanced Micro Devices, Inc.: Thomas Skornia, Vice President, Corporate Services

Aegis Venture Funds: Ted R. Dintersmith, General Partner

Altera Corp.: David Laws, Vice President, Marketing

American Electronics Association (AEA): Edward Ferrey, Former President

American Electronics Association: Pat Hubbard, Vice President, Engineering, Education, and Management

American Electronics Association: Ralph Thompson, Senior Vice President, Public Affairs

Amdahl Corp.: John Lewis, President and Chief Executive Officer

American Microsystems, Inc. (AMI): Ralph Jensen, Manager, Administrative Services and Facilities

American Research and Development Corp.: Charles Colter, Managing Director

Apple Computer, Inc.: Jim Bilodeau, Director, Worldwide Materials

Apple Computer, Inc.: Tina Marquez, Manager, Strategic Planning

Applied Materials, Inc.: James Morgan, Chief Executive Officer

Avid Technology: Jim Ricotta, Software Engineering

Banyan Systems Inc.: David C. Mahoney, President

Bell-Mason Group: C. Gordon Bell, Director

Boston Technology, Inc.: Paul W. DeLacey, Vice President, Operations

Burr, Egan, Deleage: Bill Egan, Partner

Chips and Technologies, Inc.: Gordon Campbell, President and Chief Executive Officer

Chips and Technologies, Inc.: Douglas L. Peltzer, Director, Process Development

Chips and Technologies, Inc.: Hans Schwarz, Director, Product Marketing Systems Logic

Congdon Associates: Jim Congdon, President

Conner Peripherals, Inc.: William J. Almon, President and Chief Executive Officer

Cypress Semiconductor: T. J. Rogers, President and Chief Executive Officer

Cypress Semiconductor: Lowell L. Turriff, Vice President, Sales and Marketing

Data General Corp.: Edson de Castro, President and Chief Executive Officer

Dataquest Inc.: Jim Riley, Senior Vice President

Dataquest Inc.: Sheridan Tatsuno, Industry Analyst, Japanese Semiconductor Industry Service

Dataquest Inc.: Fred Zieber, Executive Vice President, General Manager, Technology Operations

Digital Equipment Corp. (DEC): Samuel H. Fuller, Vice President, Research

Digital Equipment Corp. (DEC): Tom Furlong, Manager, RISC Workstations, Palo Alto

Digital Equipment Corp. (DEC): Bruce Holbein, Director, Government Affairs

Disk/Trend: James N. Porter, President

Fairchild Camera & Instrument Corp.: Charles Smith, Vice President and General Manager

Flextronics Corp.: Dennis P. Stradford, Senior Vice President, Marketing and Sales

Flextronics Corp.: Robert J. Todd, President and CEO

Hewlett-Packard Co.: Sara Beckman, Manager, Strategic Manufacturing Planning

Hewlett-Packard Co.: John Brown, Corporate Site Planning

Hewlett-Packard Co.: Harold Edmondson, Vice President, Corporate Manufacturing

Hewlett-Packard Co.: Jack Faber, Materials Manager

Hewlett-Packard Co.: Robert Kirkwood, Vice President, Government Affairs

Hewlett-Packard Co.: Dick Love, General Manager, Computer Manufacturing Division

Hewlett-Packard Co.: Brian Moore, Manager, Systems Planning/Manufacturing

Hewlett-Packard Co.: Dean Morton, Chief Operating Officer

Hewlett-Packard Co.: Peter M. Will, Director, Design Strategy Product Generation Team

Integrated Device Technology, Inc.: Larry Jordan, Vice President, Marketing

International Disk Equipment Manufacturers Association: Bruce Hokansen, President

International Microelectronic Products: George Gray, Chairman of the Board and Chief Executive Officer

Intel Corp.: Scott Darling, Product Marketing

Intel Corp.: Gerald Diamond, Corporate Site Selection

Intel Corp.: Robert Noyce, Vice Chairman

Lam Research Corp.: Roger D. Emerick, Chairman and Chief Executive Officer

Linear Technology Corp.: Robert Swanson, President and Chief Executive Officer

Litronix: Douglas Fraser, Site Selection Team, Public Relations

Litronix: Gary Hile, Site Selection Team, Marketing

Litronix: Andrew Mann, Site Selection Team

Logistix: Katie Nosbisch, Director, Marketing

LSI Logic Corp.: Bruce Entin, Vice President, Investor Relations

LSI Logic Corp.: William J. O'Meara, Vice President, Marketing and Sales

LSI Logic Corp.: Rob Walker, Vice President and Chief Engineering Officer

MasPar Computer Corp.: Jeffrey Kalb, President

Massachusetts Center for Technology Growth: Gregory Sheldon, Director

Massachusetts Computer Software Council: Joyce Plotkin, President

Massachusetts Institute of Technology: David R. Lampe, Assistant Director, Industrial Liaison Program

Massachusetts Institute of Technology: John T. Preston, Director, Technology Licensing Office

Massachusetts Institute of Technology: Edgar Schein, Professor, Sloan School of Management

Maxtor Corp.: Leon Malmud, Vice President, Disk Drive Products

Measurex Corp.: David Bossen, President and Chief Executive Officer

Merrill, Pickard, Anderson & Eyre: Stephen E. Coit, General Partner

Micronix Corp.: Sam A. Harrell, President

Micro Power Systems: John Hall, President

MIPS Computer Systems, Inc.: Joe DeNucci, Vice President, Entry Systems Group

MIPS Computer Systems, Inc.: Carleen LeVasseur, Director, Public Relations

MIPS Computer Systems, Inc.: Stratton Sclavos, Director, Customer Marketing

MIPS Computer Systems, Inc.: Skip Stritter, Vice President, Development Programs

MK Global Ventures: Jim Riley, Partner

Mohr, Davidow Ventures: William Davidow, Partner

National Semiconductor Corp.: Gregory Harrison, Corporate Administrator

National Semiconductor Corp.: Ed Pausa, Vice President, International Manufacturing

National Semiconductor Corp.: Charles Sporck, President and Chief Executive Officer

Novellus Systems, Inc.: Robert F. Graham, President and Chief Executive Officer

ON Technology: Mitch Kapor, President

Open Software Foundation: Ira Goldstein

Performance Semiconductor Corp.: Tom Longo, President and Chief Executive Officer

Powersoft Corp.: Mitchell Kertzman, President and Chief Executive Officer

Precision Monolithics Inc.: Anthony Steimle, Vice President, Manufacturing

Pittiglio, Rabin, Todd, and McGrath: Maxwell Hall, Director

Pittiglio, Rabin, Todd, and McGrath: Jack Moore, Director

Pyramid Technology Corp.: Joseph Bookataub, Vice President, Operations

Pyramid Technology Corp.: Lori A. Hawker, Purchasing Supervisor

Regis McKenna Associates: Andrew Rothman, Principal

Rolm Corp.: Ken Oshman, Former CEO

San Jose Mercury News: Evelyn Richards, Technology Editor

Santa Clara County Manufacturing Group: Peter Giles, President

Santa Clara County Planning Department: Cathy Remson-Lazarus, Planner

Seeq Technology, Inc.: J. Daniel McCranie, President and Chief Executive Officer

Semiconductor Equipment and Materials Institute, Inc.: Lisa Anderson, Director of Public Relations

Semiconductor Equipment and Materials Institute, Inc.: Susan Newman, Technical Programs Coordinator

Semiconductor Equipment and Materials Institute, Inc.: Bill Reid, Executive Director

Sequoia Systems, Inc.: Gabriel P. Fusco, Chairman and Chief Executive Officer

Silicon Valley Bank: Allyn C. Woodward, Jr., Director, East Coast

Silicon Valley Group, Inc.: Papken S. Der Terossian, President and Chief Executive Officer

Silicon Graphics, Inc.: Edward R. McCracken, President and Chief Executive Officer

Solectron Corp.: Winston Chen, President and Chief Executive Officer

Stanford University: Ferril McGhie, Dean, Engineering

Stratus Computer, Inc.: William E. Foster, President and Chief Executive Officer

Sun Microsystems, Inc.: Tod Basche, Vice President, Sparcstation Group

Sun Microsystems, Inc.: Linc Holland, Corporate Operations

Sun Microsystems, Inc.: Ellen Kokos, Marketing Director, Sun Desktop Software

Sun Microsystems, Inc.: Susan Levine, Electronics Commodity Manager

Sun Microsystems, Inc.: Scott Metcalf, Director of Materials

Sun Microsystems, Inc.: Cheryl Vedoe, Vice President, Marketing, Software

Sun Microsystems, Inc.: David M. Weishaar, Senior Director, East Coast Operations

Sun Microsystems, Inc.: Anthony West, Director, Business Development, Intercontinental Operations

Sun Microsystems, Inc.: Peggy Williams, Manager, Corporate Purchasing

Tandem Computers, Inc.: Don Fowler, Vice President, Strategic Planning

Tandem Computers, Inc.: Todd A. W. Frohnen, Corporate Materials Manager

Tandem Computers, Inc.: John Sims, Director, Materials and Purchasing

Teradyne, Inc.: Alex d'Arbeloff, Chairman and President

The Technology Research Group: Andrew S. Rappaport, President

TA Associates: Stephen J. Gaal, Partner

TA Associates: Kenneth T. Schiciano, Associate

TS Associates: Rowland Chen, Director

TS Associates: Bruce Janis, Director

U.S. Venture Partners: Jack Carsten, General Partner

U.S. Venture Partners: Irwin Federman, General Partner

Varian Associates Inc.: Larry Hansen, Executive Vice President, Corporate Technology

Varian Associates Inc.: Thomas Moreno, Vice President, Corporate Development

Vitelic Corp.: Alex Au, President and Chief Executive Officer

VLSI Technology Inc.: Henri Jarrat, President and Chief Executive Officer

VLSI Technology Inc.: James N. Miller, Vice President, Sales and Marketing

VMX Opcom: Dave Evans, Vice President, Product Marketing

Weitek Corp.: Art J. Collmeyer, President

Weitek Corp.: John F. Rizzo, Vice President, Marketing

Xerox Corp.: Cary A. Kimmel, Manager, Business Development

Xilinx Corp.: Bernard Vonderschmitt, President

The Yankee Group: Howard Anderson, President

3Com Corp.: Les Denend, Vice President and General Manager, Federal Systems

3Com Corp.: William L. Krause, Chairman and Chief Executive Officer

3i Ventures Corporation: James G. Bass, Vice President

Acknowledgments

▶ This book reflects longstanding personal as well as intellectual interests. I grew up in the Boston area during the 1950s and 1960s surrounded by relatives and neighbors who worked in the emerging Route 128 technology industry. I discovered Silicon Valley many years later, while in graduate school at the University of California at Berkeley, and wrote a master's thesis on the region's urbanization. When I returned to the East Coast to complete a doctorate at the Massachusetts Institute of Technology (MIT), I began reflecting on the differences between the two regions, but I continued to focus my research on Silicon Valley. It was only several years after completing my dissertation that I began the formal comparison of the two technology regions that culminated in this book.

As with any project that has such a long incubation, I have many debts. My advisors at MIT deserve first mention. Charles Sabel has influenced this book in more ways than I can list here. He taught me how to think in a new way about regional economics and politics and generously gave of his time and friendship throughout the project. Suzanne Berger taught me the value of comparative analysis and offered encouragement and material support at just the right moments. And while we sometimes disagree, Bennett Harrison has been a source of enthusiastic feedback and advice for more than a decade.

My closest friends from graduate school, Gary Herrigel and Richard Locke, have provided a rare combination of intellectual and personal camaraderie. I only hope that I am able to return to them what they have given to me over these years. I also want to specially thank Robin Broad, Martha Cooley, and Erica Schoenberger for contributing to this project in ways that only dear old friends can.

Many colleagues at the University of California at Berkeley have been supportive of this work. I would like particularly to thank Michael Teitz, Peter Hall, Manuel Castells, Ed Blakeley, Gillian Hart, Judy Innes, Roger Montgomery, and Dick Walker. Ann Markusen left Berkeley many years ago, but she still holds a special place in the Department of City and Regional Planning for inspiring so many students, including me, to study regional development.

Other friends and colleagues offered valuable comments on drafts of this manuscript or its earlier incarnations, including Paul Adler, Meric Gertler, Mark Granovetter, Carol Heim, Susan Helper, David Levine, Charles Perrow, Michael Piore, Evelyn Richards, Philip Scranton, Lenny Siegel, and Michael Storper. I was also privileged to have first-rate research assistance on both coasts. Karl Goldstein stands in a class by himself, but Tim Sturgeon, Erin Fraher, Yuko Aoyama, Steve Wiengarten, and Grant Emison each contributed in important ways to this book. I returned to MIT for a year in 1990–1991 to do research on the Route 128 region. Don Lessard at the Sloan School of Management generously provided an institutional affiliation, and Suzanne Berger arranged the use of a spectacular office. The staffs at the Department of City and Regional Planning at Berkeley and the Department of Political Science at MIT also—as usual—played an absolutely critical, if often invisible, role in making things happen.

This book could not have been written without the time and insights that the engineers and executives from the two regions generously provided. I am sorry that I can't thank them all individually here; their contribution to this project may be self-evident, but the extent of my gratitude is not. Special thanks also to Michael Aronson at Harvard University Press for his enthusiastic support of the book, and to Camille Smith for a superb editing job.

Marty Manley has been a true partner throughout this project. His intellect, energy, and love have shaped the book, and its author, in more ways than he can imagine. I look forward to many future collaborations.

INDEX